FASCISM AND CRIMINAL LAW

Fascism was one of the twentieth century's principal political forces, and one of the most violent and problematic. Brutal, repressive and in some cases totalitarian, the fascist and authoritarian regimes of the early twentieth century, in Europe and beyond, sought to create revolutionary new orders that crushed their opponents. A central component of such regimes' exertion of control was criminal law, a focal point and key instrument of State punitive and repressive power. This collection brings together a range of original essays by international experts in the field to explore questions of criminal law under Italian Fascism and other similar regimes, including Franco's Spain, Vargas's Brazil and interwar Romania and Japan. Addressing issues of substantive criminal law, criminology and ideology, the form and function of criminal justice institutions, and the role and perception of criminal law in processes of transition, the collection casts new light on fascism's criminal legal history and related questions of theoretical interpretation and historiography. At the heart of the collection is the problematic issue of continuity and similarity among fascist systems and preceding, contemporaneous and subsequent legal orders, an issue that goes to the heart of fascist regimes' historical identity and the complex relationship between them and the legal orders constructed in their aftermath. The collection thus makes an innovative contribution both to the comparative understanding of fascism, and to critical engagement with the foundations and modalities of criminal law across systems.

Fascism and Criminal Law

History, Theory, Continuity

Edited by Stephen Skinner

·HART·
PUBLISHING

OXFORD AND PORTLAND, OREGON
2017

Hart Publishing
An imprint of Bloomsbury Publishing Plc

Hart Publishing Ltd
Kemp House
Chawley Park
Cumnor Hill
Oxford OX2 9PH
UK

Bloomsbury Publishing Plc
50 Bedford Square
London
WC1B 3DP
UK

www.hartpub.co.uk
www.bloomsbury.com

Published in North America (US and Canada) by
Hart Publishing
c/o International Specialized Book Services
920 NE 58th Avenue, Suite 300
Portland, OR 97213-3786
USA

www.isbs.com

HART PUBLISHING, the Hart/Stag logo, BLOOMSBURY and the
Diana logo are trademarks of Bloomsbury Publishing Plc

First published in hardback, 2015
Paperback edition, 2017

British Library Cataloguing-in-Publication Data
A catalogue record for this book is available from the British Library.

ISBN: PB: 978-1-50991-411-1
HB: 978-1-84946-552-6

Typeset by Compuscript Ltd, Shannon
Printed and bound in Great Britain by
Lightning Source UK Ltd

PREFACE

This collection brings together a range of critical perspectives on the nature, operation and functions of criminal law and aspects of criminal justice under Italian Fascism and other authoritarian and repressive regimes. It is mainly the fruit of four panels that I convened at the second biennial conference of the European Society for Comparative Legal History in Amsterdam, July 2012, under the broad banner of 'Fascist Criminal Law'. My aim with the panels was to bring together colleagues working on the history of criminal law and its connections with political tyranny, in order to try to open some comparative conversations and, as far as possible, explore some of the related critical currents in legal history scholarship. The focus was on criminal law due to its particular significance under what may be described as generically fascist regimes, in terms of reflecting their ideological values and constituting a central component of their power structures, and in that light the panels addressed questions of historical interpretation, comparative significance and especially continuity with previous and subsequent criminal legal orders. Seven of the panel members have contributed to this volume, together with two additional scholars who subsequently joined us to provide the chapters on Spain and Brazil. A particular objective of this collection was to combine established and emerging voices in the field, and to include a range of systemic perspectives, both within and beyond Europe. As some contributors have occasionally needed to remind each other, this work is more of a beginning than an end, the start of something hopefully bigger, and one criterion of achievement is to open further avenues for research. Above all it is hoped that the collection will feed into ongoing work on a period of history that must not be forgotten, and underline the need for constant questioning of the genesis, substance, form and deeper discursive dimensions of (criminal) law, which may be an instrument of justice and protection, but has too often been a tool of power, control and repression.

Many thanks and acknowledgements are due for the support and encouragement I have received as this project took shape. I wish to thank from the project's earliest stages Michele Papa, Richard Ireland, Dirk Heirbaut and Cosmin Cercel; as the project developed, David Fraser, Thomas Watkin, Michael Stolleis and Karl Haerter; as the conference panels moved from suggestion to reality, Setu Masferrer and Jan Hallebeek; all participants in the conference panels themselves and those who came to listen and ask questions; and all contributors to this volume. In preparing the collection I am very grateful to the numerous expert reviewers across three continents who read and commented on draft chapters, but who must as agreed remain behind the veil of anonymity. Specifically in relation to my own chapter, I am grateful to the British Academy for the Small Grant funding that enabled me to undertake research in 2011–12 at the University of Florence Social Sciences Library, the Max Planck Institute for European Legal History, Frankfurt and the British Library; I also thank the staff of those institutions for their assistance, and Cosmin Cercel, Catherine Dupré, David Fraser, Jenny McEwan and my external reviewer for their comments on various drafts. My thanks also go to Richard Hart, Rachel Turner and the rest of the team at Hart Publishing for their interest, support and assistance. Finally, I thank from the bottom of my heart Catherine Dupré, for everything, but more precisely her patience. The usual editorial caveat applies.

CONTENTS

LIST OF CONTRIBUTORS

Elizabeth Cancelli is Associate Professor of Brazilian History at the University of São Paulo and Research Fellow with the Brazilian National Council of Research. She has a PhD in History from the State University of Campinas, 1991 and has published numerous works, including *Carandiru: a prisão, o preso e o psiquiatra* (University of Brasília Press, 2005); *A cultura do crime e da lei no Brasil, 1889–1930* (University of Brasília Press, 2001); and *O mundo da violência: a políciana Era Vargas* (University of Brasília Press, 1993).

Cosmin S Cercel is a Research Fellow at the University of Nottingham, UK. He completed his doctorate in Comparative Legal Studies at Panthéon-Sorbonne (Paris I) University in 2012, entitled *Le Droit Saisi par la Politique: L'Expérience Communiste Roumaine*. His main research focuses on genealogies of law and politics, especially in twentieth-century Romanian legal history, and the theoretical and historiographical assumptions related to European legal dynamics. His recent publications include articles on legal theory and Romanian legal history, and he is currently developing projects in both these areas.

David Fraser is Professor of Law and Social Theory at the University of Nottingham, UK. His primary research interest is in legal and jurisprudential aspects of the Shoah and National Socialism. Professor Fraser's key recent publications include *Law After Auschwitz: Towards a Jurisprudence of the Holocaust* (Carolina Academic Press, 2005) and *The Fragility of Law: Constitutional Patriotism and the Jews of Belgium, 1940–1945* (Routledge Cavendish, 2009).

Luigi Lacchè is Professor of the History of European Law, Faculty of Jurisprudence, University of Macerata, Italy. His research focuses on the history of criminal law and justice in nineteenth- and twentieth-century Europe. He is the founding editor of the *Journal of Constitutional History* and his recent publications include (with Jean Marc Berlière and Xavier Rousseaux), *Histoire de la Justice Militaire en Europe aux XIX et XX Siècles* (Editions de la Maison de l'Homme, 2012); (with Monica Stronati), *Beyond the Statute Law: the 'Grey' Government of Criminal Justice Systems* (eum, 2011); and (with Massimo Meccarelli), *Storia della Giustizia e Storia del Diritto: Prospettive di Ricerca in Ambito Europeo* (eum, 2011).

Michael A Livingston is Professor of Law at the Rutgers-Camden School of Law, Rutgers University, USA. He attended Cornell University, Yale Law School, and the WUJS Institute Program in Arad, Israel. He has published extensively in tax law, comparative law, and related fields. He is the author of *The Fascists and the Jews: The Italian Race Laws, 1938–43* (Cambridge University Press, 2014) and is the chief editor of Cappelletti, Merryman and Perillo, *The Italian Legal System*, 2nd edn (Stanford University Press, forthcoming). He is currently working on a book about the phenomenon of Holocaust memory in Italy, Israel, and the USA.

Emilia Musumeci is a postdoctoral researcher at the University of Catania, Italy. Her primary research interests are in the history of criminology, history of medicine, and legal history. She is a member of several research organisations including Groupe Européen de Recherche sur les Normativités (GERN) and the Society for the Social History of Medicine (SSHM). Recent publications include *Cesare Lombroso e le Neuroscienze: un Parricidio Mancato. Devianza, Libero Arbitrio, Imputabilità tra Antiche Chimere ed Inediti Scenari* (Franco Angeli, 2012); and 'New Natural Born Killers? The Legacy of Lombroso in Neuroscience and Law' in P Knepper and PJ Ystehede (eds), *The Cesare Lombroso Handbook* (Routledge, 2013).

Pascual Marzal Rodriguez is Professor of Legal History at the University of Valencia, Spain. He has published numerous articles and books on the history of legal doctrines, the administration of justice during the Second Republic, and the history of criminal law. These include *El Diputado Casas Sala: una aproximación biográfica* (Centre d'Estudis del Maestrat, Castellón, 2010); *Magistratura y República: el Tribunal Supremo 1936–1939* (Editorial Práctica de Derecho, 2005); and 'Cuestiones sobre el delito de estelionato en el derecho histórico español', *Estudios jurídicos en memoria del profesor Dr. D. José Ramón Casabó Ruiz*, vol II (Valencia, 1998) 283–99.

Hiromi Sasamoto-Collins is a lecturer in the Department of Asian Studies at the University of Edinburgh, and formerly lecturer in modern Japanese history at Durham University, 2004 to 2007. Her PhD (University of Edinburgh, 2005), entitled 'Three Modern Japanese Dissenters: Minobe Tatsukichi, Sakai Toshihiko and Saito Takao', was a study of individual contributions to the defence and dissemination of key civil and political principles in early twentieth-century Japan. Her book, *Power and Dissent in Imperial Japan: Three Forms of Political Engagement* (NIAS, 2013), discusses fascist trends and their critics in imperial Japan, 1868–1945.

Stephen Skinner is a Senior Lecturer in Law at the University of Exeter, UK. He has a PhD in legal history (European University Institute, 1998) and his research interests span comparative criminal law and history, legal theory, and European human rights law. He has published numerous articles in these fields, including 'Violence in Fascist Criminal Law Discourse: War, Repression and Anti-Democracy' (2013) 26(2) *International Journal for the Semiotics of Law* 439–58; and 'Tainted Law? The Italian Penal Code, Fascism and Democracy', (2011) 7(4) *International Journal of Law in Context* 423–46. He is currently focusing on anti-democratic ideology and criminal law under Fascism, and developing research on lethal force and the right to life.

Introduction:
Fascism and Criminal Law, 'One of the Greatest Attributes of Sovereignty'

STEPHEN SKINNER

Fascism has been described as 'the major political innovation of the twentieth century, and the source of much of its pain'.[1] Emerging in post-First World War Italy as the name of the political movement, and then self-styled totalitarian regime led by Benito Mussolini, as well as their ideological amalgam, 'fascism' soon became a term used to describe other similar authoritarian and repressive movements and regimes elsewhere.[2] Although fascism's history and meanings continue 'to launch a thousand books',[3] the specificities of its systemic construction and operation remain a rich vein for research, especially with regard to its legal order and from critical and comparative perspectives. This collection therefore seeks to provide new insights into the relationships between fascism and what is arguably the central component of state repressive power, namely the power to prohibit and punish, and the means for doing so through criminal law and institutions of criminal justice. These are fundamental dimensions of state–individual relations, and areas of inquiry that serve to highlight the ways in which fascist and closely related politico-legal orders conceived and determined the nature and boundaries of wrongdoing, the protection of state interests, and the limits of individual freedom. Indeed, as the Fascist Minister of Justice, Alfredo Rocco, famously observed when outlining Italy's new draft penal code in 1930:

> In the new legislation the penal reform excels not only for its intrinsic grandiosity, but also for its indubitably superior importance in relation to any other legislative reform.

---

[1] RO Paxton, *The Anatomy of Fascism* (London, Penguin Books, 2005) 3.

[2] As discussed below: see text relating to nn 8–23. Following the general convention, capitalised Fascism is used here to mean the Mussolini regime, while uncapitalised fascism is used to indicate a more generic sense.

[3] RJB Bosworth, 'Introduction' in RJB Bosworth (ed), *The Oxford Handbook of Fascism* (Oxford, Oxford University Press, 2009) 1–7, 1.

> The power to punish is in fact one of the greatest attributes of sovereignty, such that our ancestors considered it to be one of the most essential manifestations of imperium.[4]

The chapters in this collection thus provide a range of perspectives on fascism and criminal law in terms of their historical development and significance, theoretical dimensions, as well as their continuities and connections with previous, contemporaneous and subsequent legal orders. The first part focuses on aspects of criminal law and criminal justice under and after Italian Fascism, while the second part addresses questions of criminal law and justice under other regimes, covering interwar Romania, Franco's Spain, Vargas's Brazil, and interwar Japan, with comparative regard to conceptual models of generic fascism. The collection does not directly address issues of criminal law under the German National Socialist (Nazi) regime, partly because that system has been the main object of inquiry of the major recent studies of law and the 'darker past',[5] and partly because of its distinct approach to law, and other much-debated systemic differences.[6] Before outlining each chapter, it is necessary to look a little more closely at the nature of Fascism/fascism, how it is considered here in relation to the wider politico-legal landscape of the twentieth and twenty-first centuries, and why criminal law is particularly important.

First, any engagement with forms of fascism inevitably encounters the minefield of conceptual meanings and conflicting schools of thought that have developed in this area. Although a full critical review essay on the theoretical and historiographical terrain of debate about the meanings and historical significance of fascism is not possible here, an outline of some key axes of discussion may be useful.[7] As noted above, Fascism first took shape in post-First World War Italy.

---

[4] A Rocco, 'Relazione a sua Maestà il Re del Ministro Guardasigilli (Rocco) Presentata nell'udienza del 19 Ottobre 1930-VIII per l'approvazione del testo definitivo del Codice Penale' in Ministero della Giustizia e degli Affari di Culto, *Lavori Preparatori del Codice Penale e Del Codice di Procedura Penale, Vol VII, Testo del Nuovo Codice Penale con la Relazione a Sua Maestà il Re del Guardasigilli (Rocco)*, (Rome, Tipografia delle Mantellate, 1930) 7–28, 7. Author's translation.

[5] C Joerges and N Singh Ghaleigh (eds), *Darker Legacies of Law in Europe: the Shadow of National Socialism and Fascism over Europe and its Legal Traditions* (Oxford, Hart Publishing, 2003) and D Fraser, *Law After Auschwitz. Towards a Jurisprudence of the Holocaust* (Durham NC, Carolina Academic Press, 2005).

[6] On criminal law under Nazism see T Vormbaum (M Bohlander ed, M Hiley trans), *A Modern History of German Criminal Law* (Berlin, Springer-Verlag, 2014) 172–208; J Rückert, 'Strafrecht zwischen Nationalsozialismus und Demokratischer Rechtsstaatlichkeit' in F Lanchester and I Staff (eds), *Lo Stato di Diritto Democratico dopo il Fascismo ed il Nazionalsocialismo* (Milan, Giuffrè, 1999) 159–211 and L Klinkhammer, 'Was There a Fascist Revolution? The Function of Penal Law in Fascist Italy and Nazi Germany' (2010) 15.3 *Journal of Modern Italian Studies* 390–409. On generic fascism, the possible distinction between fascism and Nazism, and Marxist/Communist interpretations, compare AJ Gregor, *The Ideology of Fascism: The Rationale of Totalitarianism* (New York, The Free Press, 1969) ix–xiv; Z Sternhell with M Snajder, and M Asheri, *The Birth of Fascist Ideology: From Cultural Rebellion to Political Revolution* (David Maisel trans) (Princeton NJ, Princeton University Press, 1994) 3–5; SG Payne, *Fascism: Comparison and Definition* (Madison, University of Wisconsin Press, 1980) 191–212; and R Griffin, *The Nature of Fascism* (London, Routledge, 1993) 1–25.

[7] See further Paxton, *The Anatomy of Fascism* 221–49; Griffin, *The Nature of Fascism* 4–15; and Bosworth, 'Introduction' 3–6.

Mussolini's *fasci di combattimento*[8] initially constituted an eclectic political movement with mixed ideas and motives, drawing on the support of war veterans, futurists and nationalists to become the first totalitarian regime, which rose to power in 1922 and held onto it violently until 1943.[9] However, although Fascism was a particular product of interwar Italy, it was not solely rooted in that period, nor did it dominate it utterly. As outlined below, Fascism's origins can also be traced back to earlier influences that link it with deeper currents of early twentieth-century modernity.[10] Moreover, as historical studies have shown, the connections and distances between the regime and lived realities in Italy at the time indicate the limits of its totalitarian rhetoric.[11]

Identifying the essence, or core tenets, of Fascism, and considering whether or not a generic label of fascism may be extended to other, similar regimes is a complex matter and an area of semantic, theoretical and ideological disagreement. Aside from its historically and system-specific Italian application, fascism has both a broadly indicative (and abused) sense, and a more narrowly defined political meaning. Broadly, as most commentators observe, the term fascism has become a general, pejorative term for any system, or exercise of power, that is contested for apparently dictatorial qualities and for critical purposes associated, however exaggeratedly, with fascism's historical manifestations of brutal authoritarianism.[12] Consequently, in popular usage the term has to some extent been hollowed out.

However, fascism is also generally agreed to have a generic application to certain sorts of – predominantly, but not only, historical – authoritarian political order, of which the specific nature and meaning are nevertheless debated.[13] In this regard, the term fascism may be used to describe systems that are characterised by a distinctively strong ideological basis,[14] and that are authoritarian, tyrannical or totalitarian, generally militaristic, revolutionary or reactive, and violent, although whilst each of these attributes may be a necessary element of fascism, they are not alone sufficient[15] or even consistent.[16] Whereas some leading scholars prefer to

---

[8] Paxton notes the origin of the term in the Italian *fascio*, meaning group or bundle; but it also draws on the Latin word for the lictor's symbol of a bundle of rods surrounding an axe, to represent unity and discipline, *The Anatomy of Fascism* 4. Also RJB Bosworth, *Mussolini's Italy: Life Under the Dictatorship* (London, Penguin Books, 2006) 121–22 and Griffin, *The Nature of Fascism* 64.

[9] Especially Paxton ibid and Bosworth ibid. The regime's totalitarian nature is also debated: with regard to law see especially P Costa, 'Lo "stato totalitario": un campo semantico nella giuspubblicistica del fascismo' (1999) 28 *Quaderni fiorentini per la storia del pensiero giuridico moderno* 61–174.

[10] For example M Neocleous, *Fascism* (Buckingham, Open University Press, 1997). Key (somewhat controversial) Italian studies include R De Felice (B Huff Everett trans) *Interpretations of Fascism* (London, Harvard University Press, 1977) and E Gentile, *Le origini dell'ideologia Fascista, 1918–1925* (Bologna, Il Mulino, 1996).

[11] Especially Bosworth, *Mussolini's Italy*.

[12] For a recent example of this criticism see R Griffin 'What Fascism is not and is. Thoughts on the Re-inflation of a Concept' (2013) 2 *Fascism* 259–261; also Griffin, *The Nature of Fascism* 1–4.

[13] Paxton, *The Anatomy of Fascism* 14–21; Griffin, *The Nature of Fascism* 4–15; Payne, *Fascism: Comparison and Definition* 191–212.

[14] Especially Griffin, *The Nature of Fascism* 15–19, 30–32.

[15] Paxton, *The Anatomy of Fascism* 216.

[16] Payne, *Fascism: Comparison and Definition* 5.

use the term fascism in a more open-textured way,[17] in effect encapsulating most of the above attributes, others underline a set of key dimensions and attributes, focusing on the perceived threats to, and needs and priorities of fascist movements.[18] Other commentators adopt a much narrower and more specific definition, which constitutes what is said to be the 'new consensus' interpretation, emphasising fascism's focus on the idea of revolutionary rebirth through the concise formula of 'a genus of political ideology whose mythic core in its various permutations is a palingenetic form of populist ultranationalism'.[19] The terrain of fascist studies therefore provides some common ground of predominant characteristics, but is also marked by significant variations on a theme and is fraught with terminological and conceptual peril. For the purposes of this collection's predominantly legal focus, the regimes considered in the second half are not approached in terms of a single definition, and each chapter engages with the issue of how to situate the system it addresses by drawing on elements of fascism studies to different degrees.[20]

Secondly, given this collection's critically oriented focus on fascism and criminal law, the deeper politico-legal nature of the triangular nexus among fascism, law, and pre- and post-Second World War liberal and democratic orders (which are themselves terms with shifting meanings from the late nineteenth into the twentieth centuries) also needs to be considered. The principal argument is that the forms of fascism and authoritarianism considered here, although constituting new extreme forms of polity, were nevertheless not entirely exceptional 'Others'. Despite such regimes' many differences from, and self-construction in opposition to, liberal and democratic orders, the general view here is that all of these types of system shared similarities and were related to each other, in terms of their origins, the various factors shaping them in the early twentieth century, and the means and strategies of power they adopted.[21] This is largely due to the ways in which all politico-legal systems – democratic and anti-democratic – in that period were influenced by and developed through the forces of crisis, rising nationalism and populism, technology and industrialised militarism, economic breakdown, war and modernism, which was itself moulded by the philosophical and experiential contexts of the end of the nineteenth century, and acutely crystallised by the First World War.[22] In that light, forms of fascism were not completely aberrant or dis-

---

[17] Especially Bosworth, 'Introduction' 1–7.

[18] Paxton, *The Anatomy of Fascism* 218 and 219–20; Payne, *Fascism: Comparison and Definition* 4–7.

[19] Griffin, *The Nature of Fascism* 26–52, 26. For Griffin, similar regimes that share this ideological core but which develop less radical pathways to power should be described as proto-fascist (ibid 50–51), and similar regimes that appear to imitate fascism as para-fascist (ibid 121). Also R Griffin, 'Introduction' in R Griffin (ed), *International Fascism: Theories, Causes and the New Consensus* (London, Arnold, 1998) 1–20.

[20] Although an aim here is to identify similarities and core concerns, as Paxton recalls from Marc Bloch, comparison may primarily serve to highlight differences: Paxton, *The Anatomy of Fascism* 20.

[21] Compare Bosworth, 'Introduction' 6.

[22] Neocleous, *Fascism* x–xi, 59–62; Griffin, *The Nature of Fascism* viii; R Griffin, *Modernism and Fascism: The Sense of a New Beginning under Mussolini and Hitler* (Basingstoke, Palgrave Macmillan, 2007).

connected eruptions, but products of the early twentieth century, interlinked with the web of influences and developments that were constituting modernity including, as discussed in some of the chapters in this collection, similar modes of governance through law. That is not to deny fascism's bloody impact on human history and individual lives, or to seek to whitewash it through relativisation, but to indicate its disturbing similarities and proximities.

Furthermore in this regard, although fascism appears to be a predominantly historical concern, as a relatively short-lived form of repressive and destructive political system that largely ended with the Second World War, understanding its origins and dynamics is still significant today. This is arguably most important where fascism was a key part of a specific state's history, and has left traces and shadows in its socio-political and legal order,[23] but fascism's broader connections with other forms of political system, especially democracy,[24] and thus its relevance for all such states, also demand attention.[25] Moreover, fascism is of concern today both because it is echoed, even emulated, in far right movements across the world, and because it lurks as a critical point of comparison at the edges of all states' repressive practices. This is not to say that fascism is the only 'dark past' or negative comparator, for democracies also have other shadows in their histories and have engendered their own forms of pain (such as slavery, empire, state violence, internal conflict and corruption), but it nevertheless remains a key point of reference.

In this light, turning to the third point addressed here, the collection's focus on criminal law is grounded on factual and theoretical reasons. In factual terms, the Fascist and other regimes discussed here all used criminal law and related judicial procedures to assert control, repress opposition and consolidate their power. As such, the nature and role of criminal law and criminal courts in fascist orders are core aspects of the latter's systemic actuality and methods of governance. In addition to its central role as an attribute of sovereign power and in more theoretical terms, criminal law also has a powerful representative and instrumental function. As David Garland emphasised in relation to processes of punishment more generally, 'official penal practice is particularly laden with social and cultural significance'[26] and operates together with other factors of an economic and

---

[23] With regard to law specifically see Joerges and Ghaleigh (eds), *Darker Legacies of Law in Europe* and for example L Garlati (ed), *L'Inconscio Inquisitorio. L'Eredità del Codice Rocco nella cultura processualpenalistica Italiana* (Milan, Giuffrè, 2010).

[24] Such connections include both historical similarities among fascism and other political systems, and fascism's influence as a negative stimulus to later legal developments. This issue is apparent in the constitutional law of many European states, as well as in the genesis of foundational democratic normative safeguards, such as the European Convention on Human Rights. It is also apparent as a spectral antithesis in legal orders elsewhere: for example M Raymond, 'Rejecting Totalitarianism: Translating the Guarantees of Constitutional Criminal Procedure' (1998) 76 *North Carolina Law Review* 1193–1263 and R Primus, 'A Brooding Omnipresence: Totalitarianism in Postwar Constitutional Thought', (1996–97) 106 *Yale Law Journal* 423–57.

[25] Compare generally Fraser, *Law After Auschwitz*; Neocleous, *Fascism* x–xii; and Joerges and Singh Ghaleigh, *Darker Legacies of Law in Europe* ix for a distillation of the Habermasian rationale for engaging with the constitutive force of history.

[26] D Garland, *Punishment and Modern Society: A Study in Social Theory* (Oxford, Clarendon Press, 1991) 255.

political nature in 'a complex, aggregative process of world-making'.[27] Consequently penality and criminal or penal law are symbols and tools of power, and their forms and functions provide significant 'windows' into a political order's constitutive elements and objectives.

With regard to forms, Ernst Fraenkel argued in his major study of the 'dual State' under dictatorship, focusing on Nazism, that that regime generally operated through a parallel system of laws and prerogatives.[28] However, whether and how exactly this concept of duality worked in other systems, and the extent to which the distinction between law and prerogative was clear-cut, has been questioned in subsequent studies.[29] With regard to law specifically, authoritative commentary shows that whereas Nazism sought to circumvent law to maximise the regime's power (through, for example, the erosion of legal certainty via analogical reasoning and the *Führerprinzip*), Italian Fascism sought to use law to achieve the regime's ends.[30] Recurrent issues in this collection are thus the forms of criminal law and courts, especially whether and if so how Fraenkel's duality – or something similar – operated.

In terms of how criminal law and courts were used, or rather, what perhaps were their objectives and functions, although Fascists claimed to prize violence and action above ideas and theories, the Mussolini regime had identifiable ideological ambitions and strategies of power, which had significant legal and institutional dimensions. This included its repressive laws and related Special Tribunal for the Defence of the State introduced in the mid-1920s, as well as subsequently the 1930 Penal Code and Code of Penal Procedure.[31] A leading figure in relation to all of these developments was the nationalist ideologue and Fascist Minister of Justice, Alfredo Rocco, whose ideas about the 'strong State' were particularly influential.[32] However, as with the nature of the regime in general, the extent to which such developments in criminal law were distinctive, innovative or even revolutionary, and what roles they played under the regime, are matters of debate, which are taken up in the first part of this collection.[33] Similarly, the second half

---

[27] Ibid 265–66.

[28] E Fraenkel, *The Dual State: A Contribution to the Theory of Dictatorship* (New York, Oxford University Press, 1941). Also Paxton, *The Anatomy of Fascism* 119–22.

[29] For example Klinkhammer, 'Was There a Fascist Revolution?' 405.

[30] Vormbaum *A Modern History of German Criminal Law* 172–208, 184; also Klinkhammer, 'Was There a Fascist Revolution?' 398.

[31] On other related issues see for example M Canali, 'Crime and Repression' in Bosworth (ed), *The Oxford Handbook of Fascism* 221–38, which concentrates on policing and political offences, and J Dunnage, *Mussolini's Policemen: Behaviour, Ideology and Institutional Culture in Representation and Practice* (Manchester, Manchester University Press, 2012).

[32] AJ Gregor, *Mussolini's Intellectuals: Fascist Social and Political Thought* (Princeton NJ, Princeton University Press, 2005); G Neppi Modona and M Pelissero, 'La politica criminale durante il fascismo' in L Violante (ed), *Storia d'Italia. Annali, vol 12: La Criminalità* (Turin, Einaudi, 1997) 759–847; S Skinner, 'Violence in Fascist Criminal Law Discourse: War, Repression and Anti-Democracy' (2013) 26 *International Journal for the Semiotics of Law* 439–58.

[33] Generally Klinkhammer, 'Was There a Fascist Revolution?'; M Sbriccoli, 'Giustizia criminale', in M Fioravanti (ed), *Lo Stato Moderno in Europa: Istituzioni e diritto* (Rome-Bari, Laterza, 2004) 163–205; G Neppi Modona, 'Diritto e giustizia penale nel periodo fascista' in L Lacché, C Latini, P Marchetti

discusses how criminal law and aspects of criminal justice reflected the values and priorities of the regimes considered there, how they were utilised in the consolidation of power, and how they might elucidate the deeper forces at stake in the emergence of fascism and its connections with new (modern) legal paradigms.

Furthermore, the criminal law sphere is significant not only because of the way it can help to indicate the key features of individual fascist orders, but also the nature and extent of their similarities to each other and to non-fascist systems, before and after the interwar period. Although fascist orders' self-perception and self-definition included a significant element of opposition to democratic liberalism, fascist and nominally democratic orders in this period were not entirely substantive opposites in the legal field. This includes matters of proximity in the forms, techniques and substance of penal law, as well as its very 'lawness', which all reveal disturbing contiguities among fascism's predecessors, apparent opponents and successors. In relation to the latter, criminal law has been both an instrument of change and justice in the aftermath of fascist violence, and a site of conflict in that transition, revealing problematic doctrinal, procedural and institutional tensions and continuities up to the present.

Turning to the chapters themselves, the collection's exploration of the relationships between fascism and criminal law is structured by system, broadly chronologically, and considers the criminal law field from three main angles. First, in six of the eight chapters (Chapters 2, 3, 5, 6, 7 and 8) the criminal law of four systems is considered in normative and substantive terms, together with its ideological and theoretical foundations, specifically under the regime in question and comparatively with regard to other contemporaneous orders. Secondly, in four chapters (1, 6, 7 and 8) criminal law is discussed in a broader criminal justice sense, involving the systemic and procedural dimensions of courts and judicial processes across four systems. In particular, these chapters consider the fascist technique of establishing parallel and overlapping criminal justice institutions and procedures, and the reasons why such regimes chose to rely on the mechanisms of law. Thirdly, three chapters (3, 4 and 8) relating to two systems, consider the role of criminal law in the transition from fascism to democracy, as well as an object of discursive reflection of, and on, that process. This involves especially the extent to which the connections between fascism and criminal law have been expunged, denied or recast retrospectively as part of broader post-war processes of political reconstruction and identification. A brief summary of each chapter suffices to highlight these perspectives and lines of argument.

In the collection's opening chapter, 'The Shadow of the Law: the Special Tribunal for the Defence of the State between Justice and Politics in the Italian Fascist Period', Luigi Lacché focuses on the establishment and role of the Special Tribunal for the Defence of the State, the court established by the regime in 1926 to try political offences and bolster its power. Lacché considers the symbolic

and M Meccarelli (eds), *Penale Giustizia Potere. Metodi, Ricerche, Storiografiche. Per ricordare Mario Sbriccoli* (Macerata, Edizioni Università di Macerata, 2007) 341–78.

significance of courts and the trappings of law, questioning how and why the Fascist government sought to use a mechanism of justice in order to enforce injustice. To this end, he explores the nature of political justice under the preceding liberal order in terms of what he calls the paradox of freedom – that is, the problem faced by states that guarantee individual and public freedoms, in that such freedoms may be used against the state itself – in response to which the liberal system developed authoritarian and repressive tendencies. However, although the liberal order nevertheless recognised the need for freedoms, Fascism adopted its predecessor's authoritarian practices, especially the recourse to emergency powers, but crushed individual liberty under totalitarianism. Ultimately, this chapter argues that the regime's use of the Special Tribunal reveals the importance of legal frameworks to a totalitarian regime, as a device for apparently justifying repression by constructing a narrative of threats to the state, and presenting the masses with an exercise of state power through apparently legitimate means anchored in the previous politico-legal order.

This issue of Fascism's difference and its connections with preceding forms of criminal law is similarly the focus of the following chapter, 'The Positivist School of Criminology and Italian Fascist Criminal Law: a Squandered Legacy?'. In this study, Emilia Musumeci discusses the influence on the 1930 Penal Code of the much-criticised social and biological theory of criminal responsibility developed by Cesare Lombroso in the 1870s. Whereas Italy's 1889 Penal Code, the so-called Zanardelli Code, had adhered to classical criminological principles in its focus on individual responsibility based on free will, positivist theory found favour in the 1920s in the proposals to revise the Penal Code, led by Enrico Ferri, which would have diminished the influence of free will and focused more on positivist concepts of biological determinism and social dangerousness. However, Fascist criminal theory purported to favour the so-called 'technical-legal' approach, which aimed to place legal authority above contamination by other disciplines and to move away from both classical and positivist theories, so it was claimed that the development of the 1930 Penal Code under Alfredo Rocco set criminal law on a new course. Yet the actual terms of the 1930 (Rocco) Penal Code appeared to be a strange hybrid of classical and positivist influences, including an emphasis on the latter's concepts of social dangerousness and the need for individual security measures. As Musumeci argues though, the appearance of positivist elements in the 1930 Code did not mean that it really adhered to Lombrosian principles, but rather used such elements instrumentally and against positivism's original aims, subverting Lombroso's intended progressive and secular objectives in order to fashion an instrument of Fascist repression.

The third chapter, 'Fascist by Name, Fascist by Nature? The 1930 Italian Penal Code in Academic Commentary, 1928–46', also questions the nature of criminal law under Fascism by examining how the Rocco Code was received and understood by foreign commentators in contemporaneous, democratic systems, from its inception to the early post-Second World War years. This chapter, my own contribution, starts by noting that the Rocco Code was not replaced or radically reformed after the fall of Fascism, largely due to the influence of a post-war academic anti-reform movement in Italy, whose interpretation and representation of the Code effectively minimised its Fascist influences. The chapter then explores how foreign academic analysis sought to grasp the significance of this new code, in relation to the violent regime under which it was formulated and the broader historical context in which that regime and its penal code emerged. Arguing that there was a crucial relationship between commentators' analytical and comparative methods and their evaluations of the Code, the chapter shows that while the approach of the Italian anti-reform writers was not unique to Italy, some foreign scholars were acutely aware of the Code's anti-democratic roots. The chapter thus casts a new critical light on the foundations of the Italian anti-reform movement and the Code's longevity. However, in so doing, the chapter argues that commentators' reception of and engagement with the Rocco Code nevertheless underline its uncomfortably close relationship with non-Fascist criminal law.

The closing chapter of the collection's first part on Italian Fascism, entitled 'Criminal Law, Racial Law, Fascist Law: Was the Fascist Era Really a "Parenthesis" for the Italian Legal System?' reflects on the supposed uniqueness of the Fascist era and considers criminal law within the broader context of Italian law under and after Fascism. In this regard Michael Livingston pays particular attention to the ways in which post-war scholarship in Italy has tended to emphasise the new Republic's democratic credentials, and downplay its anti-democratic, Fascist origins, especially with regard to the ways in which some aspects of the legal system are clearly rooted in Fascism. Concentrating on re-evaluation of the Fascist racial laws, Livingston shows how recent research has demonstrated that those laws were home-grown and, rather than being an externally imposed anomaly unsupported by most 'good Italians', were in fact tolerated or even supported by the population, as well as by rather ambivalent interpretation by lawyers and judges. The chapter outlines how, in the post-war era, the Italian legal system, in practice and academic doctrine, has moved on from pre-war (Kelsenian) positivism in order to embrace a more active, politically aware democratic approach to law. Ultimately, the chapter underlines the universal problem of facing 'painful episodes in a nation's past' and the continuing importance of seeking to evaluate their impact on law.

Part II of the collection opens with 'The Enemy Within: Criminal Law and Ideology in Interwar Romania', a historical and theoretical reading of the relationship between Romanian criminal law and fascism in the 1930s. In this analysis, Cosmin Cercel situates and connects the emergence of a new legal paradigm, in the form of the state of exception and unlimited authority, with the rise of fascism in the interwar period as a time of crisis. Through a critical interpretation of the interconnectedness of (legal) text and (contestable historical) context, Cercel argues that the 1936 Romanian Penal Code both reflected immediate political influences on criminal law under the royal dictatorship, and demonstrated deeper shifts in legal thought typical of this period of modernity. Focusing on the Code's offences against the constitutional order and state security, this chapter shows how the Code represented the royal dictatorship's effort to suppress political opposition, including the fascist Iron Guard, in order to defend the state, but in so doing adopted aspects of ideology present within fascism, and constructed a new legal order sanctioning the very state violence that subsequent Romanian author-itarian regimes would employ. Consequently, by tracing these elements of the 1936 Code and its turn from classical concepts of lawfulness to concepts of excep-tion to be determined and addressed in terms of state-centrism, the chapter argues that that Code was thus 'both an object and an archive' of the interwar politico-legal dynamic, which engendered fascism and enabled the lawful channelling of state violence.

Moving from Eastern to Southern Europe, the next chapter, 'Criminal Law under the Francoist Regime: the Influence of Militarism and National-Catholicism' discusses the major influences on institutional and substantive dimensions of criminal law in Spain under Franco. In this chapter, Pascual Marzal identifies two key institutional attributes of Francoist criminal law, namely the reliance on military justice through special courts, anchored in the experience of civil war and the regime's classification of its opponents as dangers to society, and the regime's creation of special jurisdictions reflecting its ideological priorities, especially the repression of communism and freemasonry. In substantive terms, Marzal outlines how the Francoist Penal Code of 1944 was developed as a repres-sive tool with increased punishments, and offences protecting the Catholic faith and targeting matters reflecting Catholic and Francoist values, particularly in rela-tion to the family, fertility, marriage and sexual morals. In these respects, the chapter highlights significant modes and norms of criminal law, similar to those used under Italian Fascism, and traces the continuity of such features of Spanish criminal law through the long life of the Franco regime until its end in the 1970s. The chapter thus indicates some dimensions of criminal law whose historical shadows and residues still await closer examination.

The last two chapters in Part II both turn to dimensions of the topic of fascism and criminal law beyond Europe. Elizabeth Cancelli's chapter, 'When Law and Prerogatives Blend: Generic Fascism in Getulio Vargas's Brazil, 1930–45' presents the view that, even though some commentators have dismissed Vargas as a weak dictator rather than a fascist,[34] this authoritarian dictatorship can nevertheless be seen as a manifestation of generic fascism, by tracing its core ideological founda-tions and examining its power structures. Emphasising the Vargas regime's posi-tivist preferences, the chapter outlines how he sought to structure his authority through a combination of law and prerogative powers. Illustrating these factors with examples drawn from criminal law, Vargas's reconstruction of the constitutional order, the regime's treatment of foreigners and 'undesirable' elements in society, its repression of left-wing movements, and its control of police and prisons, the chapter argues that this regime demonstrated core 'fascist' ideologies of rebirth and ultranationalism, and sought to bring 'progress with

---

[34] Griffin, *The Nature of Fascism* 148 and Paxton, *The Anatomy of Fascism* 193.

order'. Overall, the chapter argues that Vargas's use of normative and prerogative dimensions of power enabled him to manage the contradictions apparent in his form of fascism, and to maintain control over and through key instruments of repression in the criminal sphere, especially a directly controlled police force and special court.

The final chapter, 'Facilitating Fascism? The Japanese Peace Preservation Act and the Role of the Judiciary' reflects on the nature and meaning of fascism in interwar Japan and its relationship with criminal law by examining the case of the Peace Preservation Act, the authoritarian regime's principal tool for repressing opposition from 1925 until 1945. Here, Hiromi Sasamoto-Collins engages with the main lines of discussion about the essence and historiography of Japanese fascism, highlighting its complex roots in cultural modes of communal behaviour, ingrained militarism and the cult of the emperor, and placing it within the early twentieth-century global trend of authoritarian reactions to new and disturbing socio-political developments. The chapter argues that the Japanese regime's use of law was central to its erosion of the constitutional order from within, and thus its consolidation of authority. The chapter analyses the Peace Preservation Act, focusing on the role of the judiciary in its implementation in order to demonstrate how law was used to subordinate individuals and their rights to collective interests in the form of absolute state power. Tracing the origins of the Act to concerns about labour and social protest movements, especially communism, Sasamoto-Collins shows how flexible judicial interpretation of the Act, together with incremental revisions, were used to make it increasingly repressive. This chapter thus focuses on the centrality of law and legal process to fascist power in Japan, a relationship that has only recently begun to be re-evaluated by the courts, thereby confirming the need for ongoing critical engagement with the legal shadows of the fascist past both within and beyond its European heartlands.

Lastly, the collection closes with a short conclusion that identifies and brings together some points of common ground and the major themes that emerge from the chapters. Briefly identifying some of the shared values and priorities that recur in substantive criminal law under the regimes considered, the conclusion also notes the role of the military and, importantly, of lawyers and judges in both shaping and realising the regimes' aims in the criminal legal sphere. The conclusion then focuses on three principal themes in the chapters, namely the forms of criminal law and justice, with particular reference to the concept of duality; the instrumentalisation and functions of criminal law and related institutions; and the connections and continuities that the chapters address and reveal. This thematic outline serves both to highlight links among the contributors' key arguments and to suggest possible avenues for further research.

I

Criminal Law and Italian Fascism

1

The Shadow of the Law: the Special Tribunal for the Defence of the State between Justice and Politics in the Italian Fascist Period

LUIGI LACCHÈ*

It is not by chance that Otto Kirchheimer, at the start of his great book on *Political Justice*,[1] quotes the following stimulating remarks by Alexis de Tocqueville:

> The great end of justice is to substitute the notion of right for that of violence and to place intermediaries between the government and the use of physical force. It is a strange thing what authority the opinion of mankind generally grants to the intervention of courts. It clings even to the mere appearance of justice long after the substance has evaporated; it lends bodily form to the shadow of the law.[2]

Power, in other words, seeks out justice (as language, frame or technical procedure) even when it is intent upon devising and fashioning its contrary, injustice. I propose here to analyse certain aspects of the *Tribunale speciale per la difesa dello Stato* (Special Tribunal for the Defence of the State) established by the Fascist regime in 1926, reading it through this Tocquevillean lens. I will therefore be primarily concerned with the relationship between justice and politics in a totalitarian regime, focusing on the establishment of the Special Tribunal, and on the role it played, especially at the outset. The Special Tribunal was established at the end of 1926 and it is the new institution that most vividly characterises the transformation of the Fascist regime. This Tribunal had to deal with an emergency (some failed attacks against Mussolini in 1926 and, more generally, widespread opposition to Fascism), but it was first and foremost the repressive guardian of the regime, and as such, vested with a real constitutional significance. Although a good number of studies of its activities and effects have been published, in my

---

* Unless otherwise indicated, all translations are my own.

[1] O Kirchheimer, *Political Justice – The Use of Legal Procedure for Political Ends* (Princeton NJ, Princeton University Press, 1961).

[2] Ibid 3 quoting A de Tocqueville, *De la Démocratie en Amérique* (Paris, Gallimard, 1951) vol 1, ch 8, 141–42. Kirchheimer's and my translation.

opinion there is a need to pay more attention to the judicial and symbolic position of the Special Tribunal within the whole repressive system.

My argument unfolds in four distinct stages. First, I endeavour to understand what kind of connection may be established between political justice in the liberal order and in the Fascist period. More particularly, my argument is that the liberal state is characterised by what I would call the 'paradox of freedom'. In my view, emphasis upon this same paradox enables us to grasp the elements of continuity and discontinuity between those two orders. In my argument's second stage I will analyse the establishment of the Special Tribunal as an explicit overcoming of liberal political justice. In its third stage my essay is designed to show how Fascist political justice is intrinsically linked to the political nature of the new regime. Finally, I will conclude with some observations regarding the explicitly symbolic level of the Special Tribunal in the context of Fascist political justice. The aim of the present chapter is not so much to give an account of cases[3] heard by the Special Tribunal, but rather to attempt a comprehensive interpretation of the *position* of the new Tribunal within the strategies and policies of Fascist repression.

Political Justice in the Liberal Order and the Paradox of Freedom

It is difficult to speak about justice and politics in the Italian Fascist criminal system without addressing the issue of continuity and discontinuity as regards the era of the preceding liberal state. This sort of consideration has a general validity but is of particular relevance to the question of the repression of political dissent. The central question might be phrased as follows: how much of the system of Fascist justice is genuinely new?[4] In other words, does the innovation of the Fascist regime account for most of that system or, also and above all, is such innovation apparent in the 'texture' of the repression?

In order to answer this question it is necessary to consider certain aspects of the concept of political justice in the liberal state. First, what do I mean by political justice in the liberal order? I mean by this phrase the manner in which the political institutions of government oppose dissent. Liberal regimes are based on what I call the 'paradox of freedom'. Such regimes affirm individual and public freedoms (a free press, freedom of association, freedom of assembly, the right to form parties, etc). At the same time, however – and herein lies the paradox – those same freedoms can be used against the liberal government, and may threaten the very

---

[3] I will give an account of only one particularly paradigmatic case, namely the trial of the Communist leaders in May 1928.

[4] G Melis reflects on this question in 'Le istituzioni durante il fascismo: alcune riflessioni' in E Gentile, F Lanchester and A Tarquini (eds), *Alfredo Rocco: dalla crisi del parlamentarismo alla costruzione dello Stato nuovo* (Rome, Carocci, 2010) 193–203.

existence of the state. Public liberties are fundamental, but they also pose the problem of a structural tension between order and freedom.

In 1990 I published a volume dedicated to the issue of preventive detention in the liberal state. The Italian title, *La giustizia per i galantuomini*,[5] was designed to evoke this original aporia of liberal thought and practice determined by the above-mentioned tension between order and freedom. The gap between the rhetorical safeguarding of guarantees enshrined in statute law and the mechanisms ensuring the effective functioning of the penal system is based, above all, on two functional relationships: ordinary/extraordinary; rule/exception. It was at the turn of the eighteenth century that the abstract principle of legality was formulated. However, at the same time a second level of legality – tending to separate prevention and social danger from the 'normal' juridical order – gained ground. This second level often operates beyond statute law, even though the latter ought theoretically to shoulder the burden of judicial guarantees in their entirety. It is not rare to find this other level being swept under the 'carpet of legality', much like all those things which from time to time are nonchalantly hidden from view in even the most elegant of middle-class sitting rooms.

Mario Sbriccoli has described the existence of different levels of legality as a 'permanent feature' of the liberal legal system.[6] The distinction between two tiers of legality – a distinction that throws the idea of the principle of legality construed as a unitary and indivisible bloc into crisis – helps us to identify the tensions which arise among that concept's different forms and dimensions: the codes and the statutes of public safety, the codes and the statutes of emergency, the general and universal statute law, and concrete and specific applications of law. This same concept of a dual level of legality describes the mechanisms whereby political opportunity may sometimes prevail over juridical rule and over 'principles', compressing rights and guarantees. From being an *internal* and integrated tool, the exception becomes an *external* element, the 'space of suspension of the juridical order'.[7]

So it is that the 'grey areas' in a penal system built around the principle of legality[8] reveal a more complex and problematic landscape destined to maintain an

---

[5] L Lacchè, *La giustizia per i galantuomini. Ordine e libertà nell'Italia liberale: il dibattito sul carcere preventivo (1865–1913)* (Milan, Giuffrè, 1990).

[6] On the concept of the dual level of legality see M Sbriccoli, 'La penalistica civile. Teorie e ideologie del diritto penale nell'Italia unita', currently in M Sbriccoli, *Scritti di storia del diritto penale e della giustizia. Scritti editi e inediti (1972–2007)* (Milan, Giuffrè, 2009) I, 524. Sbriccoli also noted that '[t]he dual level of legality distinguishes "gentlemen" from "scoundrels", destining them to two different punitive *filières*, and makes political opportunity prevail over juridical rule, the aim over the law. It allows the achievement of politically desirable objectives by way of the compression of rights, prerogatives and guarantees, keeping out of sight those who are juridically and politically responsible for such compression', in M Sbriccoli, 'Caratteri originari e tratti permanenti del sistema penale italiano (1860–1990)', ibid 596–97, also 647, 654–55.

[7] M Meccarelli, 'Paradigmi dell'eccezione nella parabola della modernità penale. Una prospettiva storico-giuridica' (2009) 44.2 *Quaderni storici* 501.

[8] This question was addressed by M Pifferi, 'Difendere i confini, superare le frontiere. Le 'zone grigie' della legalità penale tra Otto e Novecento' (2007) 36 *Quaderni fiorentini per la storia del pensiero giuridico moderno*, 743–98. See also L Lacchè and M Stronati (eds), *Beyond the statute law: the 'grey'*

important role in the development of that penal system as well as justice in democratic societies. The liberal state, in order to oppose adversaries and disruptive elements, operates on the borderline, creates grey areas, 'free zones' (that is to say, free with respect to the postulates of the liberal safeguarding of guarantees), which nonetheless continue to have the principle of legality as a dialectical term. It is thereby possible to maintain a link between penal law and public liberties, a controversial link certainly, yet one located within an inclusive juridical order.

In the liberal state we can observe a series of strategies and tools. Likewise, in what are defined as 'grey areas' we can discern a plurality of gradations. For example, I have in mind here the readiness of the liberal state to resort to special criminal cases, illegal arrests, the modification of the terms of prescription, the retroactive application of laws. However, the normal way of suspending the juridical order was, during the Italian liberal period, the recourse to the political state of siege. Even at its birth the Italian State came very close to assuming full and extraordinary powers. The stamp of emergency upon the Pica Law, approved in 1863 to combat brigandage in southern Italy, is all too visible. The logic may be paraphrased as follows: the exceptional nature of a situation (brigandage, but in later years, various subversive movements linked to a range of different social and political conflicts) legitimised the declaration of the political state of siege. In the absence of any legal disciplining of the latter, the principle *necessitas facit legem* and the analogy with the military state of siege prevailed.[9] Despite criticism of the legal doctrine, this model was applied on several different occasions.

As Kirchheimer has noted,[10] the government in a liberal and democratic state cannot completely control public opinion and the judicial power. It is assize courts that have jurisdiction over those accused of political crimes or common crimes committed in the context of popular uprisings. Yet sometimes jurors show sympathy for this kind of defendant, and it is therefore hard to predict the outcome of political trials. The public and adversarial process may fail and even inadvertently promote the ideas of the oppositional movements. The political trial in the liberal state may become a trap so far as the authorities are concerned.

Finally, we should recall that the First World War brought about a marked restriction of public liberties.[11] The liberal state had bequeathed the Fascist State

government of criminal justice systems. History and Theory in the modern age (Macerata, Edizioni Università di Macerata, 2011).

[9] J Davis, *Conflict and Control: Law and Order in Nineteenth-Century Italy* (Basingstoke, Macmillan, 1988); see especially C Latini, *Governare l'emergenza. Delega legislativa e pieni poteri in Italia tra Otto e Novecento* (Milan, Giuffrè Editore, 2005); L Martone, 'Le forme giuridiche dell'emergenza penale nelle scelte dei governi del regno d'Italia' in L Martone (ed), *Aspetti del sistema penale liberale e fascista tra leggi speciali e garanzie processuali* (Turin, Giappichelli, 2007) 3–27.

[10] O Kirchheimer, 'Politische Justiz', in O Kirchheimer, *Funktionen des Staats und der Verfassung. Zehn Analysen* (Berlin, Suhrkamp Verlag, 1972 [1955]) 147.

[11] See G Procacci, 'Osservazioni sulla continuità della legislazione sull'ordine pubblico tra fine Ottocento, prima guerra mondiale e fascismo' in P Del Negro, N Labanca, A Staderini (eds), *Militarizzazione e nazionalizzazione nella storia d'Italia* (Milan, Unicopli, 2006) 83–96; G Procacci, 'La limitazione dei diritti di libertà nello Stato liberale: il piano di difesa (1904–1935), l'internamento dei cittadini nemici e la lotta ai "nemici interni" (1915–1918)' (2009) 38.1 *Quaderni fiorentini per la storia*

an ambiguous legacy, one characterised by the paradox of freedom. On the one hand, there is the affirmation of individual liberties and constitutional safeguards (the rule of law). On the other hand, there is a tendency or propensity to limit these guarantees when they threaten the state and public order. The affirmation of liberties and grey areas of repression thus coexist.

The Special Tribunal for the Defence of the State as an Overcoming of the Liberal Paradox of Freedom

Between 1924 and 1925 – and especially after the Matteotti crisis[12] – Fascism went beyond the paradox of freedom of the liberal order. Mussolini steered straight towards the so-called dictatorship.[13] In his famous speech of 3 January 1925 to the Chamber of Deputies, the head of government assumed political and moral responsibility for Matteotti's murder. Political freedoms were then curbed or cancelled. The Albertine Statute – said Mussolini in June 1925 – could not be 'a hook upon which all generations should be hung'.[14] In the space of two short years, political pluralism was destroyed.

The result was the passing of the *Leggi fascistissime*, the complex of so-called 'ultra-Fascist laws', which bolstered the powers of Mussolini and reinforced the policies serving to check and to repress all forms of opposition to the regime. Not by chance, in November 1926, 124 deputies belonging to the opposition parties were dismissed, and immediately afterwards the Chamber of Deputies approved the eight articles of Law No 2008, Provisions for the Defence of the State. This was the statute that established the Tribunal for the Defence of the State, a newly created Special Tribunal composed of officers from the regular army and the volunteer militia for national security.[15] The Court was appointed by the minister of war; it had to apply the rules of criminal procedure governing the army in time of war, and its judgments were not subject to appeal and cassation. Law No 2008 imposed harsher sentences and reintroduced the death penalty for a range of different political crimes.[16] Moreover, an attempt to commit a specified crime was treated the same as the crime itself, the intention being to strike even tacit

del pensiero giuridico moderno 601–52; C Latini, *Cittadini e nemici. Giustizia militare e giusitizia penale in Italia tra Otto e Novecento* (Firenze, Le Monnier, 2010) 303 ff.

[12] See A Lyttelton, *The Seizure of Power. Fascism in Italy 1919–1929* (London, Weidenfeld and Nicolson, 1973). The Socialist Deputy Giacomo Matteotti was kidnapped and murdered on 10 June 1924 by a group of *squadristi*.

[13] A Aquarone, *L'organizzazione dello Stato totalitario*, 2nd edn (Turin, Einaudi, 1965) ch 2.

[14] Quoted by S Lupo, *Il fascismo. La politica in un regime totalitario* (Rome, Donzelli, 2000) 191.

[15] For a general bibliography about the Special Tribunal see Latini, *Cittadini e nemici* 342. On the voluntary militia for national security see C Poesio, *Reprimere le idee abusare del potere. La milizia e l'instaurazione del regime fascista* (Rome, Aracne, 2010).

[16] About the death penalty during the Fascist regime, see G Tessitore, *Fascismo e pena di morte. Consenso e informazione* (Milan, Angeli, 2000).

expressions of political dissent. The reintroduction of the death penalty was designed to intimidate, but also to serve an important symbolic function.[17] By contrast with the 'weak' liberal state of the Zanardelli Code (1890),[18] Fascism sought to reassert the authority of the state.

A decree of 1926 gave further effect to the Provisions for the Defence of the State.[19] This text laid down a number of specific rules of procedure. For example, the presiding judge could exclude civilian lawyers, or deny counsel the right to view documents at the preparatory stage. All the most serious crimes against the personality of the state were brought within the competence of the Special Tribunal. Furthermore, the accused could not be granted bail, and proceedings could be reopened whenever there was fresh evidence.[20]

It is also important to recall that during 1925–26 Mussolini survived a number of assassination attempts unscathed, some of them (above all, Zamboni's attack) remaining shrouded in mystery.[21] The new Special Tribunal can also be understood as part of the government's response to these events, together with the new public security law. The latter (Law No 1848 of 6 November 1926) reorganised policing, with a view to eradicating all forms of opposition and subversion. The former, the Special Tribunal, was on the other hand an ad hoc creation designed to curb all political crimes against the state and the Fascist regime. Prevention and repression were two sides of the same coin.[22]

Alfredo Rocco, Minister of Justice between 1925 and 1932, was probably the most influential jurist and politician during the phase of the so-called Fascist revolution.[23] The rise of Fascism was revolutionary above all because it produced – according to Rocco – the transformation of the State, in that the Fascist State finally broke with the tradition of the weak, liberal democratic state. Indeed, for Rocco the years 1925 and 1926 'mark a decisive step towards the transformation of the State'.[24] Rocco was all too well aware of his major role as architect of the

---

[17] S Skinner, 'Tainted law? The Italian Penal Code, Fascism and Democracy' (2011) 7.4 *International Journal of Law in Context*, 429. See C Schwarzenberg, *Diritto e giustizia nell'Italia fascista* (Milan, Mursia, 1977) 88 ff.

[18] L Lacchè, 'Un code pénal pour l'Unité italienne: le code Zanardelli (1889). La genèse, le débat, le projet juridique' in R Levy and X Rousseaux (eds), *Le pénal dans tous ses états. Justice, Etats et Sociétés en Europe (XIIe–XXe siècles)* (Bruxelles, Publications de l'Université Saint-Louis, 1997) 303–19.

[19] Royal Decree of 12 December 1926, No 2062, Rules for the implementation of the Law of 25 November 1925, No 2008, Provisions for the Defence of the State. This decree was modified in 1928 with the introduction of additional rules about the public prosecutor's office.

[20] See C Longhitano, 'Il Tribunale di Mussolini: Storia del Tribunale Speciale 1926–1943' in *Quaderni dell'Associazione Nazionale Perseguitati Politici Italiani Antifascisti* (Rome, 1995) 75 ff; Tessitore, *Fascismo e pena di morte* 220–29, 303–08.

[21] See n 37 and n 38 below.

[22] Aquarone, *L'organizzazione* 95–101. See also W Eder, *Das italienische Tribunale Speciale per la Difesa dello Stato und der deutsche Volksgerichtshof* (Frankfurt am Main, Peter Lang, 2002) 65 ff.

[23] G Vassalli, 'Passione politica di un uomo di legge' in A Rocco, *Discorsi parlamentari* (Bologna, Il Mulino, 2005) 41 ff.

[24] A Rocco, *La trasformazione dello Stato. Dallo Stato Liberale allo Stato Fascista* (Rome, La Voce, 1927) 7. This volume, compiled by Rocco and entitled *The transformation of the State. From the Liberal State to the Fascist State*, brought together the speeches he had delivered in parliament and the reports he submitted as minister in support of the new legislation. See also E Gentile, 'Violenza e milizia nel

regime, because the machinery of justice (prevention and repression) was essential to this transformatory process. It was not, though, just a matter of changing legislation; it was equally important to affirm the constitutional relevance of the 'new' kind of justice.[25] The *Stato forte* (strong state)[26] had to be built as a new 'totalitarian' state. This was a programme that, in the history of Fascism, must be compared with reality.

In his report to the Chamber of Deputies, the Minister of Justice, Alfredo Rocco noted that legislation alone was inadequate to forestall crimes and to satisfy public opinion 'with a reasonable and severe punishment of the crimes committed'.[27] Public opinion, or the general public – Rocco said – wanted extraordinary measures. On 9 November 1926, an MP by the name of Manaresi, when presenting to the Chamber of Deputies the draft law Provisions for the Defence of the State, commented as follows: 'The regime, attacked in what it holds most sacred, defends itself.'[28] Consequently, during November 1926, Mussolini was able to achieve his *18 Brumaire*[29] and establish the Fascist regime on firm foundations.

Otto Kirchheimer wrote in his first essay, 'Politische Justiz', that:

> According to our Western concepts, the historical image is produced by public opinion in a collective process. Western political processes, which are more effective, but at the same time highly problematic, are of course fully aware of the power of public opinion.[30]

I hold this point to be germane to our understanding of the nature of political justice under the Fascist regime, with regard to at least two major elements, namely the question of the relationship with the theory and practice of the liberal state, and the nature of Fascism in its guise as a totalitarian regime.

There is no doubt of there being continuity between Fascism and the liberal state, at least so far as the latter's authoritarian aspect was concerned. As I have already pointed out, the liberal state had had its unequivocally authoritarian episodes and practices. The Fascist regime thus consolidated existing preventive and repressive techniques and tools. However, while the liberal political order has always recognised the dialectic between freedom and authority, the Fascist political order, especially after 1925–26, considered this dialectic to have been

---

fascismo alle origini del totalitarismo in Italia' in Gentile, Lanchester and Tarquini (eds), *Alfredo Rocco* 39.

[25] Vassalli, 'Passione politica' 49; G Simone, *Il Guardasigilli del regime. L'itinerario politico e culturale di Alfredo Rocco* (Milan, Angeli, 2012) 181.

[26] For further elements of Rocco's politico-legal programme see P Ungari, *Alfredo Rocco e l'ideologia giuridica del fascismo* (Brescia, Morcelliana, 1963); R D'Alfonso, *Costruire lo Stato forte. Politica, diritto, economia in Alfredo Rocco* (Milan, Angeli, 2004); S Battente, *Alfredo Rocco. Dal nazionalismo al fascismo, 1907–1935* (Milan, Angeli, 2005); F Lanchester, 'Alfredo Rocco e le origini dello Stato totale' in Gentile, Lanchester, Tarquini (eds), *Alfredo Rocco* 27.

[27] Parliamentary proceedings, Chamber of Deputies, Legislature XXVII, first session, discussions, 9th November 1926, vol VII, 6380.

[28] Ibid 6389.

[29] R De Felice, *Mussolini il fascista. L'organizzazione dello Stato fascista, 1925–1929* (Turin, Einaudi, 1995) 220–21.

[30] Kirchheimer, 'Politische Justiz' 169.

overcome. In the so-called 'ethical State' the individual is absorbed into a political body – that is to say, the state – which expresses the whole. Only compliance, or total subjection to the regime, is now possible.[31] Although this concept of the 'Totalitarian State' constitutes a very broad and complex semantic field,[32] the Fascist regime itself employed this expression, shaped in part by the science of public law. In 1923 the liberal Giorgio Amendola spoke first about the totalitarian spirit of Fascism and then in 1925 Mussolini said that the Italian nation had to be 'made Fascist' (*fascistizzata*). Some scholars emphasised the composite character of the Fascist State: dictatorial, authoritarian, but above all corporatist and with a number of totalitarian elements.[33] The Fascist State thus 'took advantage of all the elements of authoritarianism present in the existing state, [while also] introducing new elements such as Caesarism and totalitarianism'.[34]

Political Justice and the Political Nature of the Fascist Regime

The Fascist policies of prevention and repression were composite.[35] Between 1925 and 1926, 'Fascist legality' incorporated emergency into its ordinary way of working.[36] As noted above, the numerous failed attacks against Mussolini (1925–26) prompted the idea of a strategy of tension. The first attack occurred at the end of 1925 when a former MP of the Socialist Party, Tito Zaniboni, organised a conspiracy but was betrayed by one of his collaborators. 1926 marks the apogee of the attacks. On 7 April a 62-year-old Irish woman, Violet Gibson, fired a gun at Mussolini, slightly wounding him in the nose. On 11 September the anarchist Gino Lucetti threw a bomb at the *Duce*'s car. On 3 October, in Bologna, a man fired a revolver at Mussolini, who was once again unhurt. Anteo Zamboni, 15 years old and held responsible for this attack, was lynched by a group of Fascists. Violet Gibson was declared insane and deported. Zaniboni and Lucetti were sentenced to 30 years in prison. The final two of this sequence of attacks (those of Lucetti and Zamboni) offered a convenient pretext for enacting special laws for

---

[31] About the Fascist discourse on violence and repression see S Skinner, 'Violence in Fascist Criminal Law Discourse: War, Repression and Anti-Democracy' (2013) 26 *International Journal for the Semiotics of Law* 439–58.

[32] P Costa, 'Lo 'Stato totalitario': un campo semantico nella giuspubblicistica del fascismo' (1999) 28 *Quaderni fiorentini per la storia del pensiero giuridico moderno* 61–174.

[33] See generally S Cassese, *Lo Stato fascista* (Bologna, Il Mulino, 2010) 25–32.

[34] Ibid 29.

[35] See generally G Neppi Modona and M Pelissero, 'La politica criminale durante il fascismo' in L Violante (ed), *Storia d'Italia. Annali 12: La criminalità* (Turin, Einaudi, 1997) 757–847; M Sbriccoli, 'Le mani nella pasta e gli occhi al cielo. La penalistica italiana negli anni del fascismo' (1999) 28 *Quaderni fiorentini per la storia del pensiero giuridico moderno* 817 ff.

[36] See E Fraenkel, *The Dual State. A Contribution to the Theory of Dictatorship* (Oxford, Oxford University Press, 1941).

the defence of the State.[37] Thus the identification of Fascism (and its *Duce*, Mussolini) with the state gave rise to the Special Tribunal. Any threat to the life of Mussolini was already seen as being tantamount to a threat to the life of the state. The new King's two bodies[38] posed the problem of conserving and stabilising the new regime.

Fascism depicted the situation in a lurid light in order to justify unleashing a more violent strategy of repression against all categories of opponent, and the Special Tribunal was created to overcome the emergency. The use of military justice had been by no means unknown during the liberal period, even in peacetime, to combat political dissent. It was not by chance that Minister of Justice Alfredo Rocco, in his report to the Chamber of Deputies presenting the Provisions for the Defence of the State (9 November 1926), evoked the Pica Law of 1863, the liberal state's anti-brigand statute mentioned above. As in 1863, the new Fascist State needed to adopt necessary and urgent measures to combat the violent anti-Fascist reaction.[39] Rocco declared that the enemies of the regime, though politically defeated, persisted in their criminal activities against Mussolini. For this reason, more efficient repression necessitated the adoption of new measures in criminal law and the use of the death penalty.[40]

However, the establishment of a Special Tribunal – albeit, at the outset, for a fixed term of five years – reflected a changing idea of political justice. Indeed we must not overlook the fact that the Special Tribunal had a military character, although after 1928 a good number of prosecutors and investigating judges came from the ordinary judiciary. This structure may well have made the Tribunal more efficient, but that is a point requiring further analysis.

During the Fascist period some jurists considered that the new Special Tribunal was indeed a special court rather than an extraordinary court, and thus in accordance with the Albertine Statute (Article 71), which prohibited the establishment of extraordinary tribunals or commissions. In the Tribunal itself, Enea Noseda, the military advocate general, stated in its inaugural session that the Tribunal was special only as regards its competence and not as regards its subject.[41]

In 1931 the life of the Tribunal was prolonged for a further five years. Together with this five-year extension we can also observe two very important changes. First, the head of the Special Tribunal was no longer the minister of war, but rather the head of government, Mussolini, and it was he who directly appointed the judges. Moreover, the new Penal Code subsumed all crimes covered by the

[37] See M Franzinelli, 'Attentati al Duce' in S Luzzatto and V De Grazia (eds) *Dizionario del fascismo* (Turin, Einaudi, 2002) 1, 111–14.

[38] Regarding the attacks on Mussolini and the fate of his body see S Luzzatto, *The body of Il Duce: Mussolini's corpse and the fortunes of Italy* (New York, Metropolitan Books, 2005). On the attacks and the reintroduction of the death penalty see Tessitore, *Fascismo e pena di morte*, 93 ff.

[39] A Rocco, 'Legge sulla difesa dello Stato. Relazione' in *La trasformazione dello Stato* 101.

[40] A Rocco, 'Provvedimenti per la difesa dello Stato. Discorso al Senato' (20 November 1926) in *La trasformazione dello Stato* 122.

[41] 'La seduta inaugurale del Tribunale speciale per la difesa del Regime' in *Il Popolo d'Italia*, 2 February 1927, 2, quoted by L d'Alessandro, 'I dirigenti comunisti davanti al tribunale speciale' (2009) 2 *Studi storici* 485.

law of 1926. So in 1931 we find political crimes featuring in the ordinary penal code, and the Special Tribunal becomes the 'natural' judge of such crimes. This court had offered an opportunity to try out some policies with regard to crime that the new Rocco Penal Code of 1931 was then able to systematise, and to see how the instruments of repression might be coordinated. In 1931 the coming into force of the new Penal Code and the Code of Criminal Procedure entrenched the policies tested by the Special Tribunal. We could therefore say that the provisions surrounding the new Special Tribunal established in 1926 served to place the authoritarian criminal policy of Fascism on a firm footing. This change was also backed by the Grand Council of Fascism,[42] which was the main guarantor of the Fascist revolution.

In May 1931, during the parliamentary debate about the extension of the Special Tribunal for a further five years, an MP by the name of Caprino asked for it to be made permanent, on the grounds that only a judicial power that was essentially political could judge political crimes.[43] In 1934 the President of the Tribunal, Guido Cristini, proposed to Mussolini that the Special Tribunal be turned into the ordinary court for all the most serious crimes, political and common alike because, Cristini claimed, the assize courts were not efficient. The *Duce* did not accept the proposal[44] and the Special Tribunal was suppressed only after the fall of Fascism, on 29 July 1943.[45]

In 1935 the Special Tribunal was viewed as a 'revolutionary' and political court engaged in a fight against anti-Fascism. As one jurist observed, the court was supposed to have become 'an usual and permanent court of the regime'.[46] Fernando Verna argued that the court had lost its attributes of being a 'special' and 'temporary' court, to become simply the Tribunal for the Defence of the State, the only tribunal dedicated to combating opposition and political crimes in a centralised manner. In that same year Silvio Longhi[47] spoke about a *permanent* Special Tribunal, although in a formal sense the court owed its continuing existence to a series of five-yearly extensions.

The court passed nine death sentences in peacetime. If we compare the Fascist Tribunal with other courts, such as the Nazi *Volksgerichtshof,* which in total condemned about 5200 persons to death, we must acknowledge that it was not unduly sanguinary. Out of around 5600 defendants before the Special Tribunal, some 4600 were given prison sentences, serving on average five years in jail. Of course, the Special Tribunal was only one element in the Fascist strategy of combating

---

[42] The *Gran Consiglio del Fascismo* was the supreme body of the Fascist regime. Created in 1923 as the de facto 'Chamber of Deputies' of the new political regime, consisting of the main representatives of Fascism, it was constitutionalised by Law No 2693, of 9 December 1928.

[43] Parliamentary proceedings, Chamber of Deputies, Legislature XXVIII, first session, discussions, 20 May 1931, 4809 ff. About this debate see Tessitore, *Fascismo e pena di morte* 309–16.

[44] Aquarone, *L'organizzazione* 102–03.

[45] Although it was reintroduced by the RSI (*Repubblica Sociale Italiana*) regime until April 1945 in the territories occupied by the German Army in the North of Italy.

[46] See F Verna, 'Difendere lo Stato' (1935) VI *Rivista Penale* 459.

[47] S Longhi, 'Tribunale speciale permanente' (1935) VI *Rivista Penale* 817–19.

and eradicating political dissent, in Italy and elsewhere, directed above all against the so-called '*fuorusciti*'.[48] The use of violence was systematically directed from the beginning against opponents of the regime. The creation of a strong and efficient network of secret police, the so-called OVRA,[49] served to bolster the Fascist regime as a totalitarian regime. After 1925–26 the anti-Fascists became in a formal sense enemies of the Italian nation, who could thus be deprived of Italian citizenship. Exiles and expatriates for political reasons were no longer Italians. Fascist criminal policy also broke with the liberal tradition of attributing a patent of nobility to political crime, according to the principle of *favor rei*.

The establishment of the Special Tribunal might be taken to imply that the regime did not control the judicial power.[50] In reality, Fascism had followed in the footsteps of the liberal state, being able to 'refine' an existing model whereby the executive power held sway over the judiciary. 'Purges', discipline, stronger hierarchisation, and carefully weighed professional 'advancements' paved the way to the Fascistisation of the judiciary, above all after Alfredo Rocco had become Minister of Justice. The regime may well have had its doubts about some judges, but it had the necessary instruments to supervise and control the judicial power. Addressing the Chamber of Deputies, the Minister of Justice, Alfredo Rocco could recall in 1929 the strong presence of the spirit of Fascism within the judiciary.[51]

---

[48] '*Fuorusciti*' (exiles) generally designates those who emigrated from Italy during the Fascist period for political reasons. From the legal point of view, exiles were those who had forfeited, according to the Law of January 1926, Italian citizenship (being 'bad Italians') and suffered the confiscation of their property. Article 274 of the 1930 Criminal Code introduced the offence of anti-national activities, as perpetrated by citizens abroad. See F Colao, '"Hanno perduto il diritto di essere ancora considerati figli d'Italia". I "fuorusciti" nel Novecento' (2009) 38 *Quaderni fiorentini per la storia del pensiero giuridico moderno* 653–99.

[49] OVRA was probably an acronym for *Organizzazione Vigilanza Repressione Anti-Fascismo* ('Organisation for Vigilance and the Repression of Anti-Fascism'), but this is not sure. See M Canali, 'Crime and Repression', in RJB Bosworth (ed), *The Oxford Handbook of Fascism* (Oxford, Oxford University Press, 2010) 221–38. See also Aquarone, *L'organizzazione* 105–10; P Carucci, 'L'organizzazione dei servizi di polizia dopo l'approvazione del testo unico delle Leggi di pubblica sicurezza nel 1926' (1976) 1 *Rassegna degli Archivi di Stato* 82–114; F Fucci, *Le polizie di Mussolini. La repressione dell'antifascismo nel 'Ventennio'* (Milan, Mursia, 1985); G Tosatti, 'La repressione del dissenso politico tra l'età liberale e il fascismo. L'organizzazione della polizia' (1997) 1 *Studi storici* 232 ff; M Franzinelli, *I tentacoli dell'OVRA. Agenti, collaboratori e vittime della polizia politica fascista* (Turin, Bollati Boringhieri, 2000); M Giannetto, '"Conoscenza e controllo": la faticosa elaborazione dell'istituto di polizia politica' (2002) 1 *Giornale di storia contemporanea* 50 ff; L Verdolini, *La trama segreta. Il caso Sandri fra terrorismo e polizia politica fascista* (Turin, Einaudi, 2003); M Canali, *Le spie del regime* (Bologna, Il Mulino, 2004).

[50] Especially in some showcase trials against opponents of the regime: D Zucàro (ed), *Il processone* (Rome, Editori Riuniti, 1961) 13 ff.

[51] See the works of G Neppi Modona: 'La magistratura e il fascismo' in G Quazza (ed), *Fascismo e società italiana* (Turin, Einaudi, 1973), 143 ff; 'Diritto e giustizia penale nel periodo fascista' in L Lacchè, C Latini, P Marchetti and M Meccarelli (eds), *Penale Giustizia Potere. Metodi, Ricerche, Storiografie. Per ricordare Mario Sbriccoli* (Macerata, Edizioni Università di Macerata, 2007) 373–78; 'Principio di legalità e giustizia penale nel periodo fascista' (2007) 36 *Quaderni fiorentini per la storia del pensiero giuridico moderno* 983–1005. For a recent framework see L Klinkhammer, 'Was there a Fascist Revolution? The Function of Penal Law in Fascist Italy and in Nazi Germany' (2010) 15.3 *Journal of Modern Italian Studies* 391–93; A Meniconi, *Storia della magistratura italiana* (Bologna, Il Mulino, 2012) 145 ff.

Can the Special Tribunal be Seen as a Constitutional Instance of Fascist Political Justice?

The establishment of the Special Tribunal in 1926, composed of military personnel and above all members of the Fascist militia, suggests other explanations. The regime sought to respond immediately to the attacks on Mussolini, creating a military tribunal with an avowedly political purpose. As we have seen, the regime could call upon other policies of repression apart from the Special Tribunal. The procedure of the Special Tribunal was *ad modum belli*. The judges followed the provisions of the Military Penal Code in time of war. Article 441 gave the President immense powers; during trials, he could do whatever was necessary to discover the truth. The procedure was cursory and sharply curtailed the rights of the defence counsel. Yet in 1944, after the fall of Fascism, a commentator such as Mario Berlinguer, while acknowledging the repressive and sectarian nature of the Special Tribunal, conceded that there had been certain elements of 'moderation'.[52]

The liberal order based on the rule of law had to use a composite strategy to affirm a system of political justice. Lutz Klinkhammer has said of the Special Tribunal that 'in effect, it was a showcase that was used for the conviction of defendants or deeds interpreted as particularly dangerous and/or important in order to scare the public and deter imitation'.[53] It is true that this Tribunal became an important 'hub' for the Fascist strategies of repression. The investigating judges (*giudice istruttore* or *commissione istruttoria*) of the Special Tribunal were empowered to divert many cases to the ordinary tribunals, or to acquit certain defendants. We are concerned here with a court that was allowed to 'rationalise' and grade repression, in line with the regime's general orientation. In this sense, the Tribunal was not only a 'showcase' but also a sort of 'control room' of the Fascist police and judicial power. It was the summit of the repressive pyramid, and as such it altered the entire repressive system. Important though it was to repress anti-Fascism, ultimately only one-third of those denounced appeared before the court. Of these 5619 defendants, 80 per cent (4596) were sentenced,[54] but this was only a part of the repressive machinery at the regime's disposal. We must not forget that over 12,000 people were subjected to 'confinement by the police' (*confino di polizia*), the 'silent weapon' of the regime, an administrative measure subtracted from the penal law regulations.[55] This intimidating measure, together

---

[52] M Berlinguer, *La crisi della giustizia nel regime fascista* (Roma, Migliaresi, 1944) 11.

[53] Klinkhammer, 'Was there a Fascist Revolution?' 395.

[54] G De Luna, 'Tribunale speciale per la difesa dello stato' in S Luzzatto and V De Grazia (eds) *Dizionario del fascismo*, 2, 738–41.

[55] See A Dal Pont and S Carolini (eds), *L'Italia al confino. Le ordinanze di assegnazione al confino emesse dalle Commissioni provinciali dal novembre 1926 al luglio 1943* vol IV (Milan, La Pietra, 1983); D Petrini, *La prevenzione inutile. Illegittimità delle misure praeter delictum* (Napoli, Jovene, 1996); P Carucci, 'Confino, soggiorno obbligato, internamento, sviluppo della normativa' in C Di Sante (ed),

with official warnings from the police (*ammonizione*) and special surveillance (*sorveglianza speciale*), applied to 160,000 persons and constituted the everyday implementation of Fascist policy. So, the Special Tribunal is important above all as a *space* in which the regime and its armed wing – the political police[56] – implemented flexible strategies depending on various elements: the dangerousness and quality of the opposition, its ideological nature, and its international echoes.

Important though the numbers are, they do not tell the whole story. In 1925–26 the regime sought not only to repress its opponents but also to change itself. The most obvious response to the attacks against Mussolini was the Special Tribunal. Yet this same Tribunal was also a strategic tool, serving to highlight the *political* nature of the regime, its *revolutionary* nature.[57] I would venture to say that the Special Tribunal had a pronounced *constitutional relevance*. Granting the importance of its actual function, namely, combating and stifling dissent, equal weight should be given to its 'symbolic' aspect. Using legal procedures for political purposes is to found an idea whereby justice (and its opposite, injustice) is part and parcel of a strategy of representation.

After 1925, the regime was not afraid to assert and to display its political nature. Where justice is concerned, there is a huge difference between a liberal state and an authoritarian state with totalitarian tendencies. The liberal state lives the paradox of freedom; its judicial space is based on publicity, orality, cross-examination. In Italy, the assize court was used particularly to try crimes of a political nature, beginning with offences relating to the press. A public hearing in an assize court would involve a jury which, in continental Europe, was introduced as a constitutional body in response to distrust of the judiciary.[58] In a case involving a political crime, this kind of trial might become a sort of 'boomerang' whereby the state uses the trial to repress some political ideas but the trial (public and by jury) becomes a good occasion to attack the state. The jury might favour the defendant, or the defence might play an important role in the public hearing. A trial held with a view to stifling political dissent (for example, the social movements, socialists, anarchists)[59] could become a kind of political theatre, one that threatens to

---

I campi di concentramento in Italia: dall'internamento alla deportazione 1940–1945 (Milan, F. Angeli, 2001) 5–20; Klinkhammer, 'Was there a Fascist Revolution?' 399–402; and especially the recent work of C Poesio, *Il confino fascista. L'arma silenziosa del regime* (Rome-Bari, Laterza, 2011).

[56] Verdolini, *La trama segreta* 308–09.

[57] PA Cavaliere, *Il diritto penale politico in Italia dallo Stato liberale allo Stato totalitario. Storia delle ideologie penalistiche tra istituzioni e interpretazioni* (Rome, Aracne, 2008) 438.

[58] L Lacchè, 'Un luogo "costituzionale" dell'identità giudiziaria nazionale: La Corte d'assise e l'opinione pubblica (1859–1913)' in F Colao, L Lacchè and C Storti (eds), *Processo penale e opinione pubblica in Italia tra Otto e Novecento* (Bologna, Il Mulino, 2008) 77–120.

[59] M Sbriccoli, 'Il diritto penale sociale, 1883–1912' (1974–75) 3–4 *Quaderni fiorentini per la storia del pensiero giuridico moderno* 587–94. See also M Sbriccoli, 'Dissenso politico e diritto penale in Italia tra Otto e Novecento. Il problema dei reati politici dal Programma di Carrara al Trattato di Manzini' (1973) 2 *Quaderni fiorentini per la storia del pensiero giuridico moderno* 617; F Colao, *Il delitto politico tra Ottocento e Novecento. Da «delitto fittizio» a «nemico dello Stato* (Milan, Giuffrè, 1986); Cavaliere, *Il diritto penale politico*. For a European outlook, compare K Härter and B de Graaf (eds), *Vom Majestätsverbrechen zum Terrorismus. Politische Kriminalität, Recht, Justiz und Polizei zwischen Früher Neuzeit und 20. Jahrhundert* (Frankfurt am Main, Klostermann, 2012).

overturn the liberal order. In some cases, recourse to the assize court might be dangerous.

Governments in liberal states cannot predict with any certainty the outcome of trials for political crimes for, generally speaking, they are unable to control the actors (judges, juries, lawyers, public opinion). For this reason, in some cases the strategy was to change the kind of judicial space. Governments might strive to 'eliminate' political dissent, but they cannot deprive other groups of legal procedures, by means of which they can influence public opinion.[60] During the period of the liberal state, the strategy in Italy went in two main directions. First, it could prove useful to evade the assize court, namely, trial by jury. How? By resorting in some cases to so-called *correzionalizzazione,* or 'correctionalism'. This 'mechanism' allowed the prosecution (*Sezione d'accusa*), at the end of the investigation period, to declassify the crime indicted. In this case another court became juridically competent: the correctional court (*tribunale correzionale*), sitting without the assistance of a jury.[61] The logic is: better a milder conviction than to risk acquittal in the assize court. The second, more important, strategy was to establish a 'state of emergency'. A declaration of the state of siege has the great advantage of dealing swiftly with emergency, using the tools and techniques of military justice.

In Germany the Nazis established the People's Court after the trial of the alleged perpetrators of the *Reichstag* fire.[62] This trial, staged in Leipzig, was a 'breaking trial':[63] the defendant, Dimitrov, a Bulgarian communist accused of having burnt down the Parliament building, showed how ridiculous the charges were. It was evident that the fire was the result of a Nazi plot. There was no option but to acquit Dimitrov.

A totalitarian order, even when it is based on due legal process, is not afraid to display the logic of absolute power. In this context, the new state uses trials managed by a permanent special tribunal to justify the elimination of the actual or symbolic enemy. An absolute power can easily eliminate its enemies by administrative means, but it needs to build a link between the regime and the masses. The purpose of these trials is to promote alternative truths about actions that are more or less dangerous. Propaganda in the guise of political justice seeks to show which and how many dangers may threaten the embattled state. The sentence is important but it is the trial in itself that serves as a special ritual, as we can see in the case of the Stalinist show trials in Central and Eastern Europe,[64] before and after the Second World War, and in the Nazi trials.

---

[60] Kirchheimer, *Political Justice* 14–15.

[61] Lacchè, *Un luogo «costituzionale»* 83 ff.

[62] Eder, *Das italienische Tribunale* 85 ff.

[63] According to J Vergès, *De la stratégie judiciaire* (Paris, Les Editions de Minuit, 1968), a 'breaking trial' is basically one that refutes and ridicules the system of justice.

[64] About the Stalinist trials, see HJ Berman, *Justice in Russia: An Interpretation of Soviet Law* (Cambridge MA, Harvard University Press, 1950); Kirchheimer, *Political Justice;* R Conquest, *The Great Terror: Stalin's Purge of the Thirties* (London, Macmillan, 1968); A Kriegel, *Les grands procès dans les systèmes communistes. La pédagogie infernale* (Paris, Gallimard, 1972); GH Hodos, *Show Trials: Stalinist Purges in Eastern Europe, 1948–1954* (New York-London, Praeger, 1987); M Flores, *L'età del sospetto. I processi politici della guerra fredda* (Bologna, Il Mulino, 1995).

The new Special Tribunal sent an important message. It was a pillar of the 'totalitarian experiment':

> The objective was to establish monopolist control over all forms of political power. Once that had been achieved by legal and illegal means, the aim was to destroy or radically transform the existing political system in order to create a new state organized around a single political party, flanked by the apparatus of a police state, and by the systematic use of terror to prevent or repress all forms of opposition and dissent.[65]

In 1939 Giuseppe Maggiore would point out that 'the ultimate meaning of the totalitarian state is the totality of *politics*'.[66] Whatever defines itself as 'totalitarian' needs to perform a role. It is not an oxymoron to say that enemies have rights. The 'anti-Fascists' – insofar as they were construed as enemies of Italy – were the consequence of a political construction. Justice as political action is a very important space within which to affirm a regime's truth. Unlike the liberal state, the New Order could tackle and neutralise its enemies not only through forms of extraordinary justice, but also by affirming a special justice that could use old tools to establish a new political context. The Special Tribunal likewise asserted the primacy of politics in the domain of justice. The attacks against Mussolini called for more brutal repression. As a result, the regime took complete control of the Court: a 'totalitarian' tool that it could mould to its own purposes and which used a number of different strategies.

By way of comparison, we can observe the rapidity with which Germany under Hitler changed its policies regarding law and justice.[67] Whereas Italian Fascism modified the state constitution over a period of years, Nazism lost no time in deciding which strategies to adopt. The Emergency Law (*Ermächtigungsgesetz*) thus established in March 1933 a constitutional 'tool' that would serve as a wedge in order to 'deconstruct' the *Rechtsstaat*. Likewise, the People's Court (*Volksgerichtshof*) was established in April 1934 after Adolf Hitler had been dissatisfied with the outcome of the Reichstag fire trial. According to Piero Calamandrei, Nazism and Fascism both attacked the rule of law, but whereas the Nazis openly destroyed legality, the Italian Fascists set out to falsify it.[68] The difference lay in the relative intensity and scope of the action taken.

---

[65] E Gentile, 'Fascism in power: the totalitarian experiment' in A Littelton (ed), *Liberal and Fascist Italy* (Oxford, Oxford University Press, 2000) 139–74. For a critical appraisal see RJB Bosworth, *The Italian Dictatorship. Problems and Perspectives in the Interpretation of Mussolini and Fascism* (London, Arnold, 1998) 9–10.

[66] 'Per concludere, diremo che il senso ultimo dello Stato totalitario è la totalitarietà della *politica*': G Maggiore, 'Diritto penale totalitario nello Stato totalitario' (1939) 11 *Rivista italiana di diritto penale* 140–61, then in Schwarzenberg, *Diritto e giustizia nell'Italia fascista* 279.

[67] L Lacchè, *Due lezioni (per il presente)*, Foreword to T Vormbaum, *Diritto e nazionalsocialismo. Due lezioni* (Macerata, Edizioni Università di Macerata, 2013) 8–10. Compare AJ de Grand, *Fascist Italy and Nazi Germany. The 'Fascist' Style of Rule* (London, Routledge, 1995).

[68] P Calamandrei, 'La crisi della legalità' (1944) in P Calamandrei, *Costituzione e leggi di Antigone. Scritti e discorsi politici* (Florence, La Nuova Italia, 1996) 6–7.

In a recent study that also includes unpublished documents on prosecutions[69] against communist leaders before the Special Tribunal (the so-called *Processone*, or 'Big Trial'), Leonardo D'Alessandro reconstructed the strategies adopted by the repressive apparatus.[70] The preliminary investigation and police documentation show how the objective was increasingly becoming that of 'formulating' accusations against the communists, specifically their leaders. Charges for crimes of conspiracy and incitement to hatred between social classes (Articles 134 and 247 of the Zanardelli Penal Code) culminated, after three successive arrest warrants, in the most serious of charges – following the terrible bomb attack on 12 April 1928 at the Milan Exhibition Centre (the case remains unsolved) – of seditious association (Article 251) and incitement to civil war and devastation, pillaging and massacre (Article 252). The strategy here was to tighten up the repressive dimension, and as a consequence the subsequent terms of imprisonment.

Yet the evidence still had to be identified, collected and sifted. During the course of the investigations, the powerful chief of police, Arturo Bocchini, had expressed his doubts as to the possibility of bringing the trial before the new Special Tribunal on facts or conjecture dating back to November 1926, at which date the regime had proclaimed the dissolution of parties and political associations. Before then the Communist Party had operated under a regime of formal legality, and later too it remained difficult to establish juridically the threshold of illegality.[71] Even the investigating judge, Enrico Macis, during meetings with the communist leaders, Umberto Terracini and Antonio Gramsci, had expressed his perplexity with regard to tightening up criminal procedures. The two leaders then used Macis's 'revelations' in the course of their trial. Terracini intervened several times during the preliminary investigation of 1927, protesting at the lack of evidence, at the use of materials obtained using dubious procedures, and at the presence of many anomalies. On 16 July 1927 the preliminary investigation was declared formally closed. From this moment onwards, in view of the impending trial, international mobilisation in support of the accused began. Public Prosecutor Giuseppe Ciardi proposed that the preliminary investigations be split, thereby creating two different trials, one of the founding members of the party, and the other of its principal leaders. Everything, however, centred around the issue of consistent evidence. In order to sustain the crime of conspiracy against the state authorities, the prosecutors made the most of newspaper material and police reports in particular. The accused responded with various petitions.[72]

---

[69] For trials before the Special Tribunal see Zucàro, *Il processone*; A Dal Pont, A Leonetti, P Maiello and L Zocchi, *Aula IV. Tutti i processi del Tribunale speciale fascista* (Rome, Associazione Nazionale Perseguitati Politici Italiani Antifascisti, 1962); A Dal Pont and S Carolini (eds), *L'Italia dissidente e antifascista. Le Ordinanze, le Sentenze istruttorie e le Sentenze in Camera di consiglio emesse dal Tribunale speciale fascista contro gli imputati di antifascismo dall'anno 1927 al 1943* vol II (Milan, La Pietra, 1980). The army history office of the Ministry of Defence has also published the decisions issued by the Special Tribunal 1927–43 in 19 volumes (Rome, Ufficio storico, Stato maggiore dell'esercito, 1980–99).

[70] D'Alessandro, 'I dirigenti comunisti davanti al tribunale speciale'.

[71] Bocchini's words are recounted in D'Alessandro, ibid 551.

[72] Zucàro, *Il processone* 131–46.

The trial of Terracini and the others, which began on 28 May 1928, was one of the major trials held in the *Aula IV* (Hall 4 of the Special Tribunal). In this kind of trial, publicity was guaranteed, since a number of family members of the accused were present, as were correspondents from the *Manchester Guardian*, the *Petit Parisien* and the Soviet news agency *Tass*.[73] The stages of the trial were recorded in an extremely concise manner, and yet the testimonies of the lawyers, collected immediately by the Communist Party, reflect the threatening and intimidating atmosphere created by the judges and the prosecution. A judge is purported to have said to the lawyer Nicolai after his statement for the defence: 'You, Sir, are right, but you have forgotten one thing: that we are a political tribunal.'[74]

Terracini intervened several times during the trial to dispute the statements recorded by police officers making the accusations. Of particular importance, however, was the speech[75] made by Terracini himself in his own defence, as 'spokesperson' of the accused, in which he denounced the radically political nature of the trial and the covert government involvement in all that the Tribunal did: 'Because the Government willed it so and the judges obeyed'.[76] Terracini criticised the lack of evidence and the improper manner in which it had been obtained, calling the trial a 'sham'. Yet the communist leader also wanted to respond politically:

> Your Honour; I ask at least to be permitted, as we reach the end of this trial, a trial which originates and finds its reason for being exclusively in causes and necessities [dictated by] a political agenda, I ask to be permitted, even if only for a moment, to do what has for six days been forbidden: to speak politically![77]

Terracini observed that the strategy of the Communist Party was not violent, that the attempts made on the *Duce's* life were the fruit of individual actions of subjects who, as had been demonstrated, had nothing whatsoever to do with the party.

> Oh, here then is the powerful State, the defended State, the totalitarian State, the extremely heavily-armed State! This State feels that its solidity is under threat, and more, its security, simply because before it there rises up this small Party, despised, harried and persecuted, which has seen the best of its militants killed or imprisoned, forced to go into hiding in order to salvage its ties with the working masses for whom and with whom it lives and fights.[78]

Terracini had also said a little earlier:

> We need to gather as many elements as we can to expose the impudence of the Trib[unal]. We have not yet set out our strategy for the trial; I think we should seek to

---

[73] D'Alessandro, 'I dirigenti comunisti davanti al tribunale speciale' 536. See G Fiori, *Vita di Antonio Gramsci* (Bari, Laterza, 1981) 266–70.
[74] Quoted by D'Alessandro, ibid 536.
[75] Published in its entirety in D'Alessandro, ibid 545–51.
[76] D'Alessandro, ibid 546.
[77] D'Alessandro, ibid 549.
[78] D'Alessandro, ibid 550.

sabotage the mask of legality as deeply as possible, refusing to respond unless they charge us with concrete crimes.[79]

In the end, the accused received some of the harshest sentences (from 20 to 22 years' imprisonment) – aside from the death penalty – imposed by the Special Tribunal in its 17 years of activity. In the guise of some of its historic leaders this trial convicted the Italian Communist Party – the most organised underground opposition – and initiated the progressive dismantling of its apparatus. Yet the complex story relating to the possible (and from 1927 on, frequently mooted) release of Gramsci and Terracini, in exchange for some Catholic priests held in the Soviet Union (even if they at the same time thought, mistakenly as it proved, they were facing the death penalty) reveals the international aspects of the case. This also explains why Mussolini followed so closely the stages of the preliminary investigation, and later the trial. The reasons for his interest related to domestic politics but also to diplomatic relations with the Soviet regime. The important politico-judicial role of the investigating judge Macis – an emissary of Mussolini – should be viewed in this light.[80]

Adopting the terminology used by Jacques Vergès, I would argue that this kind of trial cannot be viewed as a 'breaking trial',[81] because it was impossible in such a context to exert any influence upon public opinion. The defendants were wholly at the mercy of the regime and the trial simply branded them as defeated. The court could thus reaffirm, by manipulating police investigations, judicial evidence and finally the defendants themselves, that the trial was 'fair'; it could try to combine legality and a 'sense of justice'. In this case, the judgment was written in advance and the most important thing was the process of legitimation:

> Neverthless, political justice without risks remains a contradiction in terms. It is the totalitarian corollary of the figment of total political security. Just as the latter manages to produce only a languishing political establishment, the political trial with predetermined results misses a pre-eminent goal; the images it creates are worth neither more nor less than the authority that ordered them. In this sense the trial planned with a view toward establishing a priority program becomes just another avenue to communicate to the population at large the official message.[82]

Indeed, Fascism was not wholly successful in its bid to depict the communist leaders under trial as deluded fanatics. The defendants in some cases made trouble for the 'official' witnesses by quizzing them about evidence that was patently false.[83] At the same time, the trial of the communists became for the victims a way of 'talking' to a particular part of 'public opinion' formed by the clandestine struc-

---

[79] D'Alessandro, ibid 504.

[80] D'Alessandro, ibid and G Vacca, *Vita e pensieri di Antonio Gramsci 1926–1937* (Turin, Einaudi, 2012) 63–74, 93. This reconstruction, as demonstrated by D'Alessandro and Vacca, sheds a partially new light on Ruggero Grieco's famous letters to communist leaders in prison. About this aspect see also L Canfora, *Gramsci in carcere e il fascismo* (Rome, Salerno, 2012) 50–55.

[81] Vergès, *De la stratégie judiciaire*.

[82] Kirchheimer, *Political Justice* 426.

[83] Zucàro, *Il processone* XIII.

ture of the Communist Party in Italy and abroad, and likewise to the international solidarity movements. However, the final indictment (Terracini's *J'accuse*) was also a speech for the future, a rallying cry that might echo down the ages.

This kind of justice is admittedly 'political justice'. Political justice is a form of contradictory relationship between politics and justice, especially in periods of transition. The Special Tribunal for the Defence of the State was the special frame that Fascism established in order to legitimate its politics, though without a total break from the criminal policy of the liberal state. Devised as a temporary expedient, this court became an institution of Fascism affirming a New Order in which justice was to be permanently political. The Special Tribunal presents us with the image of a narrative and symbolic level of political justice. Such a tribunal had an important role to play in the strategy of repression of the Fascist State, and yet it is probably equally important to grasp what it was that Fascism sought to communicate. The symbolic value of the Special Tribunal is a topic meriting closer scrutiny. Future research will no doubt rest upon a better understanding of the complex political anthropology informing the Fascist regime's use of justice as repression.[84]

---

[84] About this methodological perspective, see L Lacchè, *'Richtet nicht!'. Anthropologie der Justiz und Formen der öffentlichen Meinung im 19. und 20. Jahrhundert* (Berlin, Lit Verlag, 2012).

2

The Positivist School of Criminology and Italian Fascist Criminal Law: a Squandered Legacy?

EMILIA MUSUMECI*

Cesare Lombroso: a Dangerous Method?

The Positivist School of criminology was officially established in 1876,[1] with Cesare Lombroso's publication of *Criminal Man* (*L'Uomo Delinquente*) in Italy. Although Lombroso is recognised as 'the father of criminology',[2] over the course of the last century he has been accused of a number of misdeeds. It suffices to recall the judgement expressed at the end of the 1970s by historian George Mosse, who mentioned Lombroso's born-criminal theory as the inspiration behind the Final Solution,[3] notwithstanding Lombroso's Jewish heritage. A few years later, American palaeontologist Stephen Jay Gould blamed Lombroso for his pseudo-scientific theories, inception of racism and biological determinism.[4] Both judgements were 'without appeal', characterising Lombroso as a veritable icon of evil or biological racism. Moreover, according to established opinion, the Positivist School, founded by Lombroso and later headed by his pupils Enrico Ferri, Raffaele Garofalo and Eugenio Florian, was distinguished for its illiberal, or in some cases, racist, traits that had distinctly influenced the authoritarian turn of Fascist criminal law and, in particular, the 1930 Rocco Penal Code.

---

* All translations from Italian are my own with assistance from the editor.

[1] See generally FT Cullen and PK Wilcox (eds), *Encyclopedia of Criminological Theory* vol I (Thousand Oaks CA, Sage, 2010) 476 and F Colao, 'Le scuole penalistiche', supp VIII *Enciclopedia Italiana Treccani* (Rome, Istituto della Enciclopedia Italiana, 2012) 349–56.

[2] On the scientific and cultural biography of Lombroso see D Frigessi, *Cesare Lombroso* (Turin, Einaudi, 2003); S Montaldo, *Cesare Lombroso. Gli scienziati e la nuova Italia* (Bologna, Il Mulino, 2011) and, more recently, P Knepper and PJ Ystehede (eds), *Cesare Lombroso Handbook* (London, Routledge, 2013) and P Marchetti, 'Cesare Lombroso', supp VIII *Enciclopedia Italiana Treccani* ibid 366–70.

[3] GL Mosse, *Toward the Final Solution. A History of European Racism* (New York, Howard Ferting, 1978).

[4] SJ Gould, *The Mismeasure of Man* (New York, Norton, 1981).

This belief was masterfully expressed by Luigi Ferrajoli, the well-known Italian theorist of a 'minimal criminal law', who did not hesitate to define Lombroso's thesis as a degeneration of Darwinism 'in a moralistic and racist way',[5] accusing the Positivist School of introducing the 'security measures' (or supplementary detention provisions) of the Italian legal system. In particular, he defined positivist thought as an 'ambiguous substantialist doctrine, masked by a humanitarian progressivism, enacted by the Fascist legislator, which has translated it into a doubly oppressive penal system, completely disconnected from the principle of rule of law and its corollaries'.[6]

Despite specifying the untenability of the position that considers authoritarian instances of the Rocco Code merely as a 'legacy of positivism', even the late legal historian Mario Sbriccoli claimed that the philosophical background of positivism, from which Fascism had drawn, was clearly imbued with 'illiberal and authoritarian statism'.[7] But did all authoritarian traits of Fascist legislation derive from Lombroso's theories? To answer this question, it is necessary to analyse the legacy of the Positivist School of criminology in Italian Fascist criminal law, in order to understand whether and how there was continuity or discontinuity between positivist legal doctrine and Fascist legal theory.

For this purpose, this chapter will first investigate the authentic aim of Lombroso and his School, which, through a direct study of criminal man and his world, tried to deconstruct criminal law entirely, leading to an individualised system of punishment inspired by the biological and socio-psychological characteristics of the offender. Second, the present study will analyse the debate in the field of criminal law that developed following the publication of *Criminal Man* in Italy, involving Positivist and Classical Schools of criminology in the definition of one of the key issues of criminal law: free will as the legal and philosophical foundation of criminal responsibility. This debate, which reached unprecedented peaks of acrimony, was the basis of the preparatory work for the Rocco Code adopted in 1930, which aimed to overcome the irreconcilable positions supported by the two schools in order to 'build' a new law for a new regime. In addition to the 'free will battle', a necessary antecedent of the Rocco Code was the codification project undertaken by Enrico Ferri, one of the foremost figures, and more or less loyal follower, of the Positivist School. An evaluation of this project will be useful in order to understand its elements of novelty or continuity in relation to the Rocco Code and, more generally, with respect to the Positivist School's teaching.

Finally, once the basic values of the Positivist School are understood, both as originally expressed by Lombroso and as developed, more or less faithfully, by Ferri, the middle and end of the chapter will focus on a detailed analysis of the pivotal points of the Rocco Code in its original formulation, examining on the

---

[5] L Ferrajoli, *Diritto e ragione*, 9th edn (Rome-Bari, Laterza, 2008) 543.
[6] Ibid 812.
[7] M Sbriccoli, 'Le mani nella pasta e gli occhi al cielo. La penalistica italiana negli anni del fascismo', in M Sbriccoli (ed), *Storia del diritto penale e della giustizia. Scritti editi e inediti 1972–2007* vol 2 (Milan, Giuffrè, 2009) 1015.

one hand the 'General Part' of the Code, which is dedicated to the common principles of the theory of crime, punishment and the offender, and on the other hand the 'Special Part', dedicated to individual offences. This analysis is undertaken with the aim of investigating not only whether the Rocco Code was a champion of the fundamental values of 'Fascist ideology',[8] but also whether its authoritarian principles were derived from the Positivist School's precepts, and whether the principle of the rule of law was a real or only an illusory brake against a more authoritarian turn in the Fascist penal system. Answering these questions means not only understanding whether the Rocco Code constitutes a breakage or a continuity of the Italian legal-historical paradigm, but also comprehending the reasons behind the enduring existence of a Code raised under a dictatorship (with the exception of the interventions and changes since 1948), in a democracy based on the constitutional guarantees of the rights and freedoms of citizens.

A Multifaceted 'Criminal Man'

Rethinking studies already conducted in the areas of craniology and phrenology, and strongly influenced by scientific positivism, Lombroso decided to investigate the phenomenon of deviance by analysing it through an experimental method that accepted as fact only what could be rigorously established, measured and catalogued by scientific means.[9] Lombroso believed in a 'religion of the facts', which attempted to certify scientific differences not only between criminals and 'normal' people,[10] but also between different types of criminal.[11] Believing that physical monstrosity[12] must also reflect moral monstrosity, he embarked on an intensive search through the bodies and faces of prisoners and the mentally incapacitated, in order to find the stigmata of deviance – the unmistakeable, irrefutable evidence that a criminal is predetermined to commit evil acts because he is biologically different from any other human being.

---

[8] The question of whether or not Fascism had a peculiar ideology has been the object of much debate among scholars. In many cases, the existence of an out-and-out 'Fascist ideology' is contested, viewing Fascism as only a 'practical phenomenon'; on the other hand, it is argued that Fascism did have its own ideology, characterised by its own myths (like for example that of 'romanity'). On this topic see S Luzzatto, 'The Political Culture of Fascist Italy' (1999) II *Contemporary European History* 322; E Gentile, *Fascismo. Storia e interpretazione* (Rome-Bari, Laterza, 2002) 78; and more recently A Tarquini, *Storia della cultura fascista* (Bologna, Il Mulino, 2011) 105–09.

[9] On the relationship between medicine and criminology in the late nineteenth and early twentieth centuries, see especially P Becker and RF Wetzell (eds), *Criminals and Their Scientists. The History of Criminology in International Perspective* (New York, Cambridge University Press, 2006).

[10] C Lombroso, *L'uomo delinquente in rapporto all'antropologia, giurisprudenza e alle discipline carcerarie. Aggiuntavi la teoria della tutela penale del Prof. Avv. F. Poletti*, 2nd edn (Turin, Bocca, 1878) 50.

[11] C Lombroso, *L'uomo delinquente in rapporto all'antropologia, alla giurisprudenza ed alle discipline carcerarie*, 5th edn, vol I (Turin, Bocca, 1896) 274–78.

[12] On the concept of monstrosity in Lombroso's work, see E Musumeci, 'Le maschere della collezione "Lorenzo Tenchini"' in S Montaldo and P Tappero (eds), *Il Museo di Antropologia criminale 'Cesare Lombroso'* (Turin, Utet, 2009) 75–76.

The most emblematic example of this belief is provided by the famous 'discovery'[13] attributed to Lombroso of the 'median occipital fossa' in the skull of Giuseppe Villella, a 70-year-old brigand from Calabria under suspicion of robbery, who died in prison. In 1872, during a 'cold grey November morning' (as his daughter, Gina Lombroso, remembered it),[14] while he was examining the skull, Lombroso found a strange anomaly: on the occipital part, where the spine would normally be found on a human skull, there was instead a distinct depression that he called the median occipital fossa.[15] This anomaly, which Lombroso described as the 'birth certificate'[16] of criminal anthropology, explained the existence of crime through atavism[17] (from Latin *atavus*, or ancestor), coinciding with the return to an ancestral and lower stage of evolution, and becoming the emblem of a new legislative framework designed to frame a real science of the abnormal. After that, Lombroso theorised the inborn physical and psychological characteristics of criminals, asserting that a criminal was, since birth, 'a miserable variety of man . . . more pathological than the insane'.[18] According to Lombroso, this is the evidence that in criminals there are 'frequent monstrous regressions that approach man to the lowest of animals',[19] which is the premise of his theory of the born criminal.

However, it is a simplistic reading of Lombroso's theories to reduce his work excessively and solely to the attempt to identify criminals through their external aspects or atavism. In reality, the 'criminal man' imagined by Lombroso was more complex and multifaceted than a 'primitive man', or a sort of walking museum piece. Indeed, considering the overall articulation of Lombroso's work, it is understandable that atavism constituted a milestone in his research, but it was not the ultimate solution to the ambitious question about the origins of crime. In particular, atavism especially influenced only the first edition of *Criminal Man*, which was modified and amended many times before Lombroso's death. By analysing the structure of *Criminal Man*, several theories on the explanation of crime have been gradually refined, according to clinical case studies that range from the initial thesis of the born criminal as a savage, to the theory of the political criminal and *mattoid* (an ambivalent kind of deviance between genius and insanity), and 'occasional criminals', defined *criminaloids*. In addition, Lombrosian research focused not

---

[13] 'This was not merely an idea, but a revelation': C Lombroso, 'Introduction', in G Lombroso Ferrero (ed), *Criminal Man, According to the Classification of Cesare Lombroso* (New York, GP Putnam's Sons, 1911) 14.

[14] Ibid 15.

[15] On the discovery of Villella's fossa, see especially M Renneville, 'Un cranio che fa luce? Il racconto della scoperta dell'atavismo criminale', in Montaldo and Tappero (eds), *Il Museo di Antropologia criminale* 107–12.

[16] C Lombroso, 'Discours d'ouverture au VI Congrès d'anthropologie criminelle', in *Comptes-rendus du VI Congrès international d'anthropologie criminelle: Turin, 28 avril–3 mai 1906* (Turin, Bocca, 1908) 6.

[17] See R Villa, *Il deviante e i suoi segni. Lombroso e la nascita dell'antropologia criminale* (Milan, FrancoAngeli, 1985) 144–49.

[18] C Lombroso, 'Esistenza di una fossa occipitale mediana nel cranio di un delinquente' (1871) 1 *Rendiconti del Reale Istituto Lombardo di Scienze e Lettere* 41.

[19] C Lombroso, 'Della fossetta cerebellare mediana in un delinquente' (1872) 18 *Rendiconti del Reale Istituto Lombardo di Scienze e Lettere* 1062.

only on criminal faces or their cranial shapes, as is usually thought, but also on all physical and psychological characteristics, eventually including their language, both verbal (slang) and body (tattoos), and even on their artefacts. In his more detailed and objective analysis, Lombroso tried to study all kinds of aberrant behaviour, from criminality to madness, with a 'body-centered social-scientific'[20] approach. His search was not limited to the bodies of prisoners and the mentally incapacitated, however. He even analysed several biographies of great writers, artists, politicians and poets, with the aim of understanding the 'secret of deviance', or rather, why some people emerged from the quiet pathways of so-called 'normality', for either negative (criminal) or positive (men of genius) reasons.

The explanation of crime proposed by Lombroso was not in fact crystallised in a theory, but was constituted instead by a composite picture in which the causes of criminal agency, while often having a biological substrate, overlapped and intersected each other: to atavism was added moral insanity and epilepsy, giving rise to a multi-faceted explanation of crime.[21] This approach is similar to that used by the FBI[22] in the United States since the 1970s, when two officers began to focus on the behaviour of the criminal, cataloguing all murderers by their characteristics, and laying the foundations of modern criminal profiling.[23] Of course today, many Lombrosian theses have been manifestly refuted by contemporary scientists, so that the most common criticism of Lombrosian theory has been its 'total lack of scientific spirit',[24] to use the words of the British criminologist, Charles Goring.[25] Despite these often justified claims, however, it is possible to argue that the biological explanation of criminality described by Lombroso,[26] at least in its essential questions, is not so far removed from the latest biological studies of crime developed by neuroscientists and geneticists for use in the courtroom.[27]

---

[20] P Knepper and PJ Ystehede, 'Introduction', in Knepper and Ystehede (eds), *Cesare Lombroso Handbook* 1–7, 4.

[21] See also M Gibson, *Born to Crime. Cesare Lombroso and the Origins of Biological Criminology* (Westport CT, Praeger, 2002) IX.

[22] See generally G Gulotta, *Breviario di psicologia investigativa* (Milan, Giuffrè, 2008) 9–14.

[23] See also BE Turvey, *Criminal Profiling: An Introduction to Behavioral Evidence Analysis*, 4th edn (San Diego CA, Academic Press, 2011).

[24] G Goring, *The English Convict* (London, HM Stationery Office, 1919) 12.

[25] Nevertheless, according to Lombroso's daughter, Goring was 'more Lombrosian than Lombroso' considering that the English criminologist's theories echoed her father's ideas. Compare M Gibson and N Rafter, 'Editors' Introduction' in C Lombroso, *Criminal Man* (Durham NC, Duke University Press, 2006) 29.

[26] Obviously, Lombroso was not (and will not be in the future) the only one to theorise the biological origins of crime, especially at a time when 'biological theories and criminology were virtually synonymous': N Rafter, *The Criminal Brain. Understanding Biological Theories of Crime* (New York, New York University Press, 2008) XI; but he was definitely the most famous in the world, thanks to them. Consider for example the British prison medical officers James Bruce Thomson and George Wilson, who theorised about the biological and hereditary nature of criminality before Lombroso, earning the appellation of 'proto-Lombrosian': see CHS Jayewardene, 'The English Precursors of Lombroso' (1963) 4.2 *British Journal of Criminology* 164–70.

[27] On the Lombrosian legacy in neuroscience and law debate see especially E Musumeci, 'New Natural Born Killers? The Legacy of Lombroso in Neuroscience and Law', in Knepper and Ystehede (eds), *The Cesare Lombroso Handbook* 131–46.

The Free Will Battle

Obviously, Lombroso's thesis had an impact on the legal science of his time; with the principal purpose of making criminal law a real social science, disengaging from the 'a priori legal syllogistic system',[28] the Positivist School was developed in Italy in the nineteenth century against the Enlightenment rationalism of criminal law, represented by the various doctrinal currents generically called the Classical School. The Classical School considered crime to be a mere consequence of the breach of a legal rule, and as an event arising from the free and voluntary human being's choice. The Positivist School was strenuously opposed to this abstract and unhistorical rationalism, which led to an 'immutable' law separated from context, the Positivists' primary intention being not only to deny scientifically the existence of free will, but also to expunge any metaphysical element from the criminal justice system, thereby delivering 'law in real life'.[29]

The main impact of the Positivist School was on the questions relating to the philosophical foundations of criminal responsibility, and the relationship between crime and punishment. It is informative to consider the ensuing intense debate over free will,[30] which involved the Classical School of Francesco Carrara, who firmly proclaimed the existence of human freedom, as opposed to the Positivist School of Cesare Lombroso, who denied it.

A. Destroying the Free Will Myth: the Proposal of the Positivist School

The aim of the Positivist School was indeed to overthrow 'the ideal type of human being shaped by a social selfishness and an a priori philosophy'[31] and to study 'man not abstractly but as existing and living in nature'.[32] Obviously, although not a legal scholar, Lombroso, who is considered the founder of the School, played a decisive role in the debate on the concept of free will,[33] the key concept of criminal liability according to the Classical School. It is not surprising that Lombroso, inspired by naturalism and scientific positivism, firmly denied the existence of

---

[28] C Lombroso, E Ferri, R Garofalo and G Fioretti, *Polemica in difesa della Scuola Criminale Positiva* (Bologna, Zanichelli, 1886) I.

[29] U Spirito, *Storia del diritto penale italiano da Cesare Beccaria ai giorni nostri*, 3rd edn (Florence, Sansoni, 1974) 25.

[30] See especially E Musumeci, *Cesare Lombroso e le neuroscienze: un parricidio mancato. Devianza, libero arbitrio, imputabilità tra antiche chimere ed inediti scenari* (Milan, FrancoAngeli, 2012) 151–73.

[31] A Tamassia, 'Prefazione', in E Maudsley, *La responsabilità nelle malattie mentali* (Milan, Dumolard, 1875) xxxviii.

[32] Ibid.

[33] But see D Velo Dalbrenta, *La scienza inquieta. Saggio sull'Antropologia criminale di Cesare Lombroso* (Padova, Cedam, 2004) 25.

free will, convinced that thoughts came from an 'ongoing molecular motion of the cerebral cortex'[34] or 'from an arid movement of molecules'.[35]

According to Lombroso, this was a grim and humiliating lesson for human beings, deleting once and for all any artificial boundary between 'good' and 'evil', 'natural' and 'immoral' categories,[36] and showing how the dominant theories in criminal law (the Classical School) were 'semi-barbarous'. Free will, argued Lombroso, was just a 'myth or *sancta sanctorum*',[37] like the indissolubility of marriage.

Once this certainty was dispelled, the criminal act was, in the eyes of Lombroso, 'an unfortunate natural production, a form of disease',[38] which as such deserved 'care and segregation', rather than 'punishment and revenge'. An improvement in the criminal justice system and in the fight against crime in the community (that had become an illusory game in which criminality was becoming ever stronger) could therefore be achieved, according to Lombroso, only if morality were thrown down from 'the frail altar of free will, to which it was elevated by metaphysicians.'[39]

The main theoretical attempt by a member of the Positivist School to deny free will and demonstrate its non-existence, and to underline its legal implications, was that of Enrico Ferri, who wrote an entire book on this matter.[40] In essence, Ferri summarised the key principles of the two schools, stating that before the advent of the Positivist School, criminal law had been based on the illusory belief that every human being is endowed with free will, as well as the concept that 'the offender has ideas and feelings, like any other man'.[41] Ferri concluded that these assumptions, taken as a standard for decades by the old doctrine of criminal law, were clearly contradicted by the new results of experimental sciences.

Ultimately, according to Ferri, criminal law would have to be reformed on the basis of the following guidelines: a) replacing criminal liability (*imputabilità*) with a form of 'social responsibility' (released from the concept of free will); b) redefining the purpose of punishment, not as compensation but as a special preventive measure in defence of society; c) individualising punishment and eliminating the maximum sentence prescribed by law; d) recognising the importance of the criminal, instead of the abstract crime.

---

[34] C Lombroso, 'Le nuove conquiste della psichiatria' (1887) 5 *Rivista di filosofia scientifica* 641–55.

[35] C Lombroso, *Genio e follia* 2nd edn (Milan, Brigola, 1864) 5.

[36] J Moleschott, *La circolazione della vita. Lettere fisiologiche di Jac. Moleschott in risposta alle lettere chimiche di Liebig, traduzione sulla quarta edizione tedesca pubblicata con consenso dell'autore dal Prof. Cesare Lombroso* (Milan, Brigola, 1869) 348–54.

[37] C Lombroso, 'Polemica', in C Lombroso et al, *Polemica in difesa* 19.

[38] C Lombroso, 'Prefazione del traduttore', in J Moleschott, *La circolazione* ix.

[39] Ibid xi.

[40] E Ferri, *La teorica dell'imputabilità e la negazione del libero arbitrio* (Florence, Barbera, 1878).

[41] E Ferri, *I nuovi orizzonti del diritto e della procedura penale* (Bologna, Zanichelli, 1881) 5.

B. Defending Freedom: the Reaction of the Classical School

Of course, the observations of Lombroso and scholars belonging to his school, who tended to deny the existence of free will, thus undermining the old legal categories as a basis of criminal law, could not be indifferent to the large group of legal scholars who were convinced that they should defend the principles deriving directly from the Enlightenment tradition. This doctrine, which until then had dominated criminal legal theory, presupposed that every human being is freely able to act and to make his or her own choices consciously and, as such, is responsible for his or her actions, even before the law. Since the 1880s, these scholars were labelled pejoratively[42] by positivists as the 'Classical School of criminology', the greatest proponent of which is traditionally considered to be Francesco Carrara, not only Professor of Criminal Law and Justice at the Royal University of Pisa, but also a Senator of the Italian Kingdom. Unlike the Positivist School, the so-called 'Classical School', also defined as 'the Italian School of criminology' by Carrara, or sarcastically as the 'Old School' by Aristide Gabelli,[43] did not have the same consistency and sense of belonging to a real 'school'. It comprised instead a group of legal scholars with different backgrounds (who in some cases were remote from each other) but who even so were united by a strong willingness to resist strenuously the 'new' concepts advocated by the positivists, after more than 30 years of hegemony.

Nevertheless, Carrara defended the Classical School's 'enlisting' among its ranks of the most influential legal scholars of the eighteenth and nineteenth centuries ('Beccaria, Filangieri, Romagnosi, Carmignani, Rossi, Haus, Nypels and others'[44]), with the aim of powerfully affirming that human beings could be legally responsible only if they were also morally free. Positivists, argued Carrara, had confused *will*, presupposing an unmotivated action, completely detached from human nature, with *freedom*, implying on the contrary the right to choose between two opposing reasons whichever seemed more suited to one's needs. In sum, Carrara warned that the tangible risk was to exchange 'spontaneity'[45] for freedom and therefore, in open dispute with the Lombrosian School, he concluded:

> For us, followers of the moral sciences, the new thermometers and telescopes are of no use, because the tools of our human knowledge do not benefit from the senses, but only from the study of man's interiority as revealed by his external acts, which have always been and will always be the same, until man is, in terms of psychological faculty, the same man who emerged from the hands of the Creator. Telescopes and thermometers

---

[42] L Lucchini, *I semplicisti del diritto penale* (Turin, Unione Tipografico-Editrice, 1886) xxiv.
[43] A Gabelli, 'Sulla "Scuola positiva" del diritto penale in Italia' (1886) XXIII *Rivista Penale* 524.
[44] F Carrara, 'Libertà e spontaneità. Prelusione al corso di diritto e procedura penale (28 novembre 1882)', in F Carrara (ed), *Reminiscenze di cattedra e foro dell'avvocato Francesco Carrara* (Lucca, Tipografia Canovetti, 1883) 517.
[45] Ibid 515.

do not help to judge whether a man is free or not. We must descend into the inner recesses of our minds.[46]

The Ferri Project

What were the effects of the 'free will battle' on the Italian penal codes? As Lombroso complained, the 1889 Zanardelli Code was approved at a time that was not yet ripe for the revolutionary theories of criminal anthropology, marking instead the victory of the Classical School. This code adopted a concept of criminal responsibility understood as moral responsibility, or rather, of crime committed by someone 'in full possession of their intellectual faculties'. In contrast, under the 1930 Rocco Code, the concept of 'freedom of action' established in the Zanardelli Code was replaced by that of *imputabilità*, or *mens rea*, understood as the 'capacity to understand and will'. Therefore, with the shift from the Zanardelli Code to the Rocco Code, the Positivist School lost a second major battle: the elimination of a concept of criminal responsibility based on free will and its replacement with a kind of 'social responsibility' or 'legal responsibility', beyond the criminal's mental health and in defence of society, that would have automatically followed from the commission of a crime.

However, we must remember that Lombroso was no longer alive during the debate on the Rocco Code, and his only followers involved were his more or less loyal pupils, including Ferri and Garofalo. In particular, Ferri attempted to circumvent the cumbersome figure of his master, by adding his own ideas to those of Lombroso in a manner that was not always consistent. It should be noted that in 1919, well before the draft of the Rocco Code, the Minister of Justice, Lodovico Mortara gave Ferri the task of directing, along with Raffaele Garofalo, a reform commission tasked with revising criminal law 'in harmony with the principles and rational methods of the defence of society against crime in general'.[47] The purpose was to enable the application of criminal sanctions based on categories of offenders (eg 'dangerous' people, minors), which had not previously been covered by criminal legislation.

This assignment was followed by feverish work, completed in 1921, on redefining crime for the defence of society, and remembered as the 'Ferri Project' for a new penal code. Eminent scholars have especially emphasised the illiberal characteristics of this project, due to the introduction of sanctions or measures of indeterminate duration.[48] However, a closer examination reveals a more complex framework that is worth analysing. The most interesting aspect is the punishment system, which appears innovative when compared to the previous model. If the

---

[46] Carrara, 'Libertà e spontaneità' 508–09.
[47] Royal Decree of 14 September 1919 No 1724 (1919) XC *Rivista Penale* 382.
[48] E Musco, *La misura di sicurezza detentiva: profili storici e costituzionali* (Milan, Giuffrè, 1978).

function of punishment under the Zanardelli Code was simple retribution, in the Ferri Project a primary role was assigned to social defence, applied in different ways, depending on the 'dangerousness' of offenders. This system, defined as 'scissors-shaped'[49] was planned on the one hand as a strong social defence against so-called incorrigible criminals and, on the other hand, as a kind of rehabilitating system of sanctions for types of criminals deemed less dangerous to society. Accordingly, penal sanctions were divided into those that were 'corrective, repressive and eliminative'. In addition to this general tripartite division, there was a further important distinction between punishment for 'common crimes' and for 'socio-political crimes', with different sanctions applicable to each, including mandatory work for the former. Thus beyond social defence, which was definitely the main purpose of criminal punishment in the Ferri Project, there was also a rehabilitative purpose, which even if less prominent, nevertheless highlights the intention of prioritising work outdoors, rather than mere segregation in prison.[50] The latter alternative made life imprisonment the 'cellular grave of living human beings', Ferri observed, quoting a pronouncement by Pasquale Stanislao Mancini in relation to the Criminal Project of the Kingdom of Italy on 25 November 1876.[51]

'Conditional sentence' and 'judicial pardon' were other elements directed toward a more lenient punishment system and a protection of civil liberties, making sanctions milder and oriented more to the rehabilitation and treatment of occasional or passionate offenders, and therefore breaking 'the abstract rigour of indissolubility in the relationship between crime and punishment, the son of the retributive conception of punishment and so strongly supported by the standard bearers of the so-called Classical School'.[52] These elements, along with the inclusion of compensation for victims of crime, were original features of the Ferri Project, opening the way to innovative forms of 'restorative justice' that were previously non-existent in the Italian penal system. In particular, damages compensation, previously considered as pertaining only to the private sphere and therefore a civil obligation, was here regarded as an obligation under public law, on the basis of suggestions made by scholars of the Positivist School, and especially by Garofalo.[53]

---

[49] A Manna, 'Le sanzioni penali nel Progetto Ferri' (2011) 2 *Diritto Penale del XXI secolo* 280.
[50] On prison in post-unification Italy, see G Neppi Modona, 'Quali detenuti per quali reati nel carcere dell'Italia liberale' in S Montaldo and P Tappero (eds), *Cesare Lombroso cento anni dopo* (Turin, Utet, 2009) 83–97; and see also, L Lacchè, *La giustizia per i galantuomini. Ordine e libertà nell'Italia liberale: il dibattito sul carcere preventivo (1865–1913)* (Milan, Giuffrè, 1990).
[51] S Messina, 'Il problema dell'ergastolo' in G Leone (ed), *Scritti giuridici in onore di Alfredo De Marsico* vol II (Milan, Giuffrè, 1961) 162.
[52] Manna, 'Le sanzioni penali' 286.
[53] R Garofalo, *Riparazione alle vittime del delitto* (Turin, Bocca, 1887).

From Positivist Revolution to Fascist Revolution: the Choice of Ferri

Unfortunately for Ferri, his project came at the wrong time, with regard to the rapid succession of events that would bring, in October 1922, the March on Rome and the seizure of power by the National Fascist Party led by Benito Mussolini. Shortly thereafter was the beginning of a new era for Italy: the dark years of the Fascist regime. The 'positivist revolution' advocated by Ferri and other followers of the Positivist School, was destined to fail miserably. If the Zanardelli Code had been issued 'too early'[54] to adopt the new theories of the Positivist School, as Lombroso complained, the Ferri Project inevitably arrived too late. As a recent commentator has emphatically observed:

> The glorious eighties of the nineteenth century – when positivist lightning seemed able to incinerate any contrary opinion instantly – were by this time a distant memory. That blinding light, so quickly exhausted, had left its mark, but it was not possible to avoid the birth within a few years of internal fractures, accompanied – through the emergence of diverse views and different interpretations of positivist teaching – by a progressive erosion of positions, together with a series of crushing defeats.[55]

After two failures, Ferri decided to adhere to Fascism in order to try to find a way at last to apply the principles of the Positivist School under the New Regime, moving from positivist revolution to 'Fascist revolution',[56] which was, in the words of the Fascist philosopher Giovanni Gentile:[57]

> a force stronger than the will and the ideas of individual men ... force, historical necessity, that has been personified in a Man endowed with singular gifts of productive

---

[54] C Lombroso, 'Troppo presto' in C Lombroso, A Berenini and V Rossi, *Appunti al nuovo codice penale*, 2nd edn (Torino, Bocca, 1889).

[55] E Dezza, 'Le reazioni del positivismo penale al Codice Rocco' (2011) 2 *Diritto Penale del XXI secolo* 421.

[56] 'Fascist revolution' was a phrase frequently used by Fascist intellectuals and politicians (like Gentile, Rocco and Mussolini himself) to define the years of Fascism's birth in Italy. Characterising moments of this alleged revolution are defined as the San Sepolcro period, the foundation of the Italian '*fasci di combattimento*' in 1919 and the March on Rome in 1922, which led to the formation of a government by Mussolini and was declared 'year zero' of the revolution. Challenged by anti-Fascist intellectuals and historians, who characterised Fascism as purely regressive and reactionary, the expression was confined to the early stage of the regime or considered as a direct result of the emphatic language used during Fascism. On this topic see R De Felice, *Mussolini il rivoluzionario: 1883–1920* (Turin, Einaudi, 1965); GL Mosse, *The Fascist Revolution: Toward a General Theory of Fascism* (New York, Fertig, 1999); P Buchignani, *La rivoluzione in camicia nera* (Milan, Mondadori, 2006) and, more recently, L Klinkhammer, 'Was There a Fascist Revolution? The Function of Penal Law in Fascist Italy and Nazi Germany' (2010) 15.3 *Journal of Modern Italian Studies* 390–409.

[57] According to ME Moss, *Mussolini's Fascist Philosopher. Giovanni Gentile Reconsidered* (New York, Peter Lang, 2004) 59, it was Gentile 'who provided the fundamental ideas and direction of the Fascist revolution'.

genius, which is creating by the hour, as if inspired and moved by a mysterious instinct, this new Italy, between the intent admiration and fearful anxiety of the world.[58]

Hence Ferri, either fascinated by Fascism or for reasons of political expediency, turned increasingly to authoritarian positions, embracing Fascist ideology and joining the Fascist Party in 1923, perhaps in order to fit the theories of the Positivist School into the new regime's legislative plans. In other words, as has been said, Ferri tried to 'hook his positivist wagon to the locomotive of Fascism'[59].

Although Ferri died in 1929, before the new penal code came to light, he still had time to sing the praises of Mussolini and his 'exceptional thyroid'.[60] However, Ferri did not stop at personal praise of the *Duce*, but also tried to identify the elements of contact between positivist doctrine and Fascist ideology. In a lengthy article published in *La Scuola Positiva* in 1926, Ferri sought to set out any and every point of contact between the Regime and the Positivist School, joined in the intention of 'social defence against crime'.[61] As if trying to justify himself, Ferri claimed that Fascism and the Positivist School diverged only if positivism is intended as a 'philosophical system'. Embracing the positivism developed by Auguste Comte or Herbert Spencer, or the most extreme forms of materialism by Ludwig Büchner, Carl Vogt or Jacob Moleschott,[62] he admitted that it was hard to find a point of contact with Fascism, which was strongly influenced by idealist philosophy. On the contrary, Ferri explained, positivism should be read not so much as a 'philosophical system', but as a 'study method' of observation of social reality, also applicable to the study of crime and punishment. Both idealism and positivism had at heart the same problem: that of criminal responsibility. Ferri did not hesitate to condemn the Enlightenment principles of the Classical School that had resulted in a frustrating protection of civil rights in such an individualistic way, to the point of sacrificing 'the equally legitimate guarantees of society faced with crime and criminals'.[63] In this regard, it was of considerable importance for Ferri that Fascism, in both sociological and political fields, was aiming for:

[58] G Gentile, *Discorso tenuto il 14 maggio 1927, per l'inaugurazione dei corsi di conferenze all'Istituto Nazionale Fascista di cultura*, in HA Cavallera (ed), G Gentile, *Politica e cultura. Opere complete di Giovanni Gentile* vol 1 (Florence, Le Lettere, 1990) 286–87.

[59] Sbriccoli, 'Le mani nella pasta' 1011.

[60] E Ferri, 'Mussolini. Uomo di Stato' (1927) 22 *Mussolinia* 12.

[61] E Ferri, 'Fascismo e Scuola Positiva nella difesa sociale contro la delinquenza' (1926) 1 *La Scuola Positiva* 241.

[62] In addition to the obvious intellectual debt to positivism, materialism served as an important cultural reference point for the Positivist School. In this sense, the books *Kraft und Stoff* (1854) by Büchner and *Bilde aus dem Tierleben* (1852) by Vogt, representative of the nineteenth-century *Materialismus-Streit*, were seminal, as was *Der Kreislauf des Lebens* (1852) by Dutch physiologist Moleschott, later translated from German into Italian by Cesare Lombroso and published with his foreword in 1869. See generally FA Lange, *History of Materialism and Criticism of its Present Importance* vol II (EC Thomas trans) (Boston, Houghton, Osgood & Company, 1880) 259–94 and G Cosmacini, 'Problemi medico-biologici e concezione materialistica nella seconda metà dell'Ottocento', in G Micheli (ed), *Storia d'Italia. Annali vol. 3. Scienza e tecnica della cultura nella società dal Rinascimento ad oggi* (Turin, Einaudi, 1980) 815–61.

[63] Ferri, 'Fascismo e Scuola Positiva nella difesa sociale contro la delinquenza' 243.

the reaffirmation of the pre-eminent and sovereign rights of the State against the excesses of democratic individualism, which has become demagogical and essentially anarchist under the 'liberal and agnostic State' – in other words inert and cowardly – of which Benito Mussolini has clearly proclaimed a dynamic obituary.[64]

In the supremacy of rights of the state versus the rights of the individual and, therefore, the primary necessity of social defence, Ferri saw the point of greatest agreement between Fascism and the Positivist School. Only together, he said, could they continue this virtuous path, which provided for the abandonment of criminal law that was totally focused on the concept of the offender's moral guilt, and more generally free will, in favour of a concept of 'legal responsibility' that could finally manage to unhook the links between crime and sin, and punishment and penance.

Toward the Fascist Criminal Code: the Contribution of the Rocco Brothers

The Ferri project was not the only antecedent of the Rocco Code. In 1910, Arturo Rocco, the brother of the future Fascist Minister of Justice, during his inaugural lecture at the University of Sassari, addressed 'the problem and the method of the science of criminal law'.[65] He declared that it was necessary to get rid of the legacy of the Positivist School established by Lombroso, which was guilty of having 'tainted' the 'purity' of criminal law, through the interference of other disciplines. Hence, the aim of Arturo Rocco's proposal was to adopt a technical-legal doctrine of criminal law capable of going beyond the debate between the Classical and Positivist Schools, which had monopolised discussion in the field of criminal law over the previous 30 years. This well known lecture is considered not only the 'manifesto' of a new technical-legal approach to criminal law, but also the theoretical basis of the Rocco Code, which according to some interpretations preserved the Code from taking on too much of a totalitarian guise. Yet what was the real contribution of the technical-legal doctrine to the Rocco Code? Was it really able to go beyond both the Classical School and the Positivist School?

In reality, scholars still wonder about the true extent of Arturo Rocco's technical-legal approach, so much so that in 2010, on the occasion of the centenary of his lecture in Sassari, distinguished professors of criminal law debated the significance and legacy of his thought.[66] Far from being a mere academic disquisition, unravelling the contribution made by Arturo Rocco might shed light on the true nature of the Rocco Code and its relationship to Italian criminal law doctrines,

---

[64] Ibid 244.

[65] A Rocco, 'Il problema e il metodo della scienza del diritto penale' (1910) 1 *Rivista di diritto e procedura penale* 497–521, 561–82.

[66] See nn 71, 72 and 75 below.

since Arturo Rocco was the president of the committee of experts appointed by the Minister of Justice to draw up the preliminary draft of the penal code and supervise the final project. The two main interpretations of Rocco's lecture come to completely different conclusions. According to a 'rehabilitating orientation',[67] the attempt by Rocco to escape a crisis that seemed irreversible is reasonable; the conditions of criminal law were miserable at that time, reduced by the Classical School to an 'absolute, immutable, universal, and divine'[68] law, and by the Positivist School to a 'criminal law . . . without law',[69] especially because the social sciences that were spuriously blended with law, like anthropology, psychiatry and criminal psychology, were 'reduced to scientific matters for directors of asylums . . . and charlatans'.[70] According to this view, Rocco's approach, with the perspicuity that always characterised his thought, was

> [a plausible] appeal to restore the centrality of the positive criminal law's object, not in order to make a fetish and passive cult of it, but to explore its roots, implications and organization in an open and flexible perspective, as long as the boundaries of positive law are the positive law itself, without leaks or evasions.[71]

This interpretation takes a positive view on Arturo Rocco's intervention, considering it almost a duty, and focusing on a conception of criminal law as a science, which puts dogmatic research at its centre, accompanied by the exegetic tools and systematic logic of the fundamental principles of positive law, but which despite criticism is not a sort of legal formalism.[72] In support of this view are the words of Rocco himself, who several times in his lecture advised against being a follower of 'empty as well as dangerous legal formalism'[73] and advocated not a divorce, but only a separation, between law and other disciplines.[74] Despite the fascination of this argument, it does not convince.

The opposite interpretation[75] of Rocco's manifesto, seeking to expose its real political implications, appears more valid for the following reasons. Despite Rocco's claim that he intended to avoid 'the hurdle of formalism',[76] it is precisely that into which he stumbled. Two key elements emerge from reading his lecture:

---

[67] See M Sbriccoli, 'La penalistica civile. Teorie e ideologie del diritto penale nell'Italia unita', in Sbriccoli (ed), *Storia del diritto penale* 573–83.

[68] Rocco, 'Il problema e il metodo' 500.

[69] Ibid 504.

[70] Sbriccoli, 'La penalistica civile' 579.

[71] T Padovani, 'Lezione introduttiva sul metodo nella scienza del diritto penale' (2010) *Criminalia* 235.

[72] See M Donini, 'Tecnicismo giuridico e scienza penale cent'anni dopo. La prolusione di Arturo Rocco (1910) nell'età dell'europeismo giudiziario' (2010) *Criminalia* 127–78.

[73] Rocco, 'Il problema e il metodo' 511.

[74] Ibid 518.

[75] Compare A Malinverni, *La scuola dogmatica del diritto penale* (Vercelli, Premiata Tipografia Gallardi, 1939); E Gallo, 'Una politica per la riforma del codice penale' (1981) 1 *La Questione Criminale* 49–65, and, more recently, G Fiandaca, 'Rocco: è plausibile una de-specializzazione della scienza penalistica?' (2010) *Criminalia* 179–206.

[76] Rocco, 'Il problema e il metodo' 577.

a cultural mentality that was cramped and stifled;[77] and a constant ambiguity. First, cleaning up the study of law from mingling with other disciplines (sociology, criminology, criminal policy) appears illusory as well as hypocritical, because it is impossible to separate the juridical purpose and political aim of a specific incriminating norm, relegating these issues to the sphere of competence of criminal policy. Furthermore, although Rocco's openings to other disciplines were always made with great caution (made evident in the constant use of formulations such as 'up to a certain point', 'but only in this way', 'to some extent', 'within certain limits', 'although only in a subsidiary way'), his wish to take them into account was apparent and also made clear by his programmatic statement, inspired by the principles of legal formalism:

> it is always true that strictly and narrowly legal investigation must be kept distinct from philosophical and political inquiry, if we want to avoid *an illicit and dangerous intrusion and mingling of philosophical and political elements in the logical clarity of legal research.*[78]

To conclude, the technical legal approach advocated by Arturo Rocco was nothing more than a moderately sweetened variety of legal formalism that enhanced the isolation of law from other spheres, entirely separating it from reality, in order to serve the alleged neutrality of the jurist. In that neutrality, under the cloak of 'technical' analysis, is hidden the inevitable subordination of the law to political power, as actually occurred under the Fascist regime.

If the criminal law scholar Arturo Rocco was responsible for the fundamental 'legal' footprint of the nascent Rocco Code, the more important 'political' imprint was provided by his brother, Alfredo Rocco, the regime's Minister of Justice.[79] The contribution of these two of the four Rocco brothers[80] (this Neapolitan family of lawyers has been described as 'a stable of thoroughbred horses'[81]) can in fact be read as two sides of the same coin.

Passing quickly from nationalism to Fascism, Alfredo Rocco soon became the architect of the radical transformation of institutions in an authoritarian way[82] and, consequently, also of the construction of the legal system that could support and defend the dictatorship. The authoritarian transformation of criminal law began in 1925, with the promulgation of the so-called ultra-Fascist laws, which

---

[77] Compare Fiandaca, 'Rocco: è plausibile una de-specializzazione' 182, who defines Rocco's approach as 'moralising legal positivist bigotry'.

[78] Rocco, 'Il problema e il metodo' 520 (emphasis added).

[79] On the importance of Alfredo Rocco as the 'legislator of the Fascist regime', as well as for his political and cultural biography, see P Ungari, *Alfredo Rocco e l'ideologia giuridica del fascismo* (Brescia, Morcelliana, 1963); M Sbriccoli, 'Rocco Alfredo', in Sbriccoli (ed), *Storia del diritto penale* 993–1000 and, more recently, G Simone, *Il Guardasigilli del regime. L'itinerario politico e culturale di Alfredo Rocco* (Milan, FrancoAngeli, 2012).

[80] The other two brothers, Ugo and Ferdinando, were respectively a professor of civil procedure in Naples, and a judge and Chair of the Council of State.

[81] I Montanelli, 'I quattro grandi giuristi della famiglia Rocco' (18 January 1998) *Corriere della Sera* 33.

[82] Compare F Lanchester, 'Alfredo Rocco e le origini dello Stato totale', in E Gentile, F Lanchester and A Tarquini (eds), *Alfredo Rocco: dalla crisi del parlamentarismo alla costruzione dello Stato nuovo* (Rome, Carocci, 2010) 15–38.

outlined the framework of an authoritarian state. Among those laws were 'laws of defence' concerning secret societies, bureaucracy and the defence of the State, and 'rules of constitutional reform' regarding the legislative power of the executive body and the powers of the head of government. Also significant for the configuration of Fascist criminal law was Law No 2008 of 25 November 1926, which reinstated the death penalty and established the Special Tribunal for the Defence of the State[83] as a supplementary instrument to the ordinary courts, against potential opponents of the regime and 'anti-Fascist subversives'. In the same manner, Law No 1848 of 6 November 1926 on public safety strengthened and expanded police powers of preventive and repressive intervention. These laws were the harbingers of the new Fascist style of criminal law, opening the way for the Rocco Code and its approach to crime in the name of defending society, and introducing what would become the cornerstones of the new penal system: an exasperated statism and the gradual elimination of individual rights. According to Mussolini's well-known motto, 'all within the State, nothing outside the State, nothing against the State',[84] one of the fundamental ideas of Fascism was the centrality of the state,[85] and the legal reform undertaken by Alfredo Rocco, with the support of Arturo Rocco and other jurists, such as Vincenzo Manzini, was directed precisely towards strengthening this idea.

What Legacy?

Just after Cesare Lombroso's death, Father Agostino Gemelli wrote a book entitled *Funeral of a Man and of a Doctrine*,[86] in which he declared that with Lombroso's passing, his theory of criminal anthropology would have to be definitively abandoned. Nevertheless, 10 years later, in the debate on the new Rocco project for the Italian Penal Code that was approved in 1930, the name of Lombroso and his Positivist School of Criminology still seemed far from dead and buried. In 1927, Enrico Ferri, commenting on the Rocco project, stated that the work initiated by Lombroso and continued by his followers that was aimed at the creation of a criminal law focused on the figure of the criminal, would ultimately be realised. Indeed, Ferri pointed out that criminal law inspired by Cesare Beccaria's thought, or rather a 'legal anatomy of crime', had finally come to an end, due to new studies of criminal man. In other words, after the resounding

---

[83] See further E Gallo, *Il Tribunale Speciale per la Difesa dello Stato e il suo ambiente politico-culturale* (Rome, Stilgrafica, 1980) and, for a comparative perspective, W Eder, *Das italienische Tribunale Speciale per la Difesa dello Stato und der deutsche Volksgerichtshof: ein Vergleich zwischen zwei politischen Gerichtshöfen* (Frankfurt am Main, Peter Lang, 2002). See also Ch 1 in this collection.

[84] B Mussolini, *Opera Omnia* (E and D Susmel eds) vol XXI (Florence, La Fenice, 1954) 425.

[85] Compare G Gentile, 'Idee fondamentali', in B Mussolini, *La dottrina del fascismo. Con una storia del movimento fascista di Gioacchino Volpe* (Rome, Istituto della Enciclopedia Italiana, 1934) 1.

[86] A Gemelli, *I funerali di un uomo e di una dottrina. 3a edizione notevolmente aumentata e completamente rifusa*, 3rd edn (Florence, Libreria Editrice Fiorentina, 1911).

defeat of the Positivist School in the 1889 Zanardelli Code, which was clearly liberal and more responsive to theories supported by the Classical School, the Rocco project seemed the first real opportunity to see Lombroso's theories applied to a criminal law in force. Ferri's position, like that of other positivists looking favourably on the Rocco project, could be seen as the almost immature happiness and satisfaction of those who 'have the last chance to battle with ghosts and proclaim themselves as winners'.[87]

Beyond Ferri's political opportunism, it would be useful to understand the real legacy of the Positivist School in the Rocco Code. At first glance, some fundamental rules of the Enlightenment legal tradition were confirmed, such as the principle of the rule of law and the prohibition of analogy. Apart from this apparent success of the Classical School, the latter's victory over the question of free will had the bitter taste of a battle only half-won; social responsibility, rejected by the adoption of the concept of criminal responsibility, clashed surreptitiously with the concept of 'social dangerousness', or rather the probability that an accused would repeat his or her antisocial behaviour. Along with this new concept, the possibility of imposing a 'security measure' (such as the obligation to work in an agricultural colony) in addition to a sentence was also introduced, with the precise purpose of preventing other crimes by the same offender, strictly connected with his or her social dangerousness. Thus a shift in the Code's centre of gravity occurred towards social dangerousness, although not to the extent hoped for by the positivists. Similarly significant are the assimilation of attempted crime with actual crime, and the elimination of different degrees of responsibility in conspiracy depending on role (ie the possibility for the judge to reduce a sentence for those who played a marginal role), as well as the different treatment of 'continuous crime'[88] (whereas before, a reduction in sentence had been almost automatic, it became purely discretionary). Moreover, circumstances were calibrated on the basis of criminal personalities, which for the first time were classified according to the categories outlined by criminal anthropology (ie born criminal, mentally insane, criminal by passion or by tendency, juvenile, etc).

Despite these obviously positivist traces in the Rocco Code, however, we cannot say that this Code represents a full realisation of Lombroso's theories. On the contrary, the attempt to go beyond the two Schools in order to create a technical law totally separated from other disciplines, as repeatedly stated by Rocco, actually resulted in a sort of monster. Onto the trunk of the 'old' liberal tradition of criminal law was grafted the foreign body of positivist theories, resulting in the creation of a strange system that failed to surrender the concept of criminal responsibility based on the offender's moral responsibility and his mental ability

---

[87] M Sbriccoli, 'Il problema penale' in Sbriccoli (ed), *Storia del diritto penale* 692.

[88] According to article 81 of the 1930 Code, crime was considered to be 'continuous' where someone committed multiple breaches of the same legal provision as part of the same criminal endeavour, even if such breaches occurred at different times and were of different degrees of seriousness. In such a case, and in derogation from the general principle *tot criminae, tot poenae*, the penalty was that applicable to the most serious offence committed, which could be increased by up to three times.

to understand and will, and yet to which at the same time was added the concept of social dangerousness,[89] wholly unconnected with mental capacity. The result was a general increase in levels of punishment that was expected neither by followers of the Classical School, nor by Positivists. This was because the availability of security measures[90] in addition to traditional punishments created the new so-called 'double-track' system,[91] or rather, an instrument capable of multiplying penalties.[92]

Fascist Criminal Law?

A. The 'Fascist' Principle of the Rule of Law

The Rocco Code was not merely a hybrid of two opposing doctrines with the necessary characteristics for the Fascist revolution. Since 1945, Italian legal scholars have debated the nature of Fascist criminal law, or rather, whether a criminal justice system could, for its intrinsic and extrinsic characteristics, be defined as exclusively adherent to Fascist ideology, and whether a penal code in force under a dictatorship could be compatible with a constitutional democracy.[93] Beyond the complex disquisition on the continuity or discontinuity[94] between the Zanardelli and Rocco Codes, the most significant element invoked is the presence in both cases of the principle of *nullum crimen, nulla poena sine lege*,[95] ie legal certainty, or the principle of the rule of law, clearly inspired by the Enlightenment. The presence of this principle has been evoked by scholars who argue that there is continuity between the two codes, especially in their general part (relating to the principles and basic concepts of criminal law).

First, it was argued that the existence of the principle of legal certainty could mitigate the authoritarianism of the Fascist-inspired Code, creating a bridge

---

[89] See generally A Calabria, 'Pericolosità sociale (voce)', in *Digesto delle discipline penalistiche* (Turin, Utet, 1995) 451–69. See also for the philosophical and historical implications of this concept M Foucault, 'About the Concept of the "Dangerous Individual" in 19th-Century Legal Psychiatry' (1978) 1 *International Journal of Law and Psychiatry* 1–18.

[90] See A Manna (ed), *Imputabilità e misure di sicurezza* (Padua, Cedam, 2002). On security measures and their comparative legal-historical analysis see Musco, *La misura di sicurezza detentiva*.

[91] See eg A Bitonti, 'Doppio binario (voce)', in *Digesto delle discipline penalistiche* (Turin, Utet, 2005) 393–414. In addition, with respect to the double-track system and its crisis see M Pelissero, 'Crisi e mutazioni del sistema doppio binario', in P Pisa (ed), *Verso una riforma del sistema sanzionatorio?* (Turin, Giappichelli, 2008) 129–59.

[92] Dezza, 'Le reazioni del positivismo' 433.

[93] See especially, S Skinner, 'Tainted Law? The Italian Penal Code, Fascism and Democracy' (2011) 7 *International Journal of Law in Context* 423–46.

[94] cf M Sbriccoli, 'Caratteri originari e permanenti del sistema penale italiano (1860–1990)', in M Sbriccoli (ed), *Storia del diritto penale*, vol I 591–670.

[95] On the 'thin boundary lines' of this principle, univocal only at first glance, see M Pifferi, 'Difendere i confini, superare le frontiere. Le "zone grigie" della legalità penale tra Otto e Novecento' (2007) 36 *Quaderni fiorentini per la storia del pensiero giuridico moderno* 743–99.

between the criminal law of the Enlightenment tradition and constitutional principles. Accordingly in 1945, when Italy was faced with the problem of having to
reform the Penal Code compromised by the Fascist regime, Giovanni Leone
argued that 'the Rocco Code had not broken away from the line of tradition (and,
therefore, from liberal theory) regarding its political inspiration'.[96]

Indeed even today, while acknowledging the obviously illiberal nature of several articles of the Rocco Code, many scholars insist on valuing the contribution
of Arturo Rocco and the jurists who collaborated in drafting it (eg Filippo
Grispigni) as commendable, not only for the quality of their legal skills, but also
for their inclusion of the principle of legal certainty. This was seen as an indispensable guarantee that made the Rocco Code appear to be the result of an elabo-
rate and cunning legal alchemy, rather than a penal code fit for the dictatorship's
purposes. Hence the reference to the existence of a 'dogmatic brake',[97] or rather a
positive role played by legal scholars and academics under the Fascist regime.
According to this view, which was asserted by some commentators after the war,[98]
the law and lawyers in general somehow held back the excesses of Fascist politics,
and avoided forms of 'degenerate law',[99] such as those issued by the Nazi regime.[100]

However, the 'brake' theory seems unconvincing, as does the aim of many legal
scholars who were active during the time of Fascism to entrench themselves in a
supposed position of 'neutrality' by adhering to the technical-legal approach.
Such action amounted to a kind of legal formalism[101] adopted by Rocco, that can
be considered a sort of loophole, or shelter behind which they could hide, in order
not to be tainted by the horrors of the regime; in other words this was 'an alibi, an
excuse to turn their eyes to heaven avoiding having to see what Fascism was doing
to Italian criminal science'.[102]

On a distinct front, and with different assertions, but reaching more or less the
same conclusions (a thesis for the generic prevalence of 'continuity'), it has been
claimed that the Rocco Code did not mark a real break with the past, because it
lacked an autonomous cultural development, a lack which consequently prevented the formation of an original and independent doctrine of criminal law.
Therefore, the Rocco Code not only adopted the principle of legal certainty, but
also 'rested on dogmatic scaffolding with a predominantly liberal basis',[103] even if

---

[96] G Leone, 'Contro la riforma del codice penale' (1945) *Archivio penale* 277.

[97] Sbriccoli, 'Il problema penale' 693.

[98] T Delogu, 'L'elemento politico nel codice penale' (1945) *Archivio Penale* 161–95.

[99] Compare B Rüthers, *Entartetes Recht* (München, Beck, 1989).

[100] On the experience in other countries, like Nazi Germany or Vichy France, see I Muller, *Hitler's Justice: The Courts of the Third Reich* (Harvard MA, Harvard University Press, 1992); M Stolleis, *Law under the Swastika: Studies on Legal History in Nazi Germany* (Chicago IL, University of Chicago Press, 1998); R Weisberg, *Vichy Law and the Holocaust in France* (New York, New York University Press, 1996); Z Sternhell, *Ni droite, ni gauche: L'idéologie fasciste en France* (Paris, Éditions du Seuil, 1983).

[101] On legal philosophical debate between formalism and anti-formalism, see generally R Cavallo, *L'antiformalismo nella temperie weimariana* (Turin, Giappichelli, 2009).

[102] Sbriccoli, 'Le mani nella pasta' 1033.

[103] G Fiandaca, 'Il codice Rocco e la continuità istituzionale in materia penale' (1981) 1 *La Questione Criminale* 69.

limited by the 1926 introduction of the Special Tribunal for the Defence of the State, with jurisdiction over political offences.

In fact, it seems more relevant to warn against viewing legal certainty and its corollaries (prohibition of analogy and non-retroactivity of criminal law unfavourable to the accused) as a sort of lifeline capable of saving the Rocco Code from its involvement with the dictatorship, even after the end of World War II.[104] Indeed, the rule of law cannot be considered as 'a magic label' that automatically ensures the transition from a dictatorship to a democracy, as if it had some real 'miraculous virtues'.[105]

Contrary to appearances, during the Fascist era the 'glorified' principle of legal certainty did not perform the same functions that it would have done in a democratic legal system. The principle provides that one cannot be subjected to penal sanctions unless these are previously provided for by law. During the Fascist regime, however, laws were issued without wide, democratic parliamentary debate, but instead as the will of a single party, the Fascist Party, which since the beginning of the dictatorship had trampled on every kind of political opposition. This then was the 'law' – legal, but not legitimate – to which the principle of legality referred. Although it was not formally abolished by the criminal justice system, it was as if the rule of law, like an imaginary pendulum, was 'suspended on the pole of authority, rather than on that of the guarantee of rights'.[106] Above all, although legal certainty was formally guaranteed, it was openly violated from a substantive point of view, as demonstrated by the number of laws aimed at the protection of abstract legal interests or vague concepts, such as the crime of *vilipendio* (contempt, or vilification). For their intrinsic vagueness, they materially violated the principle of legality, giving judges ample authority for the application of criminal law to the needs of repressive political power. Furthermore, the judicial power that had to enforce the law was completely devoid of the most basic guarantees of autonomy and independence, being entirely subordinate to the government.[107] Hence, it is more appropriate to consider that the rule of law was useful for giving the Rocco Code a veneer of 'democratic paint'. That coating of formal legality has to be scraped away in order to understand how this principle was reinvented and instrumentalised by the regime.

Political violence, one of the key elements of the so-called Fascist revolution, was shrewdly disguised as Fascist law. As Rocco himself stated, emphasising the need to spread the new Fascist spirit throughout the legal system, 'the old law

---

[104] On continuity and discontinuity between legal systems under dictatorships and after their downfall see especially, C Joerges and N Singh Ghaleigh, *Darker Legacies of Law in Europe: the Shadow of National Socialism and Fascism over Europe and its Legal Traditions* (Oxford, Hart, 2003).

[105] G Neppi Modona, 'Principio di legalità e diritto penale fascista' (2007) XXXVI *Quaderni fiorentini per la storia del pensiero giuridico moderno* 985.

[106] P Costa, 'Il principio di legalità: un campo di tensione nella modernità penale' (2007) XXXVI *Quaderni fiorentini per la storia del pensiero giuridico moderno* 17.

[107] Neppi Modona, 'Principio di legalità' 1001–05.

would be replaced by the new law: Fascist legality'.[108] In fact, Giuseppe Maggiore, one of the most enthusiastic legal scholars of the regime, pointed out in 1939 that the principle of *nullum crimen sine lege*, according to which conduct cannot be a crime unless it violates a law extant at the time of its occurrence, had to be amended, adding that 'every conduct offending the State's authority must also be considered as a crime and deserving of punishment according to the spirit of the Fascist revolution and the will of the Duce, sole interpreter of the will of the Italian people'.[109] Without this modification, Maggiore warned, the principle of legal certainty could have been a sort of '*magna carta* for criminals'.[110]

B. Journey to the End of the Law: Inside the Rocco Code

If the Fascist connotation of the Rocco Code is clearly traceable in its general part, the authoritarian tone is even more evident in its special part, which sets out specific crimes and constitutes a 'litmus test' of the new Fascist ideology that was emerging in those years. In fact, as has been argued, 'in this matter . . . the Rocco Code was undoubtedly the child of dictatorship'.[111]

For one thing, there was an increase in the quantity of offences (from 34 crimes punished by the Zanardelli Code, to 72 under the Rocco Code). Also, the layout of chapters reflected the hierarchy of values to be protected.[112] Not by chance, the first chapters addressed crimes against the personality of the state, the public administration, public policy, and all other crimes that were related to the public sphere of the state. One must turn to the 12th chapter to find crimes against the person, and after that, against property.[113] In addition, Fascist influence also appeared in the insertion of a series of crimes related to the 'Protection of the Official State Religion'. The Fascist State, indeed, had ceased to be secular, and created a strong Catholic and conservative moralism. Along with crimes related to private life were crimes connected more to the public life of 'citizens', such as offences against 'the public economy', and the whole system of political offences. From these offences clearly emerged the extremely importance role given to the state and its 'personality', which was to be respected at all times, and in which

---

[108] A Rocco, 'Legge sulla facoltà del potere esecutivo di emanare norme giuridiche' in A Rocco (ed), *Discorsi parlamentari* (Bologna, Il Mulino, 2005) 257.

[109] G Maggiore, 'Diritto penale totalitario nello Stato totalitario' (1939) 11 *Rivista italiana di diritto penale* 140–61, 160.

[110] Ibid 158.

[111] Fiandaca, 'Il codice Rocco' 73.

[112] The principal provisions of the Code's special part were structured as follows: I Crimes against the Personality of the State; II Crimes against Public Administration; III Crimes against the Administration of Justice; IV Crimes against Religious Sentiment and against Piety to the Dead; V Crimes against Public Order; VI Crimes against Public Safety; VII Crimes against Public Faith; VIII Crimes against the Public Economy, Industry and Commerce; IX Crimes against Public Morality; X Crimes against the Integrity and Health of the Race; XI Crimes against the Family; XII Crimes against the Person; XIII Crimes against Property.

[113] See eg F Colao, G Neppi Modona and M Pelissero, 'Alfredo Rocco e il codice penale fascista' (2011) 1–2 *Democrazia e Diritto* 184–85.

citizens became silent subjects or, in the case of criminal conduct, 'enemies of the State'[114] to be eradicated by every possible means, including the most violent.

Along these lines were also instated crimes of 'anti-national activities by the citizen abroad' (so-called defeatism), 'subversive association' and 'subversive propaganda or apology', all seemingly abstract, but powerful means to silence any persons who expressed dissent against the regime. Crimes were defined in terms of the protection and supremacy of the state; individual rights were protected only in connection with injury to the public sphere; and so there was, in other words, a 'publicisation' of individual interests. For example, sexual freedom was protected only as a reflection of the public life of every citizen. Thus the crime of rape was not an offence against the person, but against 'public morality and decency'. Moreover, it was certainly significant that the Code included crimes relating to 'the protection of the integrity and health of the race [*stirpe*]' and 'family protection', which were fully functional to a Fascist model of society and family, with a strong leader and breadwinner and a submissive and subordinate wife.[115]

Similarly, in regulating property crimes, while proposing the same crimes as in the old code, the Rocco Code gave greater protection to the assets of the individual, but as part of the community, due to the state's interest in economic matters. This was evidenced by an expansion of the crime of fraud, the introduction of fraudulent insolvency, and the new crime of usury (previously abolished). The individual, in other words, was protected in his person and in his property only in the broader context of protecting the integrity of the ethical Fascist State, of which he was inextricably part.

Conclusion

In conclusion, the Rocco Code took a peculiar form, veering strongly towards an extreme Statism and authoritarianism that did not mesh at all with the principles of the Positivist School. Through direct study of the criminal man and his world, the aim of Lombroso was indeed to integrate law with real life, in order to lead to an individualised system of punishment, rather than a moralist criminal law, on the one hand using scientific theories to create easy stereotypes of 'enemies', both internal and external, and on the other hand using Catholic principles to take a conservative and moralistic turn.

[114] See also P Marchetti, 'Le "sentinelle del male". L'invenzione ottocentesca del criminale nemico della società tra naturalismo giuridico e normativismo psichiatrico' (2009) 38 *Quaderni fiorentini per la storia del pensiero giuridico moderno* 1009–80; M Donini and M Papa (eds), *Diritto penale del nemico. Un dibattito internazionale* (Milan, Giuffrè, 2007).

[115] According to a general interpretation, the role of a woman during Fascism was that of 'Queen of the hearth'. Against, on the 'active' role of women during the regime, see M Freddosio, 'The Fallen Hero. The Myth of Mussolini and Fascist Women in the Italian Social Republic (1943–45)' (1996) 31.1 *Journal of Contemporary History* 99–124.

Despite the many ambiguities throughout the work of Lombroso (ie his being a socialist, yet at the same time in favour, in some cases, of the death penalty), he probably would have liked a very different society from that of the Fascist era, such as a secularised society in which science could be a means of liberation and human evolution. It suffices to recall Lombroso's criticism of the narrow-minded and chauvinist mindset that became one of the characteristics of the ideal Fascist man. Therefore, it is possible to argue that in Lombroso's work deviance, as well as the concept of monster, has an ambivalent nature, or is Janus-faced. Not surprisingly then, albeit gradually, 'normality' according to Lombroso was likely to look almost insipid: indeed the 'normal' man, even though 'biologically healthy' and 'reassuring' in his 'good sense', was also apathetic and insignificant; not only did Lombroso find him to be a misoneist (one who is afraid of or hates every kind of novelty), selfish and lacking in creativity,[116] but as he pointed out, the 'normal'[117] man 'is not even cultured, nor learned, and does nothing but work and eat – *fruges consumere natus*'.[118] This idea led Lombroso to develop an evolutionary explanation of crime, highlighting its propulsive role in society.

Moreover, the Positivist School, due to its determinism derived from the denial of free will, was opposed both by the Catholic Church and the Crocean and Gentilian idealism that formed the philosophical background of Fascism. Thus, how could such a radically scientific concept of the world supported by the Positivist School be reconciled with the principles of idealism?

Under cover of the technical approach professed by Arturo Rocco[119] and his obsession with keeping law separate from other spheres, the precise political purpose that was realised not in an attempt to adopt the positivist thesis but, on the contrary, in the strenuous fight against it, was hidden. Protecting criminal law from any possible contamination by philosophy, human, social or other sciences, also shielded it from surveys and discussions that could have shed light on the authoritarian matrix of some institutions and principles, triggering or facilitating social and political processes that were among the main concerns both of the capitalist bourgeoisie (before) and Fascism (after).

It must not be forgotten that the intent of the Positivist School was to banish the myth of crime as 'sin' and of punishment as 'atonement' replacing this approach with a criminological and sociological one. Consequently, it is surely correct to note that

> positivism was attacked first by Rocco and then by the fury of Fascism which, serving the capitalist bourgeoisie, made use of both Rocco and his technical-legal method, in

---

[116] C Lombroso, *La funzione sociale del delitto* in D Frigessi, F Giacanelli and L Mangoni (eds), *Delitto, genio, follia. Scritti scelti*, 2nd edn (Turin, Bollati Boringhieri, 2000) 911.

[117] In the first edition of *Criminal Man* Lombroso used the term 'healthy man' instead of 'normal man' (used later), but the meaning was the same in both cases: 'ordinary' or 'non-criminal' man.

[118] C Lombroso, *L'uomo di genio in rapporto alla psichiatria, alla storia e all'estetica*, 6th edn (Turin, Bocca, 1894) xiii.

[119] Compare I Stolzi, *L'ordine corporativo. Poteri organizzati e organizzazione del potere nella riflessione giuridica dell'Italia fascista* (Milan, Giuffrè, 2007) 169–70.

which Fascism found scientific justification of an authoritarian nature for its penal repression.[120]

Moreover, the legal socialism[121] of positivists had at its heart the 'social question',[122] or rather the aim of using legal science positively to transform society. Such an aim is clearly apparent from reading the titles of many works by scholars belonging to the Positivist School, such as 'The class struggle in criminal justice' (Adolfo Zerboglio), 'Social injustices in the criminal code' (Eugenio Florian), or 'Crime and the social question' (Filippo Turati).

On the contrary, the operation set out by the Rocco Code was clearly functional within the Fascist system. Fascist criminal law, fishing liberally from the 'positivist magma', used positivistic weapons in a totally instrumental and anti-democratic way. The concept of 'social dangerousness' and the creation of the double-track system can be read in this context, allowing consideration of a 'squandered legacy' of the Positivist School.

Even though it is overly simplistic to see the authoritarian traces of the Rocco Code merely as a distortion of the positivist thesis, acknowledging that the Fascist regime itself is a complex and multi-faceted phenomenon, it is nevertheless true that many fundamental principles of the Positivist School (such as that of social defence) were adopted and used by the Fascist regime for its own ends. The Fascists took from this tradition only what they needed, eliminating all progressive and secularised instances and emphasising concepts and theories in an exclusively repressive way, in order to create with every available means a terrifying new legal machine suited to the regime. This regime had nothing of the new secular world, dominated by science, of Lombroso and his followers, even though they fell into serious error and over simplification.

Perhaps for these reasons, it is crucial – as some scholars, in contrast to the prevailing doctrine, have recently highlighted – finally to abandon the demonising and biased reading of the Positivist School, discovering instead the 'real' legacy[123] of the last major foundry of ideas to have influenced criminal science in many countries,[124] and to continue to investigate the reasons behind the 'success' of the Rocco Code[125] which, even though born under a dictatorship, could be considered to be 'the last great patriarch'[126] of the 'glorious' era of codification.

---

[120] Gallo, 'Una politica per la riforma del codice penale' 54.

[121] On this complex phenomenon, see two special issues of the review *Quaderni fiorentini per la storia del pensiero giuridico moderno* (1974/75) nos 3/4, and P Grossi, *History of European Law* (Malden, Wiley-Blackwell, 2010) 123–25.

[122] See eg G Neppi Modona, 'Diritto penale e positivismo', in ER Papa (ed), *Il positivismo e la cultura italiana* (Milan, FrancoAngeli, 1985) 58–61.

[123] See especially S Vinciguerra, *Diritto penale italiano. Concetto, fonti, validità, interpretazione* vol I (Padua, Cedam, 2009) 271 and Manna, 'Le sanzioni penali' 298.

[124] Not only in Latin America, but also in Northern Europe and the United States. See eg HH Jescheck, 'Il significato del diritto comparato per la riforma penale' (1978) *Rivista Italiana di Diritto e Procedura Penale* 808.

[125] On the 'celebration' of the Rocco Code's 80th anniversary see recently L Stortoni, G Insolera (eds), *Gli ottant'anni del codice Rocco* (Bologna, Bononia University Press, 2012).

[126] Donini, 'Tecnicismo giuridico' 130.

3

Fascist by Name, Fascist by Nature? The 1930 Italian Penal Code in Academic Commentary, 1928–46

STEPHEN SKINNER*

The 1930 Italian Penal Code, introduced under the Fascist regime[1] and named after its Minister of Justice, Alfredo Rocco, was the product of a number of criminological and theoretical influences, including explicit and implicit political connections with Fascism.[2] Despite the Code's genesis and connection with the regime, after the fall of Fascism and Italy's transition to a constitutional democracy, the impetus for reform and renewal stopped short of replacing it. Instead, even though it was to undergo a lengthy process of revision, the Code remained in force.

The way in which the Code survived after the war requires close attention, and was largely due to influential Italian legal scholars in the mid-1940s, who relied on the Code's hybrid nature and its ambiguity to construct an interpretation that minimised its political connections with the totalitarian regime and emphasised its merits, thus supporting its retention.[3] This anti-reform argument focused on the Code's purportedly apolitical 'technical-legal' nature and its apparent

* This chapter is based on research undertaken with British Academy Small Grant SG101739. All translations are my own.

[1] The Fascist regime also introduced the 1930 Code of Criminal Procedure (replaced in 1988–89) and the 1942 Civil Code and Civil Procedure Code (both revised, but like the Penal Code, also still in force today).

[2] See generally EM Wise, 'Introduction' in EM Wise with A Maitlin (eds), *The Italian Penal Code* (London, Sweet & Maxwell, 1978) xxi–xlvi; S Skinner, 'Tainted Law? The Italian Penal Code, Fascism and Democracy' (2011) 7.4 *International Journal of Law in Context* 423–46; G Neppi Modona and M Pelissero, 'La politica criminale durante il fascismo' in L Violante (ed), *Storia d'Italia, Annali 12, La criminalità* (Turin, Einaudi, 1997) 759–847 and M Sbriccoli, 'Caratteri originari e tratti permanenti del sistema penale italiano (1860–1990)' in L Violante with L Minervini (eds), *Storia d'Italia, Annali 14, Legge Diritto Giustizia* (Turin, Einaudi, 1998) 487–551.

[3] See especially (regarding both the Penal Code and Penal Procedure Code) L Lacché, '"Sistemare il terreno e sgombrare le macerie." Gli anni della "Costituzione Provvisoria": alle origini del discorso sulla riforma della legislazione e del Codice di Procedura Penale (1943–1947)' in L Garlati (ed), *L'Inconscio Inquisitorio. L'Eredità del Codice Rocco nella Cultura Processualpenalistica Italiana* (Milan, Giuffrè, 2010) 271–304 and G Neppi Modona, 'Principio di legalità e giustizia penale nel periodo fascista' (2007) 36 *Quaderni fiorentini per la storia del pensiero giuridico moderno* 983–1005.

adherence in its first two articles to the principle of legality, or legal certainty.[4] Yet from the 1970s, subsequent Italian critical analysis has emphasised the narrow legal positivism of the anti-reform argument and its misreading of Fascist legality,[5] attributing such a selective view to dominant internal conditions at the time, primarily including vested professional interests, the absence of a politically strong alternative reform project, and institutional continuity for reasons of expediency in an intensely difficult socio-political context.[6] This internal Italian debate, or academic discourse, about the Code and the relationship between Fascism and criminal law can therefore be understood as both a component and a reflection of the complex processes at work in post-war Italy, whereby Fascist laws and institutional structures were not completely expunged.[7]

However, the issue of academic analysis of the Code and the perception, representation and interpretation of its roots and characteristics also raises the fundamental question of how we may grasp and understand the nexus between Fascism and criminal law, or in other words, how we can tell if a law that is 'Fascist by name' is also 'Fascist by nature', and what we then make of it. This is a concern not only in the Italian post-war discourse but also in the Code's reception by its wider interpretative community. Addressing this question in a broader systemic and temporal context provides a new critical perspective on the history of Fascism and the Rocco Code, including the latter's survival, as well as on the processes by which legal science acknowledges the relationship between law and political power, on the history of comparative law and its critical relevance, and on our comparative understanding of the legal dimensions of Fascism and its democratic opponents. With those objectives, this chapter offers an original analysis of how the Rocco Code was received in international academic publications in the period from its draft stage in 1928 to the time of the Italian post-war reform debate, and the waning of post-war comparative attention around 1946. The chapter examines a range of studies of the Rocco Code by contemporaneous legal and political scholars in the United Kingdom, the United States and (pre-Vichy) France, the major liberal democracies at the time (albeit in the relative sense of the interwar period[8]).

---

[4] A key expression of the anti-reform position was T Delogu, 'L'elemento politico nel codice penale' (1945) 1 *Archivio Penale* 161–95. See Lacché, 'Sistemare il terreno e sgombrare le macerie' 282–83; P Piasenza, 'Tecnicismo giuridico e continuità dello Stato: il dibattito sulla riforma del codice penale e della legge di pubblica sicurezza' (1979) *Politica del diritto* 261–317, 265–68; M Sbriccoli, 'Le mani nella pasta e gli occhi al cielo – la penalistica italiana negli anni del fascismo' (1999) 28.1 *Quaderni Fiorentini per la Storia del Pensiero Giuridico Moderno* 817–50, 842–50. See also G Neppi Modona, 'Tecnicismo e scelte politiche nella riforma del codice penale' (1977) 17.4 *Democrazia e diritto* 661–84.
[5] Piasenza, 'Tecnicismo giuridico e continuità dello Stato' 269–70 and 272–73; Neppi Modona, 'Tecnicismo e scelte politiche nella riforma del codice penale' and 'Principio di legalità e giustizia penale nel periodo fascista'.
[6] Piasenza ibid 315–16.
[7] See generally M Battini (SG Pugliese ed and NG Mazhar trans), *The Missing Italian Nuremberg* (Basingstoke, Palgrave Macmillan, 2007); P Ginsborg, *A History of Contemporary Italy 1943–1980* (London, Penguin Books, 1990).
[8] Skinner, 'Tainted Law?' 426.

This reading of the Rocco Code through contemporaneous academic commentary has two main methodological foundations. First, this comparative approach is inspired by similar work that has considered how German National-Socialist (Nazi) law was perceived by its wider interpretative community, before the fall of that regime.[9] Although such work has focused on the fact that Nazi law has generally been considered non-law in the post-war era – an interpretation that has not been made of Fascist law – it usefully demonstrates how reading Nazi law from the outside through contemporaneous and comparative analyses provides important perspectives on its status at that time, highlighting its problematic similarities with other systems. With regard to Fascist law, however, such an undertaking is in many ways particularly difficult, because of the absence of a retrospective law/non-law dichotomy and the fact that the Fascism-law nexus, despite some acute features, is generally more ambiguous. This is due to the ways in which Fascism sought not to subvert but to use law, apparent legal principles and legal institutions to ground and direct its authority.

The chapter draws its second methodological support for this analysis from George Fletcher's well-known argument about the critical force of comparative law.[10] In Fletcher's view, '[t]he promise of comparative law is that it enables us to get beyond ourselves to look back, with slightly alienated eyes, on the assumptions that [we] accept without reflection'.[11] This 'looking back' here involves both a critically reflexive reconsideration of the relative (perceived) identities of Fascist and non-Fascist law through external (non-Italian) commentary (in Fletcher's terms, interpretative representations[12]), and critical engagement with Fascism and criminal law through a matrix of historically contemporaneous analysis. This seeks to avoid anachronistic, retrospective appraisal in terms of post-war democratic principles and political judgement, and to situate the Italian post-war anti-reform arguments in relation to the views of the wider legal community, as well as its contextual influences, up to that period. The critical force of this sort of comparative analysis is to be found both in the ways that the studies themselves construct understanding of their object, in this case the Rocco Code, as well as in reflection ('looking back') on the studies together and in their historical setting.

On these bases, the chapter undertakes what has to be an essentially chronological and necessarily linear study of the comparative commentaries on the Italian Penal Code addressed here. Taking them in order, the chapter structures them in terms of key phases in the Code's development, their own emerging

---

[9] D Fraser, '"The outsider does not see all the game": Perceptions of German Law in Anglo-American Legal Scholarship, 1933–1940' in C Joerges and N Singh Ghaleigh (eds), *Darker Legacies of Law in Europe: the Shadow of National Socialism and Fascism over Europe and its Legal Traditions* (Oxford, Hart, 2003) 87–111; similarly, L Lustgarten has also argued that Nazi law embodied principles and concerns shared in other contemporary systems in '"A Distorted Image of Ourselves": Nazism, "Liberal" Societies and the Qualities of Difference' in Joerges and Singh Ghaleigh ibid 113–32.

[10] G Fletcher 'Comparative Law as a Subversive Discipline' (1998) 46 *American Journal of Comparative Law* 683–700.

[11] Ibid 695.

[12] Ibid 691–92.

themes, and importantly the broader context of the Fascist regime's development and reception on the world stage. In so doing, the chapter constructs three lines of argument.

First, it argues that commentators' responses to the Rocco Code and their ability to identify and engage with its political and ideological significance depended on their chosen methodology. Here the chapter shows the limited usefulness of positivist (de-contextualised, solely substantive) legal analysis in responding to the emergence of a new legal order and its problematic dimensions. In terms of comparative engagement, the chapter argues that there were four main methods of analysis apparent in the studies outlined here. These involve the construction of understanding by reference to the commentator's own system; to a system considered to be more problematic (or a paradigm 'worse case'); to standards associated with what the commentator considered to be an ideal model of criminal law (or legal principles more generally); and to actual practice. Whereas the first two sorts of approach appear to be the least useful for critical purposes, either by tending to support the identification of similarities or by concealing the Code's problematic dimensions behind references to more extreme forms of penal law, the other two approaches support more critical analysis. Consequently, the chapter argues that the response of legal scholarship in this period to the emergence of Fascism and its criminal code was best able to grasp the significance of that law where scholars had an awareness of its real implications in practice or a clear sense of fundamental values. Emphasising the latter, the chapter suggests that evaluating law's ideological subordination in Fascism requires ideologically awakened legal analysis.

Secondly, in that light the chapter argues that, although even by the end of the Second World War the nexus between Fascism and the Penal Code was still to some extent ambiguous, so that the Italian anti-reform perspective was not completely anomalous internationally, crucial dimensions of deep, political critique of the Code were by then evident in comparative scholarship. This means, it is argued, that the Code and conservative Italian doctrine's treatment of it were far more contestable than they were at the time presented as being.

Third, and perhaps most importantly, the chapter argues that this study of foreign commentaries also demonstrates the Fascist regime's reliance on recognisable criminal law, and reveals some uncomfortable similarities and connections between the Code and democratic law in the interwar period, in terms of both contextual influences and substantive elements. As such, the chapter suggests that Fascist and non-fascist law may be seen as two sides of the same coin: although there are important ideological distinctions between them, they are both manifestations of similar normative forms and functions in early twentieth-century Europe across divergent political systems.

Reading the Rocco Code in
Comparative Academic Commentary

The historical discussion of the 1930 Code is explored here primarily on the basis of commentaries by legal scholars, although some informative political and general discussions of Fascism and law from the 1930s are also included by way of contrast.[13] These commentaries are addressed in terms of three periods, which cover key stages in the history of the Code and of external perceptions of Fascism, as reflected in the commentaries themselves. The first period includes initial engagement with the Code's draft form in the late 1920s, reflecting first responses to that draft and ongoing reaction to the birth of Fascism. The second, longest period includes developing critical commentary on the Code from its coming into force in 1931 up to the eve of the Second World War, a period of rising global tensions in which Fascism was increasingly recognised to be a threat, then an enemy. The third period, in which the number of foreign commentaries markedly declines, runs from the start of the war to the year following its end: after an apparently fallow period of commentary, the first study considered in this period was published in 1943, contemporaneous with the fall of the Fascist regime, and the last in 1946, the year after the key publications in the Italian anti-reform debate. This period importantly also reflects the emergence of a new world order, in which the major threat was increasingly a different totalitarian regime, Soviet communism.

A. Initial Engagement, 1928–30

Following the March on Rome in 1922, the advent and increasingly alarming activities of the Fascist regime led to growing interest and concern abroad. Studies of public opinion in England at that time note a shift in attitudes, from relative indifference to Italian affairs after the First World War, to increasing alarm at the Mussolini regime's use of violence and declaration of imperialist plans.[14] Similarly, the rise of Fascism, the consolidation of the regime's power and its imperial

---

[13] These commentaries have been located through library catalogues, electronic databases and bibliographical references. The research is ongoing (extending to commentators from other countries) and the chapter does not at this stage purport to provide exhaustive coverage of commentaries from the chosen systems, nor does it include the work of Italian writers publishing abroad, or consideration of differences between time of writing and publication. Future research might enrich this analysis by exploring the commentators themselves in more detail, including matters such as political profile, academic background and professional connections with Italy, as well as the role of editors and publishers. Due to its focus on the Penal Code, the chapter includes only a few references to penal procedure and criminal justice more generally, which also require further attention from this perspective.

[14] A Berselli, *L'Opinione Pubblica Inglese e l'Avvento del Fascismo (1919–1925)* (Milan, Franco Angeli Editore, 1971) 11–13. See also E Fasano Guarini, 'Il "Times" di fronte al fascismo (1919–1932)' (1965) *Rivista Storica del Socialismo* 155–85.

ambitions also meant that French opinion had to start to take its 'Latin sister', previously considered a poorer, unimportant relation to the south, more serious-ly.[15] Against this background, and combined with Italy's legal reputation as a cra-dle of criminal law and criminology (due to the influence of figures such as Cesare Beccaria, Cesare Lombroso and Enrico Ferri), the development of a new penal code in the late 1920s under the Fascist regime attracted a certain amount of com-parative legal interest, notable also per se because this 'discipline' was still in its infancy at the time. In this period, what was to become the 1930 Code began with an outline project and consultation process, before moving to a draft text, which then led to the definitive final version. However, despite the increasing evidence of the Fascist regime's harsh realities, legal engagement with the draft Penal Code only briefly acknowledged its context.

An early example of commentary from this time is a short English article on the preliminary project for the Rocco Penal Code from 1928, which relates it to Justice Minister Alfredo Rocco's ideological claims about state superiority and the supremacy of force, noting its criminologically positivist tendencies, and empha-sising its apparently Fascist dimensions, in terms of the reintroduction of the death penalty and protection of the state and family values.[16] In this regard the commentator, SE Saunders, also flags the increased scope of judicial discretion over punishments, noting that:

> There are lawyers in Italy who watch the eclipse of Zanardelli's code with profound misgiving. They question what they believe to be a degradation of the lofty conception of law as the immutable centre of every legal system. In its place they find a penal code which draws the attention away from the law and focuses it on the magistrate.[17]

Recognising the importance of systemic reality, Saunders emphasises with restrained concern why this shift in favour of judicial discretion is problematic:

> [W]here one is inclined to be most skeptical about the new penal code, is perhaps in the essentially political character which the legal body assumes, since all its members have to be members of the Fascist party. In the last five years every barrister, magistrate, and judge who has been considered by the Government as insufficiently Fascist has been suspended from office. This whole problem, however, is intimately bound up with the evolution of that party into a State system; a process that is gradually going on in mod-ern Italy.[18]

This first commentary thus situates the draft code in its context and is one of the few such works to acknowledge Fascism's totalitarian aims over the legal pro-fession. Similar evidence of unease about the draft code is also apparent in a French commentary published in the same year. Louis Hugueney, a law professor at the University of Paris, begins his study by underlining the interest of examin-

---

[15] P Milza, *Le Fascisme Italien et la Presse Française (1920–1940)* (Brussells, Editions Complexes, 1987) 42–49. See also C Vivanti, 'La stampa francese di fronte al fascismo (luglio 1922 – gennaio 1925)' (1965) *Rivista Storica del Socialismo* 52–92.

[16] SE Saunders, 'The New Penal Code in Italy' (1928) 165 *The Law Times* 307–09.

[17] Ibid 309.

[18] Ibid 309.

ing the draft code in terms of Italy's heritage as the 'fatherland of criminal law' and due to the draft's merging of elements of classical and positivist criminology.[19] However, Hugueney points out that the key feature of the draft code is its Fascist genesis, stating that 'of all the Codes being renewed, none bears the mark of Fascism to the same extent as this draft penal code, which is truly the quintessential Fascist code'.[20] Its Fascist features, for Hugueney, are evident in its length, which he suggests mirrors the new grandiose Fascist ambition; its 'nationalist and internationalist' scope, covering offences against Italian interests committed by Italians and foreigners in Italy and abroad, all of which indicate the aim of 'defending at any cost Fascist Italy and Italians loyal to it'; together with its increased severity of punishment over the previous Zanardelli Code, even its at times 'draconian' nature.[21] Moreover, Hugueney cites Rocco's preliminary declarations about the draft code's special part, in which Rocco underlined that its content seeks to enhance protection of the state, the family and public morality, the race (with a focus on Italy's birth rate), Catholic beliefs, and public economic interests.[22] Hugueney concludes, like the previous comment, by noting that assessing the draft code would be premature, and that all will depend on how the actual code is applied, but also observes that it is not for a foreigner to appraise the code politically, as that is a matter of national concern only.[23]

However, some commentaries were notably more detached. A detailed but uncritical analysis of the draft code was published in French by a Dutch legal commentator the following year, 1929.[24] This monographic commentary – praised at the time by a reviewer in the *Harvard Law Review*[25] – is predominantly a technical outline of the background and contents of the draft code's general part. Despite noting the draft code's mixed positivist and classical criminological influences, and increase in punitiveness,[26] this commentary barely mentions the Fascist context – seven years into the regime – and only briefly remarks (contra Saunders) on the Code's tendency to limit judicial discretion.[27] Similarly, an article published in 1930 by a *conseiller* at the French Cour de Cassation, Pierre de Casabianca, provides a detailed outline of all of the new Italian code's provisions dealing with the responsibility and protection of minors. Although it relates these to the regime's desire to protect and nurture its youth, 'in the interest of the Nation and to assure it a greater future', it is technical in its focus and neutral in its observations.[28]

---

[19] L Hugueney, 'Le Projet de Code pénal fasciste' (1928) *Études Criminologiques* 41–49.
[20] Ibid 41.
[21] Ibid 41–42.
[22] Ibid 46–47 citing a speech by Rocco on the draft code in 1927.
[23] Ibid 49.
[24] HGJ Maas Geesteranus, *La Réforme Pénale en Italie* (Paris, Recueil Sirey, 1929), electronic copy provided by the International Institute of Social History, Amsterdam.
[25] Review by T Sellin (University of Pennsylvania), (1929) 42.8 *Harvard Law Review* 1086–88.
[26] Geesteranus, *La Réforme Pénale en Italie* 61–63, 81, 156–63.
[27] Ibid 22; also Sellin's review 1088.
[28] P de Casabianca, 'Les mineurs dans le nouveau code pénal italien' (1930) *Revue pénitentiaire et de droit pénal* 453–83, 483.

The major contemporaneous work on the 1930 Code by an English scholar is a five-part article comparing Rocco's 'definitive project', or final draft of the Code (as subsequently brought into force) with criminal law in England. First published in translation in one of the ambitious comparative studies on criminal law produced by the Italian Institute of Legislative Studies to herald the introduction of the 1930 Code,[29] the English original then came out in five parts in a leading comparative law journal starting the following year.[30] Strikingly, the author of the comparison, WTS Stallybrass, a Reader in Criminal Law and the Law of Evidence at the University of Oxford, states that his principal objective is to draw to the attention of Continental lawyers key principles of English criminal law that might inform what was then an ongoing penal codification process across Europe.[31] He specifically states that he will not interpret the draft Rocco code in terms of criminological approaches, referring to Saunders's article on this issue (even though as noted it does not say much in this regard) or in terms of Fascism, on which he refers to Italian studies, although he does ultimately make some brief critical observations in this connection, as indicated below.[32] Consequently, Stallybrass's mainly and deliberately apolitical approach focuses on comparison with his own system and treats the nascent 1930 Code as a worthy object of study on a par with English law. Most notably, he separates it from the Fascist political backdrop and context – at the time already distinctively totalitarian, given the regime's activities since 1922 and its passing of the repressive, so-called 'ultra-Fascist' laws in 1926 that brought back the death penalty and clamped down on political opposition.[33]

Stallybrass begins by focusing on Article 1 of the draft code, which as noted in the introduction above appeared to uphold legal certainty and the prohibition on arbitrary punishment, and Article 2 on the prohibition on retroactivity except to the benefit of the accused. Comparing Article 1 favourably with long-standing implicit principles of the rule of law and common law decency, Stallybrass nevertheless argues that its worth will depend on its enforceability, and in that regard he suggests that the English procedure of habeas corpus provides a valuable benchmark. With regard to Article 2, Stallybrass notes that there was no equivalent principle in English law. Although he comments that 'English law does not regard ex post facto legislation with favour', it is not 'hostile to English law' and would probably be enforced by the courts if in the public interest.[34] Similarly, he

---

[29] WTS Stallybrass, 'Paralello dei principi generali del Diritto penale inglese col Progetto definitivo del nuovo Codice penale italiano' in *Studi di Diritto Penale Comparato I: Saggi Critici, Il Progetto Rocco nel Pensiero Giuridico Contemporaneo* (Rome, Edizione dell'Istituto di Studi Legislativi, 1930).

[30] WTS Stallybrass, 'A Comparison of the General Principles of Criminal Law in England with the "Progetto Definitivo di un Nuovo Codice Penale" of Alfredo Rocco' (1931) 13 *Journal of Comparative Legislation and International Law* 203–15 (pt I), (1932) 14 ibid 45–61 and 233–43 (pts II–III), (1933) 15 ibid 77–88 and 232–41 (pts IV–V).

[31] New penal codes were also introduced or under discussion in countries including Austria, Denmark, Spain and Switzerland.

[32] Stallybrass, 'A Comparison of the General Principles of Criminal Law' pt I 204–05.

[33] PA Cavaliere, *Il diritto penale politico in Italia: dallo Stato liberale allo Stato totalitario. Storia delle ideologie penalistiche tra istituzioni e interpretazioni* (Rome, Aracne, 2008) 207–73.

[34] Stallybrass, 'A Comparison of the General Principles of Criminal Law' pt I 206–07.

notes that there was no 'provision in English law for the cessation of punishment' if an offence is repealed, and that a solution would be found on the basis that 'it can scarcely be doubted that the Government would use the prerogative power of pardon'.[35] The first two foundational principles of the draft code were thus taken at face value by Stallybrass at the time of their drafting, and generally compared favourably with the common law, in terms of both its implicit ideals and inherent flexibility. Interestingly, reading between the lines, Stallybrass also appears to have great faith in the benevolence of government, and implies that judges are the best guardians of criminal justice, only alluding to Italy's Fascistisation of the judiciary at the end of his study.[36]

The remainder of Stallybrass's lengthy analysis goes on to address the fundamental principles of liability, as set out in the draft code. In essence, three key points are worth noting here. First, Stallybrass observes that the draft code and English criminal law differ in some respects in their relative harshness and clemency. For example, whereas he observes that the draft code adopts a more severe approach to the punishment of attempted crimes, it is 'more satisfactory' in its approach to dealing with insane defendants, with set terms of confinement, as opposed to a lifetime of detention in an asylum that he notes generally followed the so-called special verdict in English law.[37]

Secondly, with regard to issues of jurisdiction, Stallybrass observes major differences between the draft code and English criminal law. Articles 7–11 of the draft code 'assert jurisdiction over offences committed abroad by Italian citizens and foreigners', which Stallybrass notes exceeds the common law understanding of the appropriate reach of criminal law under international law.[38] According to Article 7, political offences committed by Italian citizens or foreigners abroad were justiciable in Italy, including crimes against the personality of the state, crimes of counterfeiting, and abuse of office by public officials working for the Italian State.[39] For Stallybrass, 'these astonishingly wide claims' represent 'an extreme assertion of the claims of Fascism' in the name of the state's duty to protect its interests and prestige, and the regime's reaction against historical, liberal limitations of territory and jurisdiction, going beyond the tendency of Continental States to claim a wide jurisdiction over political offences.[40]

The significance of this wide jurisdictional claim is greater still due to the fact that Article 8 extended the definition of political offences to ordinary crimes committed 'wholly or in part' with 'political or social motives'.[41] The fact that Fascist Italy also opposed the exclusion of all such defined political offences from

---

[35] Ibid.

[36] Ibid pt V 235–36.

[37] Ibid pt I 212 and pt II 54–56. Stallybrass goes on to note that the draft code makes certain defences easier to rely on than English law, including intoxication and coercion by threats (ibid pt II 58–61), as well as superior orders, provocation and necessity, albeit on narrow grounds (ibid pt III 234–43).

[38] Ibid pt IV 83–84.

[39] Ibid 84.

[40] Ibid 84 and 86–87.

[41] Ibid 84.

extradition treaties (reflected in Article 13) is noted by Stallybrass as a departure from precedent. Revealingly he adds: 'This tendency is not likely to meet with much favour in England, at any rate whilst the present Soviet government is in power in Russia.'[42] At the time Stallybrass was writing, the violent and repressive tendencies of the Fascist regime had been apparent for several years but, as the latter quotation indicates, it was the Soviet menace that constituted a specific reason for his reservations about an increase in claims of state jurisdiction over extended political offences, a precursor of the sort of double political myopia that was to become even more pronounced in some later commentaries. As a last point on jurisdictional matters, Stallybrass also notes that Article 11 of the draft code allows an Italian citizen or foreigner to be tried in Italy for an offence committed on Italian territory, even if the accused has already been tried for it elsewhere. This he observes 'seems a somewhat extreme and unfortunate development of Fascist principle, and to smack not a little of the "ferment of international distrust"' that he says Rocco otherwise opposes.[43]

Thirdly, Stallybrass ends his study with some comments on punishment and some general conclusions. On punishment, Stallybrass makes two notable observations. The first of these is that:

> It was strange that at the same moment in history Italy, which not so many years ago had altogether abandoned the death sentence, should have been contemplating its introduction for some twenty different offences whilst there was a committee sitting in England to consider the abolition of capital punishment for the one offence for which for practical purposes in time of peace it is still retained![44]

By focusing on the contrast with England, this comment rather understates the importance of the reintroduction of the death penalty in Italy. Abolished under the Zanardelli Code, brought back in 1926[45] and then reintroduced in the Rocco Code, the political significance of this extreme punishment was perhaps worthy of closer consideration, especially given Rocco's own lengthy justification of it in his principal speech about the draft Code.[46] Stallybrass's relative silence on this point can usefully be contrasted with a political monograph on Fascism published at the same time as Stallybrass's papers, in which the link between the death penalty and totalitarian power was underlined as a step back from Italy's former Beccarian progressiveness.[47]

---

[42] Ibid. See further Cavaliere, *Il diritto penale politico in Italia* 513.

[43] Stallybrass, 'A Comparison of the General Principles of Criminal Law' pt IV 87–88.

[44] Ibid pt V 232.

[45] Cavaliere, *Il diritto penale politico in Italia* 513.

[46] See especially A Rocco, 'Relazione a sua Maestà il Re del Ministro Guardasigilli (Rocco) Presentata nell'udienza del 19 Ottobre 1930-VIII per l'approvazione del testo definitivo del Codice Penale' in *Lavori Preparatori del Codice Penale e Del Codice di Procedura Penale, Vol. VII, Testo del Nuovo Codice Penale con la Relazione a Sua Maestà il Re del Guardasigilli (Rocco)* (Rome, Ministero della Giustizia e degli Affari di Culto, Tipografia delle Mantellate, 1930) 7–28 at 21 and 25.

[47] The work was published by a professor of political science at Ohio State University, HR Spencer, *Government and Politics of Italy* (London, George G Harrap & Co, 1932) 222 and 230–31.

The second observation about punishment concerns the positivism-inspired security measures introduced in the draft code. Supplementary measures in addition to basic punishments, these security measures were to become a major feature of the new Penal Code's increased harshness. For Stallybrass this increase in severity is a possible model for his own system:

> The whole carefully considered proposals for the treatment of recidivists, and habitual and professional criminals, deserve the most careful consideration in England, where considerable doubts exist as to the success of our own experiments in that direction . . . the juridical systematization of 'measures of security' . . . may well afford a model for other countries.[48]

Therefore for this particular commentator, the draft code had numerous merits, the political dimensions of which attracted critical comment only in certain respects; notably, Stallybrass does not address the contents of the draft code's special parts on particular crimes. His general conclusion is that the code has 'far more in it to praise than to censure' and is welcome for 'asserting the moral responsibility of human beings, for reasserting the dignity of man'.[49] Importantly, he notes, the code rightly reaffirms the moral weight and impetus of punishment due to the fact that 'it is right to hate criminals'.[50] While this forthright comment is striking, it is apparently 'of its time' and relatively mild when compared with an earlier statement in the English textbook, *Salmond on Jurisprudence*, according to which:

> We hang murderers, not merely that we may put into the hearts of others like them the fear of a like fate, but for the same reason for which we kill snakes, namely, because it is better for us that they should be out of the world than in it.[51]

However, Stallybrass's observations, which reflect a contemporary excitement about the technical advances in the code, end with an important reservation about its overall probable impact, despite the general absence of political assessments elsewhere. Stallybrass, like Saunders before him, observes the Italian State's insistent 'Fascistisation' of the legal profession, and notes that the real test for the new code will be in its implementation.[52] As a counterpoint, Stallybrass's implied concern about the code's application was apparently not subsequently shared by Villem Pompe, a law professor at the University of Utrecht, who expresses reservations about the scope of security measures but states that the code's unclear dimensions would be addressed through its implementation, to the benefit of the

---

[48] The use of 'security measures' reflected wider positivist influences on penality in Europe during the 1920s: see for example M Ploscowe, 'An Examination of Some Dispositions Relating to Motives and Character in Modern European Penal Codes' (1930–31) 21 *American Institute for Criminal Law and Criminology* 26, which discusses (among other examples) the Zanardelli Code and the famously positivist Ferri Project of 1921, but not the Rocco Project. See also Ch 2 in this collection.

[49] Stallybrass, 'A Comparison of the General Principles of Criminal Law' V, 234 pt.

[50] Ibid 235.

[51] CAW Manning (ed), *Salmond on Jurisprudence*, (London, Sweet & Maxwell, 1930) 122.

[52] Stallybrass, 'A Comparison of the General Principles of Criminal Law' pt V 235–36.

'new and strong fascist order of State'.[53] Yet while the fact that such 'benefit' might only be one-way did not seem problematic to Pompe, its repressive potential is later noted by the American commentator, Morris Ploscowe, who shows how the Fascist system decreased procedural protections for individuals in the application of criminal law.[54] Consequently, contextual and practical awareness of the code's systemic application is an important element in the formulation of more qualified assessments of its merits and possible effects at this time, and Stallybrass's otherwise generally neutral, even positive evaluation is ultimately attenuated by this.

Stallybrass's study also appeared (as indicated above) in Italian translation as part of a significant comparative study of the draft Rocco code published in 1930–31, which included a range of technical analyses of various aspects of the draft code by international experts. Predominantly devoid of political and contextual commentary (perhaps unsurprisingly given the publication background) these studies focus on 'black letter' comparative discussions of the Italian code's provisions in relation to the law in force elsewhere – primarily commentators' own systems – treating the code as a criminologically and scientifically respectable, even leading example of criminal law.[55] Two such contributions to that collection deserve mention because of their engagement with key aspects of the draft code's general and special parts.

The first of these is a study of the draft code's provisions on justifications by JA Roux, a law professor at the University of Strasbourg.[56] Roux's analysis is noteworthy because he finds Article 57 of the draft code (which became Article 53 in the final version) on the legitimate use of arms by public officials a fair innovation to enable state agents to do their duty unopposed. This is particularly interesting as this provision is one of the few elements of the original code that are still in force today, and is a key example of a much-criticised Fascist legacy in current Italian criminal law.[57]

The other contribution is also by a French law professor, Pierre Garraud of the University of Lyon, and addresses the draft code's inclusion of offences against public morality, the family and race, as covered by provisions in its general and, primarily, special part.[58] Garraud observes explicitly that the special part of a penal code provides a reliable indication of a country's political, economic and social principles and, referring to Hugueney (outlined above), notes that the draft

---

[53] V Pompe, 'Colpa e Pericolosità nel Progetto Definitivo di Codice Penale Italiano' in *Studi di Diritto Penale Comparato II – Il Codice Rocco e le recenti codificazioni penali, Saggi Critici* (Rome, Edizione dell'Istituto di Studi Legislativi, 1931) 7–31, 31.

[54] M Ploscowe, 'La Procédure Criminelle dans L'Italie Fasciste' (C Bastide trans) (1932) 55 *Revue des Sciences Politiques* 497–523 and 'Jury Reform in Italy' (1934–35) 25 *American Institute for Criminal Law and Criminology* 576–85 at 582 and 584–85.

[55] For example R Burrows, 'Impressioni di un giurista inglese sul Progetto di Codice penale italiano' in *Studi di Diritto Penale Comparato I* 343–50.

[56] JA Roux, 'Il Progetto Rocco e la nozione d'*injuria* (a proposito degli articoli 55 e seguenti)', in *Studi di Diritto Penale Comparato I* 281–93, 283–84.

[57] Skinner, 'Tainted Law?' 430–31.

[58] P Garraud, 'La difesa della moralità pubblica, della famiglia e della razza nel Progetto definitivo di Codice penale italiano', in *Studi di Diritto Penale Comparato I* 357–93.

penal code is the epitome of a Fascist code and gives a clear insight into the values of contemporary Italy.[59]

Most significantly, Garraud emphasises that even though such matters are of central importance to the Fascist regime they are not only Fascist, but indicative of, and relevant to international approaches to, shared problems of industrialisation, urbanisation, a perceived decline in family values, concerns about demographic decline, and a perceived increase in 'egotism and violence' resulting from the moral decay brought about by economic and political upheavals, especially the First World War – an almost paradigmatically modernist *cri du coeur*.[60] Combined with what he identifies as a general philosophical reaction against the excesses of liberalism and the individualism of previous approaches to criminal law, he situates the Italian draft code as part of an international trend of penal intervention against 'indiscipline and immorality of family and social customs'.[61] Ultimately, Garraud's conclusion is particularly informative:

> As it stands, the final draft code (Progetto definitivo), which is much less excessive than the German Codes, but more daring and repressive than legislation inspired by liberal principles such as the French or Belgian Codes, constitutes, better than the 1889 [Zanardelli] Code, in which this aspect could nevertheless already have been identified, a point of transition, a bridge, between the two sorts of penal legislation. Cleared, in some respects, of a certain arbitrariness and imprecision, freed of some provisions that are inadmissible for States faithful to individualism and opposed to excessive State interference, the draft code could well be a base and a model in the undeniable movement that tends to bring closer together and unify penal legislation, inspired by Christian morals, in the area of defending public and family morality.[62]

In this light it is clear that despite certain reservations, Garraud does not consider these areas of its special part to be particularly problematic or exceptionable. Instead, they are situated within what he identifies as shared values and converging trends in criminal legislation at the time, albeit with extremes in the form of German and French law. So, as with Stallybrass's commentary, Garraud concludes that the code's value and impact will only be measurable through its application.[63]

Thus in this initial period of foreign engagement with the draft code, some of its political dimensions were already apparent but, despite the growing evidence of the Fascist regime's conduct, its nascent penal code attracted only limited critical commentary. In terms of method, most of these commentators undertook comparisons with their own systems or, in Garraud's paper, with reference to another system, in that case German law. The latter paper also placed the draft code favourably (remembering the publication context) in the broader post-world war perception of decline and threats to society, welcoming its tough stance

[59] Ibid 357–58.
[60] Ibid 359.
[61] Ibid 359, 359–60.
[62] Ibid 393.
[63] Ibid 392.

on core values. Most studies though showed at least some awareness of the importance of practice, noting that that would be the key indicator of value and significance as the draft code was put into effect. Academic perspectives began to change,
however, after the code came into force.

B. Commentary in a Time of Crisis, 1931–38

The period from the Code's entry into force to the brink of war saw a notable shift
in critical engagement with Italian penal law, against the unstated – but impossible to ignore – backdrop of rising tensions in Europe. Although in the early 1930s
Mussolini still enjoyed relatively good relations with Britain and France, from
around 1934, as he started to build his alliance with Hitler, perceptions of Italy
abroad began to change. This process was influenced also by other events, including Italy's invasion of Abyssinia in 1935, the establishment of the Rome-Berlin
Axis in 1936, and above all the impending outbreak of war in 1939.[64] In this
context, commentaries on the Code include more confident evaluation of its
substance and essence, as being in contrast to the values and principles of the
writers' understanding of democracy.

After an apparent lull in attention to the Code in the early 1930s immediately
after its introduction,[65] the first significant commentary to be considered here
addresses the odd coexistence in Italian penal law between an apparently classical
focus on individual responsibility and more criminologically positivist preventative and security measures.[66] In this study, Nathaniel Cantor, Professor of
Criminology at the University of Buffalo, and a leading commentator on penal
law at the time, notes how the Code's retention of a basis in individual responsibility is supposed to be anchored in the Fascist theory of the state's right to punish
in order to conserve and defend itself, rather than in the post-French Revolution
idea of a partial surrendering of rights by the individual.[67] This, he observes, is
combined with an 'eclectic' use of positivist security measures, which despite
Rocco's claims of a deliberate synthesis that 'transcends the various scientific tendencies into a superior unitary organ', instead results, Cantor argues, in 'inevitable confusion' in principle and practice.[68] In this regard therefore, Cantor's critical
engagement with the Code's punitive provisions focuses on inherent inconsisten-

---

[64] See RJB Bosworth, *Mussolini's Italy: Life Under the Dictatorship* (Penguin Books, London, 2005)
396–97, 400–01, 403–05.
[65] Contrast G Battaglini, 'The Fascist Reform of the Penal Law in Italy' (1933–34) 24 *American
Institute for Criminal Law and Criminology* 278–89. A professor at the University of Pavia and editor of
the *Rivista Italiana di diritto penale*, Battaglini provided an outline of selected Statist dimensions of the
new Penal Code, emphasising their merits.
[66] N Cantor, 'The New Prison Program of Italy' (1935–36) 26 *American Institute for Criminal Law
and Criminology* 216–27.
[67] Ibid 220. Cantor was also writing on German law at this time: see Fraser, 'The outsider does not
see all the game'.
[68] Cantor, 'The New Prison Program of Italy' 220.

cies in Fascist criminal philosophy, a fusion of competing approaches that Rocco's claims of unitary superiority could not in fact integrate.

Cantor's focus on the inherent tensions of Italian criminal law are more starkly evident in a subsequent article, published the following year, which only briefly touches on dimensions of the 1930 Code.[69] In a study of the brutal treatment of political prisoners of the Fascist regime, Cantor delineates the legal provisions on political crime under both the 1926 Act for the Defence of the State (one of the regime's 'ultra-Fascist' laws mentioned above) and the 1930 Penal Code, as well as the operation of the Special Tribunal for the Defence of the State (also set up in 1926) that could try such offences.[70] Noting, like other commentators (above), the inclusion of numerous political crimes against the state in the 1930 Code and its increased penalties, Cantor's study is significant because it details the treatment of those convicted, including savage torture.[71] This outline of the contextual reality beyond the Code, and the brutality of the Fascist regime, puts into stark relief the more apolitical, decontextualised approach of some earlier legal commentaries that focused on the new Code's provisions in technical isolation. Although studying the Penal Code itself is distinct from its implementation and institutional setting, the nature of the Fascist regime's conduct in the penal sphere appears retrospectively to have needed closer attention.

Around the same time as Cantor's work, a noteworthy political monograph on the Fascist State was published, which included an important observation on its law. This book, by Herman Finer, Reader in Public Administration at the University of London, discusses the scope and harshness of Italy's laws on political offences and compares them with English law. As in earlier studies, this comparison with his 'home' system serves to highlight an important similarity, but of a more disturbing nature. Finer notes that some aspects of English law on seditious libel at the time were almost as widely drawn as provisions of the Italian Penal Code punishing criticism of the state, but were he believed restrained by 'the safeguard of independent judges trained in law and justice'.[72] Sharing Stallybrass's faith in the judiciary, Finer draws attention to an important commonality in states' handling of threats to their internal security through open-textured concepts and wide discretion. However, aside from the contestable judicial safeguards he suggests, this comparison mainly indicates that the Fascist approach in this area was not so far removed from established 'democratic' practices.[73]

---

[69] N Cantor, 'The Fascist Political Prisoners' (1936–37) 27 *American Institute for Criminal Law and Criminology* 169–79.

[70] Ibid 174–77. On the 1926 Act and Special Tribunal see Cavaliere, *Il diritto penale politico in Italia*, and Ch 1 in this collection.

[71] Cantor, 'The Fascist Political Prisoners' 171 and 178.

[72] H Finer, *Mussolini's Italy* (London, Victor Gollancz, 1935) 231, 236, 241–47. Similar points are also made by HW Schneider, a political scientist, in *The Fascist Government of Italy* (New York, D Van Nostrand, 1936) 61.

[73] S Skinner, 'Crimes Against the State and the Intersection of Fascism and Democracy in the 1920s–30s: Vilification, Seditious Libel and the Suspension of Legality', forthcoming.

Soon afterwards two important articles on Fascist law in more general terms appeared in major law journals, one American and one English. In 1936, H Arthur Steiner of the University of California at Los Angeles published a theoretical article on 'The Fascist Conception of Law' in the *Columbia Law Review*.[74] Steiner provides a useful explanation of the main Fascist arguments that sought to give the regime theoretical foundations, highlighting the focus on the total State and its 'ethical' existence as a distinct, overarching entity above and beyond the law.[75] Steiner indicates briefly how this was supported in the criminal sphere by the repressive measures of the 1926 Law on the Defence of the State against political offences, and the 1930 Penal Code's measures to protect the Fascist State's interests, thus pointing like Cantor to the Code's political, state-centric characteristics.[76] This dimension of Fascist law becomes the principal point in Steiner's study, underlined in his concluding paragraph. Here, Steiner emphasises that the Fascist conception of law 'is founded upon a distinctive and conscious conception of the absolute and omnipotent State', which relegates the individual to an inferior position deprived of rights, and means that the 'function of the positive law parallels the unlimited function of the State, in its direction and control of every conceivable aspect of human and social endeavour.'[77] On this basis, Steiner concludes, Fascist law reflects the will of the state, is never subject to superior (natural law) standards and is based on an almost spiritual concept, because 'climaxing the Fascist conception of law is a characteristic element which defies verbal definition: this is its trenchant spirit of virile self-assertiveness, which must be felt to be appreciated.'[78]

In that interpretation Fascist law deviated markedly from the concepts of natural law, rationality and restraint in democratic ideas of the rule of law, becoming instead a thin veil over, and the instrument of, political power. Although Steiner does not comment explicitly on the implications for substantive law of his outline of Fascist legal theory, the implicit result is that Fascist claims about legality – especially Articles 1 and 2 of the Penal Code, outlined above, which became central to the post-war Italian doctrinal salvage operation – should not therefore have been taken at face value. Indeed, in his subsequent monograph, Steiner noted the care with which the new law codes were prepared in Fascist Italy, but that this 'was not intended to provide law codes suitable for the administration of abstract justice, but for the administration of Fascist justice' and that 'the regime regards the attainment of its political and social objectives as considerations far outweighing the "democratic" rights of individuals.'[79] These objectives were grounded on what he calls 'the cult of State worship', with law becoming 'the vehicle of the State, which knows no law or obligation apart from itself'.[80]

[74] HA Steiner, 'The Fascist Conception of Law' (1936) 36.8 *Columbia Law Review* 1267–83.
[75] Ibid 1274–76.
[76] Ibid 1276–77.
[77] Ibid 1283.
[78] Ibid 1283.
[79] HA Steiner, *Government in Fascist Italy* (New York, McGraw-Hill, 1938) 86.
[80] Ibid 26, 32.

The issue of legality in Fascist law is more directly addressed in an article published the following year by Julius Stone of the University of Leeds.[81] Stone's publication on Fascist theories of law and justice is particularly important because it begins with some explicit commentary on context and the differences between legal principle and the reality of law's application.[82] Stone insists that his study of Fascist theory is not clouded by naïve detachment from legal reality, and states that he seeks to redress the error in 'the prevailing approach to Fascism in democratic literature', which assumes its theories are advanced but its practice backward.[83] Instead he examines the ways in which four central dimensions of Fascism are derived from, and parallel to, similar developments in the history, theory and practice of democratic states, especially with regard to facing the demands of modern industrialised society. These four areas are the tight integration of the State and its focus on co-ordinating economic activity, known under Fascism as the doctrine of the corporative state; nationalism; the centrality of the strong state in theory and practice; and the emphasis on 'the notion of a government of men and not of laws', that is the idea of personal dictatorship.[84]

Noting that in broad terms the Fascist approach to these areas is not entirely new, Stone concludes by emphasising the negative distinctions between Fascism and democracy.[85] In addition to the regime's use of lawless violence, its repression of opposition, its reliance on military discipline, and the fact that the combination of a strong state with dictatorship means the Fascist Party had a monopoly of power, it is significant to note that Stone's main comments concern the Fascist State's treatment of criminals. Here he focuses on the erosion of procedural safeguards and the Fascist regime's emphasis on retribution and prevention over rehabilitation in punishment.[86]

Although Stone's closing remarks focus on Nazi Germany rather than Italy, and do not allude to the 1930 Penal Code itself, it is clear that his central concern is with the way that criminal legal powers represent the core of a state's controls over its citizens, and that in this regard the paramount difference between Fascism and democracy is the former's erosion of individual protections and 'respect for human personality.'[87] This is a striking contrast with Stallybrass's earlier observation that the Code respected human dignity.[88] At the same time, it is also important to note that Stone's focus shifts away from the original Fascist system, Italy, to a perceived 'worse case', Nazi Germany, which overshadows the former. Nevertheless, the force of Stone's analysis comes from his sense of values and principles for evaluating law, placing humanistic ideals above the normative framework of Fascist power.

---

[81] J Stone, 'Theories of Law and Justice of Fascist Italy' (1937) 1.3 *Modern Law Review* 177–202.
[82] Ibid 177–78.
[83] Ibid 178.
[84] Ibid 179–81 at 181.
[85] Ibid 182–97.
[86] Ibid 201.
[87] Ibid 201–02 at 201.
[88] See n 49 above and related text.

Soon after the works of Steiner and Stone, an especially informative study by the authoritative French criminal legal scholar (and later Nuremberg prosecutor), H Donnedieu de Vabres of the University of Paris, was published in 1938. Focusing on the criminal policies of authoritarian states, this work encompassed developments in Nazi Germany, Soviet Russia and Fascist Italy.[89] It is particularly useful because of its systematic analysis of the Rocco Code's ideological foundations and political dimensions, which Donnedieu de Vabres contrasts with the liberal principles inherent in the idealised French post-Revolutionary penal tradition, in order to grasp the essence of the Rocco Code's Fascist nature.

The study begins by identifying a division in Europe, born of the First World War, between states attached to the 'idealist, democratic and liberal' tradition of the French Revolution and states that blame it for leading to anarchy and seeking instead to restore authority.[90] On one side of this divide the author situates the 'guardians' of the liberal tradition, France and England (although English lawyers would no doubt have disputed the influence of the French Revolution on the common law), and on the other the authoritarian regimes on which his study focuses. He situates the emergence of authoritarianism in its historical context, influenced by changing economic conditions before the First World War, the collective pressures and primacy of public safety and authority engendered by the War itself, and the perceived need for a firm response to the clash of interests brought about by post-war economic crisis in order to avert anarchy.[91] On this basis, Donnedieu de Vabres argues, state authority seeks to ensure order and stability but can only assert itself through force and violence; as these are mainly directed through repression, it leads to the need to reorganise the means for doing so – that is, criminal policy and essentially criminal law. At the heart of this reorganisation, he argues, is a contrast between the liberal foundations of previous orders of criminal law and the political aims of the new authoritarian regimes, namely to reinforce state power and subordinate the individual to the general interest.[92]

In that light, Donnedieu de Vabres proceeds to set out his comparative analysis of liberal and Fascist criminal law. Beginning with the former, he considers a paradigm example of a liberal and individualist penal code – his idealised point of comparison – namely the short-lived but historically iconic French Revolutionary Penal Code of 1791.[93] In essence, he identifies the elements of that code embodying the fundamental principles of liberty, equality and fraternity: liberty in legal

---

[89] H Donnedieu de Vabres, *La Crise Moderne du Droit Pénal: La Politique Criminelle des États Autoritaires* (Paris, Librairie du Recueil Sirey, 1938). The book is based on a series of lectures given in November 1937 at the Syrian University of Damascus – the combination of topic, location and title are tragically noteworthy at the time of writing. The book includes a chapter on the Italian Penal Code and Penal Procedure Code, but the focus here is on the former.

[90] Donnedieu de Vabres, *La Crise Moderne du Droit Pénal* 5. Opposition to the values of the French Revolution was an explicit tenet of Fascism: see Rocco, 'Relazione a sua Maestà il Re del Ministro Guardasigilli (Rocco) Presentata nell'udienza del 19 Ottobre 1930-VIII' 11.

[91] Donnedieu de Vabres, *La Crise Moderne du Droit Pénal* 5–6.

[92] Ibid 6–7.

[93] Ibid 14 and 18.

certainty, non-retroactivity and the impartiality of justice; equality in application of the criminal law to all; fraternity in the humanity of punishment.[94] These roots, he argues, have remained in French criminal law and maintain its liberal character, despite subsequent influences leading to greater judicial discretion and the individualisation of penalties. These latter shifts in criminal law, however, are the issues that he identifies as characterising the fundamental differences between liberal and authoritarian criminal justice.[95]

Turning to the 1930 Rocco Code, although he notes that it was drafted in a way that combined elements of classical and positivist criminological theory into the so-called technical-legal approach, thus differentiating it from both more liberal theory and pure positivism, he argues that it was still strongly influenced by Fascist politics and ideology. Here, he identifies the essence of Fascism in three elements: its 'dynamism', focusing on action over theory and on force as both the justification and sanction of law; nationalism, another of Fascism's core ideological tenets; and its fundamental authoritarian Statism.[96]

The most important of these was the latter principle, according to which the individual is not important for his own sake, but solely as part of the total state[97] and, whereas in liberal theory law as the arbiter of justice is paramount and controls all, including the state, in Fascist theory law emanates from the state, and is primarily intended to serve the state. Emphasised by Donnedieu de Vabres and by Steiner before him, this principle's centrality was also underlined by two other noteworthy French studies published in 1938. The first, although focusing on Nazi law, stressed that the apparent respect for the principle of *nullum crimen, nulla poena sine lege* in Italian criminal law served primarily to assert the primacy of state power[98] and the second, by the leading French criminal law commentator, Marc Ancel, outlined the prevalence of political offences in the Rocco Code and similarly noted its emphasis on collective interests over individual rights.[99] Consequently, by drawing out the Code's ideological foundations, these commentators were able to identify what its Fascist 'essence' could be said to involve.

In terms of the Code's detail, Donnedieu de Vabres argues that these issues were manifested in the 1930 Code in six main ways. First, the primacy of the state above everything else, including law, meant that (as also noted by Stallybrass) the Code abandoned the liberal distinction between ordinary and political crime, and no longer treated the latter leniently.[100] Secondly, the Code dealt with crimes

---

[94] Ibid 14–17.

[95] Ibid 19.

[96] Ibid 25–27. These are similar to the key elements identified by Stone, 'Theories of Law and Justice of Fascist Italy' but without the economic dimension.

[97] Donnedieu de Vabres, *La Crise Moderne du Droit Pénal* 8–9.

[98] R Béraud, 'Le droit pénal et les dictateurs' (1938) *Revue de Science Criminelle et Droit Pénal Comparé* 672–84 at 673.

[99] M Ancel, 'Le crime politique et le droit pénal du XXe siècle' (1938) *Revue d'Histoire Politique et Constitutionelle* 87–104. Contrast his earlier article, M Ancel, 'La règle "nulla poena sine lege" dans les législations modernes' (1936) *Annales de l'Institut de droit comparé* 245–72, in which he appears to ignore this interpretation at 247 and 259.

[100] Donnedieu de Vabres, *La Crise Moderne du Droit Pénal* 27–30.

against the state's interests under the heading of 'crimes against the personality of the State' (Book II Chapter 1). This, he argues, demonstrates the extent to which the state was considered in Fascist legal theory to be a personified entity, the embodiment of sovereign power.[101] Thirdly, Fascist priorities were also evident in the Code's rigorous treatment of ordinary crimes protecting morality, the family, the race and religion, which were all deemed to be essential aspects of national 'grandeur' and of Fascism's spiritual and totalitarian core.[102] His fourth point involves drawing an important distinction between liberal and authoritarian approaches to the 'moral or psychological' element of crime, or in other words, *mens rea*.[103] Whereas, he argues, a liberal approach focuses on culpability, objectively manifested in external facts or conduct, 'an authoritarian power willingly interferes in the domain of the conscience,' including criminalising attempted crime at a very early stage.[104] Fifthly, he notes that the Code also introduced the category of 'criminal by tendency' (Article 108), an unmitigated Lombrosian element involving the assumption of innate criminality, leading to the imposition of security measures.[105] Finally, he argues that the key characteristics of the Code can be identified in terms of its major changes in relation to the previous code, primarily involving its increased punitive severity, which combined with central control over the judiciary made the 1930 Code a particularly powerful tool of intimidation and repression.[106] Again here, the Code's substance was interpreted not at face value, but in terms of its deeper motivations and objectives, and thus its ideological nature.

In his conclusion, Donnedieu de Vabres emphasises that he has sought to analyse authoritarian criminal policy but not to judge it, and suggests that history may show that the regimes he discusses were necessary to re-establish order after the shocks of the Great War – a key point of contextual specificity also made by previous commentators with regard to the need for a reassertion of state authority.[107] He also considers whether such authoritarian criminal policy may have useful lessons for the French system, in terms of realism, solidarity and severity, a comparative openness that indicates both an appreciation of the code's legal merits

---

[101] Ibid 30–32.

[102] Ibid 32–36. In the totalitarian order, families and religious beliefs were to be controlled by and absorbed into the state.

[103] Ibid 37–38.

[104] Ibid 37. In this regard he notes that the authoritarian turn towards punishing culpable intentions, exemplified in the Code by its criminalisation of attempted crime as soon as the requisite intent is identifiable, mirrors a general subjective trend in modern criminal law, but is tempered by the Code's technical-legal approach, which moderates pure positivism by retaining the classical foundation of criminal responsibility in free will.

[105] Ibid 39–40. According to this provision, if after committing an offence, even a first offence, an offender was deemed to fall into this category, a 'security measure' could be applied, leading to indefinite detention. Donnedieu de Vabres notes how this category, which was not the same as the idea of a repeat or habitual offender, apparently respected the *nullem crimen, nulla poena* principle by requiring an offence to be committed, but in fact represented a legacy of the Lombrosian idea of the born criminal, to be determined by the judge.

[106] Ibid 9, 41–43.

[107] Ibid 199.

and that it was not considered to fall outside the category of recognisable criminal law.

Nevertheless, he draws on his idealised comparison with the principles of 1789 in the criminal sphere to set out three key criticisms of Fascist criminal law.[108] Here he states that the 'complete subordination of individual rights' is against nature and elevates the state, which is an artificial construction and a means, above the individual, who is an end.[109] He also challenges the idea of racial difference and superiority, emphasising the importance of the equality of all before the law, especially criminal law.[110] Lastly, he argues that the repressive policy of authoritarian states defies reason and feeling 'fashioned by centuries of Christianity and humanism', because it is based on hatred, and 'hatred is not constructive'.[111] Consequently, this French analysis of the 1930 Penal Code (and other authoritarian criminal laws and procedures) identifies its problematic features in relation to (idealised) liberal democratic legal principles, using them to construct a critical representation of that law's authoritarian dimensions and effects, which Donnedieu de Vabres perceives as being the hallmarks of Fascism, and as more than superficial.

This crucial period from the Code's entry into force to the eve of the war thus saw the publication of a number of important studies that managed to look beyond the form and substance of penal law to its theoretical substrata and contrasts with fundamental (democratic) legal values. These studies included consideration of contextual factors and, most notably, reference to ideological values and criteria as critical benchmarks, which found expression in the last study considered here in the form of an idealised liberal model. That last study also engaged with the detail of the Code, setting out key substantive dimensions indicative of Fascism's instrumentalisation of criminal law, including the merging of ordinary and political crime, specific policy objectives, and increased repressive force. With the advent of the war and the fall of Fascism however, such critical engagement appeared to fade.

C. The Waning of Comparative Attention, 1939–46

In the third phase of commentary on the 1930 Penal Code considered here, there is a notable decline in discussion of Italian criminal law by foreign scholars, despite the outbreak of war, the regime's collapse, the controversial nature and importance of Italy's transition to democracy, and the contemporaneous debate in Italy about the Penal Code. Following an apparent gap in commentary after 1938, the first article requiring attention in this period is by Leon Yankwich, a

---

[108] Ibid 200.

[109] Ibid 200. Fascist legal theory infamously reversed this idea of ends and means: see for example S Skinner, 'Violence in Fascist Criminal Law Discourse: War, Repression and Anti-Democracy' (2013) 26.2 *International Journal for the Semiotics of Law* 439–58.

[110] Donnedieu de Vabres, *La Crise Moderne du Droit Pénal* 200.

[111] Ibid 201.

District Court judge from California, published in 1943.[112] Yankwich outlines various themes and concerns that have changed over the centuries in the area of criminal law. Like Donnedieu de Vabres, he also comments on Nazi, Soviet and Fascist criminal law, outlining their distinctive features. He emphasises that the first two of these shared a focus on concepts of harm to the state, based on judicial discretion.[113] Turning to Italy, Yankwich indicates that Fascist criminal law is an example of the approach of an 'autocratic state, which tolerates no opposition.'[114] In this regard he focuses on Fascist criminal law's severe treatment of offences against the state and its interests, and the role of preventative detention on the basis of social danger, that is the 1930 Code's security measures.[115]

Clearly bracketing it alongside the other two extreme, anti-democratic regimes of the period, Yankwich notes – like other commentators before him – the harshness and state-centrism of Fascist criminal law, but observes that its fundamental philosophy is nevertheless distinct from the approaches of Soviet and Nazi law, due to their social-impact orientation and – importantly – lack of respect for legal certainty. The 1930 Penal Code, therefore, is once more understood to be authoritarian and influenced by Fascist politics and philosophy, but not as alien to liberal legal principles as German and Russian criminal law. Yankwich thus demonstrates both the 'camouflage effect' of apparent legality in the Code and the 'occultation effect' of comparison with the two principal 'worse cases' at the time.

Also in this period, Stallybrass's earlier analysis of the draft Italian penal code was reprinted in 1945.[116] While the reprint includes some updated references to English law, given the date (although the publication was undoubtedly prepared earlier) and contemporaneous events in Italy, it is surprisingly devoid of references to that context and the fall of the regime that existed when Stallybrass first wrote his commentary. These changes, and the need for democratic reforms in the criminal justice system, are however addressed in an article by the US commentator, Ploscowe, also published in 1945, but without mention of the Penal Code itself.[117]

The Penal Code does receive some attention in a spirited article published in 1946, the last comparative commentary considered here, which discusses more generally the extent to which principles of legality were maintained in Fascist Italy and Nazi Germany.[118] In this article the author, AH Campbell of the University of Edinburgh, appears (like Yankwich) to take at face value the adherence to legal

---

[112] LR Yankwich, 'Changing Concepts of Crime and Punishment' (1943) 32.1 *Georgetown Law Journal* 1–24.

[113] Ibid 5–6.

[114] Ibid 6.

[115] Ibid 6–7. Yankwich discusses substantive criminal law and penal measures, the province of the 1930 Penal Code, but oddly footnotes a commentary on the 1930 Penal Procedure Code.

[116] L Radzinowicz and JWC Turner (eds), *The Modern Approach to Criminal Law: Collected Essays* (London, Macmillan, 1945) 390–466.

[117] M Ploscowe, 'Purging Italian Criminal Justice of Fascism' (1945) 45.2 *Columbia Law Review* 240–64.

[118] AH Campbell, 'Fascism and Legality' (1946) 62 *Law Quarterly Review* 141–51. Campbell discusses both Italian Fascism and German Nazism in terms of fascism and totalitarianism.

certainty expressed in Articles 1 and 2 of the Penal Code, in order briefly to support his conclusion that Fascism 'maintained in principle, though not always in practice, the idea of legality, of respect for law, at least in non-political cases',[119] which was in sharp contrast he argues to Nazi Germany's rejection of law and legality.[120] However, Campbell does not consider the problem facing Italy at that time of what to do with the 1930 Penal Code, or critically engage with the deeper theoretical and substantive significance of the apparent legality principle in relation to the urgent need to assess carefully the Code's Fascist and non-Fascist characteristics. Consequently, these final commentaries,[121] contemporaneous with the fall of Fascism and the end of the war, appear to limit their critical engagement through a process of relativisation with regard to Nazi and Soviet law, the major legal bugbears of the time. Thus the process and discourse of criminal law reform in Italy was left to be an internal matter.

Conclusion

So how was the Rocco Penal Code received and discussed in foreign commentary in the early years of its existence, and what does this tell us about the Code and its survival, as well as Fascism, its criminal law and academic responses to them? First, what is perhaps most striking, especially in the initial period examined here, is that the criminal law of a regime that burst onto the international political scene through violence and repression did not generally cause greater alarm or reservation, or attract more decisive critical engagement from academic commentators. Even though the regime's nature was increasingly clear at the time they were writing, some commentators adopted a 'black letter' approach, with little or no qualitative or political appraisal (such as Hugueney, Geesteranus and to a certain extent Stallybrass). Although the turn to a foreign system may be in itself indicative of some broader curiosity and political awareness, and was in itself innovative at the time, this sort of predominantly technical commentary can perhaps only reveal what it is predisposed to recognise, namely the legal objects of its own specialist field of knowledge, isolated from their broader significance. In that light, the 'technical-legal' approach of the Italian anti-reform scholars, based on the criminal law method that had prevailed in Italy under Fascism, was not particularly different from generally 'neutral' legal science elsewhere. Even though commentators selected and considered key components of the new Italian law, which could be seen to derive from its political context, as a technical approach

---

[119] Ibid 143–44.
[120] Ibid 145–51.
[121] M Ancel, 'The Collection of European Penal Codes and the Study of Comparative Law' (1958) 106 *University of Pennsylvania Law Review* 329–84, briefly notes the authoritarian character of the 1930 Italian Penal Code at 370–71 and considers its mixed criminological dimensions and innovation at 379–83. See further Ch 4 in this collection on subsequent post-war commentaries.

mainly sidestepped the law's political and ideological dimensions, it was arguably of limited usefulness when addressing the laws of an emerging extreme regime.

Looking more closely at comparative methods where they are used, commentaries on the 1930 Penal Code are constructed around what could be termed four main points of reference, or analytical benchmarks. As identified at the start of the chapter, these consist of the commentator's own system; a worse system (or systems), considered by the commentator to be a negative extreme; actual practice in the system in question; and an idealised system, represented in terms of fundamental principles valued by the commentator. Of these apparent benchmarks, comparison with the commentator's own system, as in some of the early commentaries, although not entirely devoid of critical reservations, seems mainly to be used to focus on similarities or to evaluate relative strengths. On the other hand, comparison with worse systems – primarily Nazi and Soviet criminal law – seems to result in relative occultation. This is more significant and reflects the 'bigger picture' of the international situation in this period, wherein Germany and Russia were seen as more serious threats and Italy was still deemed to be a less significant force. At the war's end, such occultation was arguably also a factor in Italy's own transition process, in which a future communist threat outweighed past Fascist misdeeds. In legal terms, this sort of comparative approach, while valuable in locating Fascism and its criminal law in relation to a larger complex of totalitarian legal systems, tended to pass over the Rocco Code's deeper significance.

More critically important are the other two points of reference, with actual practice providing a consistent caveat on the Code, even in the initial commentaries on Fascism's criminal law. Some commentators sought to evaluate the law, or recognise the limits of evaluation, in terms of systemic reality (such as Saunders, Stallybrass and Cantor). This involved both the imbrication of the Fascist Party with the judicial system and the regime's penal practices (although as noted, one apparent sympathiser, Pompe, observed that practice under the new Code would be to the benefit of the Fascist State).

Of greater significance though was critical positioning in terms of principles, which provided the strongest qualitative engagement with the Code, especially in the late 1930s.[122] In that sense, the works of Stone and Donnedieu de Vabres provide the clearest representation of the Rocco Code as conflicting with identified (democratic) values, and thus a way of recognising the ideological core of, and taking an ideological stand against, criminal law under Fascism. It is important to recall though that such evaluation shifts the focus from law per se to its ideological foundations and objectives. However, the extent to which deployment of these benchmarks and their effects were dependent on the element of commentators' own political stance remains invisible, and the influence of prevailing attitudes to Italy in the light of cultural perceptions and world affairs can only be suggested.

---

[122] Post-war critical engagement with the Code, and more generally with problematic legal systems, has of course been able to draw on the additional benchmarks of constitutional principles and norms, as well as human rights and other international legal frameworks.

Secondly, in terms of the Code itself, all commentators thought it to be worthy of study and comparable with law in their own systems, so just as Fascist law was not considered to be non-law after the war, it was clearly also deemed to be part of the criminal law family before then. As some commentators noted, it was even considered to be a strong and admirable code with some advantages over other systems. In contrast, the Code was considered by several commentators to be distinctive and problematic in terms of the ideological orientation of some of its general principles and substantive provisions, as well as its criminological inconsistency and harshness of punishments. With regard to its General Part, while the Code's apparent adherence to legal certainty was taken to be a prima facie criterion of acceptability by some commentators (Yankwich and Campbell), other observers (especially Steiner, Stone and Donnedieu de Vabres) note that its underlying theoretical framework and application in fact reveal the illusory nature of such a principle and the Code's Fascist essence. Looking at its Special Part, a consistent observation is the Code's focus on certain family and moral values, and its emphasis on the protection of state interests. Such provisions were often noted as buttresses of the strong state and its renewal of social and moral values, which were not deemed to be unusual legal priorities at the time (for example Hugueney, Garraud, Donnedieu de Vabres and Yankwich).

From that perspective, especially regarding the issues of legal certainty, the problems raised by the post-war academic representation of the Code in Italy appear to be compounded. On the one hand, when considered from a comparative perspective, the Italian anti-reform 'salvage operation' on the Code does not appear to be dramatically out of line with some foreign analyses by commentators from democratic systems. Foreign appraisals of the Code were, as shown, rather mixed. The Code's authoritarian tendencies were not always deemed to be problematically different from criminal law in democratic systems, and its identifiably Fascist values were simply noted rather than condemned. Consequently, the Italian Penal Code was not therefore entirely 'Other', or consistently deemed to be a foreign body to be rejected by democratic law.

On the other hand, however, the comparison with outside perspectives nevertheless supports the later Italian critique of the post-war anti-reform discourse and the latter's minimisation of the Code's political dimensions. Situating the anti-reform arguments in comparative perspective shows that – albeit to varying degrees – the wider legal community did have some serious concerns about both the letter and spirit of Italian criminal law. Such commentaries indicate the view that Fascism was not the sort of superficial contamination that could be simply excised from the Code and, as commentaries contemporaneous with Europe's slide towards war underlined, the regime's penal practices and subjacent, ideologically shaped legal principles were open to challenge. On that basis, the anti-reform discourse appears to be not only selective, but also dangerously introspective. It suffices to note here that the work by Donnedieu de Vabres discussed above is one of the rare foreign commentaries referred to by the leading anti-reform commentator Delogu in 1945, but very narrowly: for example,

Delogu relies on the French commentator's comments about the Code's moderate approach but ignores his other, more critical observations.[123]

Thirdly and finally, questioning the connections between Fascism and criminal law through this comparative analysis of academic commentaries also highlights some disturbing commonalities in the essence of criminal law in the modern state. In general terms, some commentators underlined shared objectives and authoritarian tendencies across criminal law systems as a result of common sociopolitical and economic conditions, namely the problems of the modern world after the First World War (as identified with different objectives by Garraud and Donnedieu de Vabres). This is significant not only because it illustrates how different systems adopted similar strategies and protected similar values through criminal law, but also because it shows the common usage of criminal law as a tool of state power in seeking to achieve social control in the specific context of the interwar period, whatever the state's political complexion.

More fundamentally, these commentators' engagement with Fascist criminal law confirm the latter's very legal identity. In other words, looking beyond the usage of criminal law to the reliance on law itself and its related concepts and structures, they show that the Fascist State deemed it worthwhile to retain a recognisable form of law and the apparent safeguards of legality as instruments of totalitarian power, rather than subverting or replacing them entirely, as some more extreme Fascist legal commentators desired and the Nazis achieved.[124] In that light, although the ideological foundations and intentions of Fascist and democratic law diverged, as some commentators indicated, there is a commonality in normative forms, functions and concerns that connects the Fascist regime and other types of state in interwar Europe. Nevertheless, as some of the last, prewar foreign studies considered above show, once that normative fabric was unpicked and its fundamental intentions and values were identified, it became possible to edge closer to Fascism's darker nature in the guise of law, and to see the subordination of law to state power.

---

[123] Delogu, 'L'elemento politico nel codice penale' 182–83.

[124] G Maggiore, 'Diritto penale totalitario nello Stato totalitario' (1939) 11 *Rivista italiana di diritto penale*, 140–61; T Vormbaum (M Bohlander ed, M Hiley trans), *A Modern History of German Criminal Law* (Berlin, Springer-Verlag, 2014) 172–208, 184 and 200.

4

Criminal Law, Racial Law, Fascist Law: Was the Fascist Era Really a 'Parenthesis' for the Italian Legal System?

MICHAEL A LIVINGSTON

Defining the Problem

The idea that Fascism, to quote Benedetto Croce, was a mere 'parenthesis' in Italian history has a persistent and obvious appeal.[1] There is a powerful human urge to remember happy episodes and repress or forget those that are less pleasant. The urge is compounded by the fact that many post-war Italian institutions – perhaps more than in other European countries – were to a large degree continuations of their Fascist predecessors. The legitimacy of the post-war Italian order, together with the sense of moral superiority reflected in the 'Good Italian' (*italiani brava gente*) myth, thus to some degree requires the minimisation of the preceding era and its influence on later events.

The problem of collective amnesia is especially powerful in the legal field. Even more so than other areas, the Italian legal system was largely continuous before and after 1945. A substantial portion of the country's laws, including both its criminal and civil codes, were written during the Fascist period. Institutional continuities were still greater: few if any judges lost their jobs in the post-war *epurazione* (purges), and many or most new law professors had been trained during the preceding regime. The antisemitic Race Laws, perhaps the single greatest outrage of the Fascist era, were duly repealed, but with relatively little effort to compensate their victims or to reinstate those who had lost their jobs or seniority.

For most of the post-war era, the prevailing approach within the Italian legal community was to ignore or soft-pedal the Fascist influence on the legal system, with several authors championing the 'democratic' virtues of post-war Italy but

[1] See B Croce (A Carella ed), *Scritti e discorsi politici: 1943–1947* vol I (Naples, Bibliopolis, 1993) 61. In fairness, Croce also referred to Fascism as a 'moral sickness' (*malatia morale*) and was himself a prominent anti-fascist, but the appellation has stuck.

few discussing the decidedly non-democratic background from which that Italy emerged. When the Fascist origins of legal provisions could not be denied, there was a tendency to downplay the degree of Fascist influence and the continuity between the pre- and post-war eras.

In recent years this has begun to change, as scholars consider both the continuities between the Fascist and post-Fascist eras, and the traumatic impact of developments, like the Race Laws, that present significant discontinuities. Yet this process is necessarily incomplete, and involves painful questions regarding the nature both of individual laws and of the overall legal system. As always, the debate has parallels to developments in other countries, particularly Germany and France, but with a particular Italian twist.

This chapter will consider these new approaches and the effort to arrive at a more balanced perspective regarding the Fascist influence on Italian law. Given the overall focus of this collection, some emphasis will be placed on the issue of Fascist criminal law, but within the broader context of national trends and tendencies. Special attention will be paid to the Race Laws which, although only partly criminal in nature, present an extreme case of the Fascist distortion of law and the post-war reaction to it. The chapter will conclude with some thoughts on the implicit as well as explicit response to the Fascist era, as reflected in Italian legal thought and institutions in the post-war era.

The 1930 Penal Code and 1942 Civil Code

The effort to 'cordon off' the Fascist era, legally speaking, is complicated by the fact that both the civil and criminal codes were drafted in this era and – in their broad essences if not in every detail – remain in effect today. This is an especially important fact because Italy, like most Continental countries, is a civil law jurisdiction in which codes are the principal, if not the only, source of law.

In the post-war period it was common to argue that at least the Civil Code was not particularly Fascist in content, and was for this reason properly retained after 1945. Thus, the first edition (1967) of Cappelletti, Merryman and Perillo's influential treatise on the Italian legal system states flatly that '[t]he 1942 Code is not a fascist document'; that much or most of it reflected ideas of increased productivity, better distribution of wealth, and the general modernisation of law that were common to numerous countries; and that Italian jurists had successfully resisted the effort to 'contaminate' the code with more Fascist ideology. While conceding that 'a price was paid' by the insertion of the 1927 Charter of Labour and other corporative norms in the Civil Code, the authors insist that these had little or no long-term effects, and that the worst of them, together with the racial/antisemitic laws (see below), 'never became organic parts of the Code. They were superficial blemishes on it, and the surgery that removed them was clean and painless.'[2] Italian language sources in the early post-war period frequently adopted a similar view.

Analyses of this type are of course not limited to Italy. Ernst Fraenkel has described Nazi Germany as a *Doppelstaat* (double state) in which antisemitic and other extreme provisions coexisted with a more or less normal juridical system that continued to function in other substantive areas.[3] Vichy France was cordoned off by post-war French officials – in the most extreme formulation, it was not recognised as 'French' at all – yet much of the regime's more quotidian legislation remained in place. Even in the United States a debate rages whether the US Constitution was fatally compromised by its acquiescence in the slave system, or whether this was a sort of secondary characteristic that does not vitiate the accomplishments of the overall document, the latter being the mainstream if not predominant view. One suspects that there is a degree of wilful amnesia in these views – it is not pleasant to believe that one's entire legal system is compromised by past misbehaviour – but also an offsetting tendency toward greater realism with the passage of time.

The Italian Penal as opposed to Civil Code is more difficult to cordon off, both because of its prevailing ideology and because the control of criminal or dangerous behaviour was central to Fascist political appeal. Even the Cappelletti treatise suggests the 'authoritarian ideology of Fascism' penetrated the Penal Code to some significant extent, although also noting post-war amendments to the Code, a process which has continued and even accelerated in the intervening years.[4] The authors made similar observations regarding the Code of Penal Procedure, which was drafted at the same time as the Penal Code but subsequently replaced in 1988.

A more in-depth study by Stephen Skinner investigates the issue of Fascist influence further. Skinner notes first that the drafting of the Penal Code was supervised by Alfredo Rocco, who was strongly identified with the regime's legal philosophy. He argues further that the Code was authoritarian both in its general theory, which substituted the idea of criminal law as a tool for state control of behaviour in place of the older idea of a contractual relationship between state and citizen, and in its specific provisions, which tended to reduce the rights of suspects as opposed to the state, often in rather dramatic fashion. Among the more dramatic examples of substantive changes were reinstitution of the death penalty, prohibition of strikes, and various 'pro-family' provisions, including imprisonment for adultery and the keeping of a mistress, a rule that it seems fair to say was not strictly enforced. However, the new philosophy pervaded the entire document: while maintaining a superficial adherence to law and legality, 'in fact

[2] M Cappelletti, JH Merryman and JM Perillo, *The Italian Legal System* (Stanford CT, Stanford University Press, 1967) 221, 218–22. The author is currently working on a second edition of this treatise.
    [3] Ernst Fraenkel, *The Dual State: A Contribution to the Theory of Dictatorship* (New York, Oxford University Press, 1941).
    [4] Cappelletti, Merryman and Perillo, *The Italian Legal System* 47.

the Fascist order meant that that principle and the very idea of law changed from their eighteenth-century sense of a guarantee of liberties and a restriction on the state's power to punish, to an authoritarian conception in which law was to be exalted as the expression of state power over its subjects.'[5] Skinner quotes Rocco himself to the effect that the previous code had made a 'fetish' of individual liberty and that '[t]he principles which inspire the present proposal . . . are in complete opposition to those which inspired the code of 1890, just as the Fascist conception of the state is opposed to the democractic-liberal conception of the State.'[6]

Skinner argues that – notwithstanding changes to numerous specific provisions – there is an essential philosophical continuity between the Rocco Code and today's Italian criminal law. He notes that the Italian codes are not unique in this respect and that indeed many current European laws have their origins in dictatorial or otherwise unsavoury regimes: his point is less to single out Italy than to raise a more general question regarding the issue of ideological contamination and the proper role of fascist-era statutes in today's democratic environment. He concludes by defining the Italian Penal Code as part of a broader species of 'tainted law,' which does not necessarily lose its validity but requires an honest engagement with its historical sources and an ongoing effort to render it compatible with democratic norms.[7]

The issue of the codes is not an isolated problem but part of a much broader question of how to treat 'Fascist law', and what precisely is meant by this term. Perhaps the leading expert on the topic, Claudio Schwarzenberg, has identified various characteristics of the Fascist approach to law. These include a preference for positivism over natural law; for legislative over judicial resolution of controversies; and (not surprisingly) for state authority to be untrammelled by individual rights.[8] Schwarzenberg has also suggested that, until a relatively late date, there was little pressure on judges to conform to a particular legal philosophy or to decide cases in a particular way: that most judges did in fact adopt a pro-Government position thus appears to have resulted from voluntary agreement and perhaps social/psychological pressure rather than overt compulsion.

The debate on the origins of the Penal Code, and its relationship to the broader policies of the regime, has of course not been limited to English-speaking scholars. There is also a lively and provocative Italian-language scholarship which considers the philosophical origins of the 1930s-era codes and other legislation, frequently emphasising that the underlying characteristics of these laws – an emphasis on groups rather than individuals, an increase in state powers, and (in the case of criminal law) an emphasis on the criminal individual rather than solely on criminal acts – were common to many countries and not limited to Italy. The

---

[5] S Skinner, 'Tainted Law? The Italian Penal Code, Fascism and Democracy' (2011) 7.4 *International Journal of Law in Context* 423–46.

[6] Ibid 427.

[7] Ibid 429–32. See also C Joerges and N Singh Ghaleigh, *Darker Legacies of Law in Europe: The Shadow of National Socialism and Fascism over Europe and Its Legal Traditions* (Oxford, Hart Publishing, 2003).

[8] C Schwarzenberg, *Diritto e giustizia nell'Italia fascista* (Milan, Mursia, 1976).

names of Guido Alpa, Guido Neppi Modona, and Marco Pelissero are especially significant in this context.[9]

It must be added that, while the record of the legal profession under Fascism is not a happy one, it is also true that Fascist law never quite departed from the mainstream Western tradition in the way that Nazi law arguably did. For example, there is no precise Italian equivalent to the *Führerprinzip* (ie the notion of Hitler's leading role in law and other matters) in Nazi Germany, and indeed a small but not insignificant number of anti-Fascist judges and scholars remained in their posts throughout the era. It is also true that much of Fascist ideology, in law and other areas, was rather more mainstream and even 'modern' in its presumptions than many in the post-war world would prefer to admit. Before reaching the question of what to do about so-called 'Fascist law' there is thus an a priori question of what we mean by this term, and whether mere association with Fascism is sufficient to discredit an otherwise valid or even admirable endeavour.

The Racial Laws

The Italian Race Laws (*leggi razziali*) were enacted in 1938 following an antisemitic campaign in the press and popular institutions. The laws resulted in the exclusion of Jewish students and teachers from Italian universities and public schools; prohibited marriages between Jews and 'Aryan' Italians even when they practised the same religion; and placed severe limitations on Jewish employment and property rights, including a ban on the practice of law, medicine, and other professions for non-Jewish clients and effective confiscation of real property in excess of specified limits. Exemptions were provided for war veterans and certain other individuals, but were generally not extended to their family members.

The degree to which the *leggi razziali* were an authentic Italian product or (alternatively) an inferior version of the German Nuremberg Laws has been debated for several decades. The emerging consensus is that while the timing of the laws was no doubt influenced by the emerging alliance with Hitler's Germany, the laws were fundamentally Italian in derivation, including many differences from the German statute and a number of original, even creative ideas and concepts of their own.[10] Most notably, the laws relied upon a series of 'tiebreaker'

---

[9] Alpa, whose work emphasises the Civil Code, attempts in particular to find a middle ground between denying the Fascist influence on Italian law and balancing it against other factors. See G Alpa, *La cultura delle regole: storia del diritto civile italiano* (Rome-Bari, Laterza, 2000) 263–303. On the Penal Code see also F Colao, G Neppi Modona, & M Pelissero, 'Alfredo Rocco e il codice penale fascista' (2011) 1–2 *Democrazia e Diritto* 184–85.

[10] See generally M Sarfatti, *Gli ebrei nell'Italia fascista: Vicende, identita, persecuzione* (Turin, Einaudi, 2000); M-A Matard-Bonucci, *L'Italie fasciste e la persecution des juifs* (Paris, Editions Perrin, 2007); MA Livingston, *The Fascists and the Jews of Italy: Mussolini's Race Laws, 1938–1943* (New York, Cambridge University Press, 2014). There is also a more focused and fascinating scholarship on the role of lawyers and the legal profession in promoting or (less frequently) resisting the Race Laws:

provisions for determining the status of the children of mixed marriages, emphasising the religious and cultural identification of the individuals in question, and did not include a *mischlinge* or hybrid category, in the manner of the German laws. Thus, although in theory adopting a 'racial' rather than a 'religious' theory of antisemitism, the laws also reflected the persistence of religious categories which in many cases pre-dated the modern era: indeed, as Guido Fubini has noted, some of the provisions were essentially identical to medieval restrictions on the Jews.[11] Exemption and other rules also differed from the German model, not always in ways favourable to the Jews in question. In this the Italian laws shared some features with the antisemitic provisions enacted by the Vichy regime in France, but with the significant difference that the Italian laws were enacted earlier than the French, and without an intervening military defeat.[12]

There is likewise an emerging consensus that – contrary to popular image – the laws were enforced with a high degree of severity, which tended to increase with the passage of time. This is true, although the economic provisions were somewhat more open to evasion than the rules relating to personal status issues, and (as always) wealthy Jews were in a better position to evade the laws, or else leave the country, than their poorer compatriots. Indeed, as various scholars have demonstrated, there was a pronounced tendency to extend the laws to areas not covered by the original legislation, so that (by 1943) almost all areas of significant endeavour were closed to Jews, as well as to reduce the number of exemptions and close off evasion strategies one after another. One of the most gratuitous provisions stripped the licences of Jewish street vendors, who were thereby left essentially destitute.

Even the most significant limitation of the Race Laws – the absence of physical as opposed to economic or moral danger to Italian Jews – was not destined to last. With the German occupation and the institution of the Republic of Salò (Italian Social Republic, RSI) in northern Italy after 1943, an even stricter series of laws was enacted, treating the Jews as enemy aliens, confiscating their remaining property, and (eventually) enabling the deportation of Jews to Auschwitz and other concentration camps, a process which was directed by the Germans but involved large-scale Italian participation and in which about 7,000 Italian Jews, a bit less than 20 per cent of the pre-war population, died.[13] Although the situation undoubtedly worsened after 1943, there was significant continuity of laws and

among the more impressive works are G Acerbi, *Le leggi antiebraiche e razziali italiane ed il ceto dei giuristi* (Milan, Giuffrè, 2011); S Falconieri, *La legge della razza: strategie e luoghi del discorso giuridico fascista* (Bologna, Il Mulino, 2011); and S Mazzamuto, 'Ebraismo e diritto dalla prima emancipazione all'età repubblicana,' in C Vivanti (ed), *Storia d'Italia annali vol 11: Gli Ebrei in Italia* (Turin, Einaudi, 1997) 1767–1827.

[11] G Fubini, *La condizione giuridica dell'ebraismo italiano*, 2nd edn (Turin, Rosenberg & Sellier, 1998).

[12] An in-depth study of the Vichy laws and their treatment by the French legal profession is R Weisberg, *Vichy Law and the Holocaust in France* (London, Routledge, 1997).

[13] See L Picciotto, *Il libro della memoria: gli ebrei deportati dall'Italia (1943–1945)* (Milan, Mursia, 1991) 29, table 1.1.e (citing a figure of 6,806 victims, not including those on the island of Rhodes, then under Italian administration).

administration before and after the German occupation, the previously existing provisions substantially weakening the Jewish community and providing detailed records regarding the identity and whereabouts of the Jewish victims. The work brigades (*precettazione al lavoro*), and a never-enacted proposal for the 'total mobilisation' of Jewish labour – effectively the internal deportation of remaining Jews – provide a further conceptual link between the pre- and post-1943 period. Indeed, the Race Laws remained at least theoretically in effect even under the so-called Badoglio Government, which took over in Southern Italy after 1943, and were repudiated only in subsequent legislation and in the post-war republican constitution.[14]

As the Race Laws were a Fascist imposition and were repealed, albeit with some delay, after the fall of the Fascist government, there is a strong temptation to treat them as an isolated event with no significance in post-war Italy. In Benedetto Croce's memorable phrase, if the Fascist era was indeed a 'parenthesis' in Italian history, then the Race Laws were a sort of 'parenthesis within a parenthesis', not worthy of special consideration.[15] This view was further supported by the so-called Resistance Myth, under which all Italians suffered under Fascism (especially after 1943) and the Jews were not entitled to special consideration. An expanded version of this myth, which has become known as the Myth of the Good Italian (*italiani brava gente*), holds that Italians – by virtue of Catholicism, Mediterranean origins, or cultural sophistication – are simply incapable of large-scale evil unless it is enforced on them by an outside source.[16] The first edition of the Cappelletti, Merryman and Perillo treatise (*The Italian Legal System*) generally follows this view, suggesting that the racial laws were a temporary aberration which left no long-standing impact on Italian legal thought.

In the past two decades an ongoing re-evalution of the Race Laws has contested many of the conclusions above. Part of this re-evaluation is historical in nature, with scholars emphasising the severity of the Race Laws and the indifference or active cooperation of most of the Italian population in their enforcement. The research of Michele Sarfatti and Liliana Picciotto of the Jewish Documentation Centre (CDEC) in Milan, the former emphasising the enforcement of the Race Laws and the latter the Italian role in the deportation process, has been especially influential.[17]

There is also a more focused scholarship regarding the behaviour of Italian lawyers, judges, and legal scholars in the Race Laws era, which suggests that the racial programme cannot so easily be separated from the greater body of Italian law.[18]

---

[14] A comprehensive source on the post-war Jewish community is M Sarfatti (ed), *Il ritorno alla vita: vicende e diritti degli ebrei in Italia dopo la seconda guerra mondiale* (Florence, Giuntina, 1997).

[15] See R Finzi, *L'Università italiana e le leggi anti-ebraiche* (Rome, Riuniti Editore, 2003).

[16] See generally D Bidussa, *Il mito del bravo italiano* (Milan, Il Saggiatore, 1994).

[17] See Sarfatti, *Gli ebrei nell'Italia fascista* and Picciotto, *Il libro della memoria*.

[18] See for example L Garlati and T Vettor (eds), *Il diritto di fronte all'infamia nel diritto: a 70 anni dalle leggi razziali* (Milan, Giuffrè, 2009); D Cerri (ed), *Le leggi razziali e gli avvocati italiani: uno sguardo in provincia* (Pisa, Edizione PLUS, 2010); D Menozzi and A Mariuzzo (eds), *A Settant'anni dalle leggi razziali: Profili culturali, giuridici, e istituzionali dell'antisemitismo* (Rome, Carroci, 2010).

For example, there appears to have been a significant debate on how to reconcile the Race Laws with the Roman law tradition, which related to each citizen on an individual basis without regard to his or her religion or ethnic background, as well as a series of sharply contested judicial decisions regarding the scope and interpretation of the laws themselves.[19] While some of these disputes reflected genuine concern for the Jews, many or most of them appear to have emphasised jurisdictional or bureaucratic conflicts, with judges and some agencies (notably the Finance Ministry) concerned about the precedent of legislation that trampled individual rights and was enforced outside normal channels. A rather technical decision by the Turin Court of Appeals in 1938, in which the judge (Peretti Griva) said that the Race Laws were a derogation from traditional legal principles and should therefore be interpreted narrowly, has been a particular focus of attention, together with a broader series of decisions regarding the pension rights of Jews dismissed under the laws.[20] It must be emphasised that these decisions were to a large degree outliers: the general judicial as well as administrative tendency was toward an expansion of the laws and a slow but steady constriction of the ability to avoid them.

The Race Laws also appear to have had a significant effect on post-war legal theory. Pre-war Italian scholars tended to emphasise a positivist approach to law and a limited role for judicial interpretation, an approach which has been credited with restraining (and at times may actually have restrained) efforts to 'bend' pre-existing laws in a pro-Fascist direction. Yet this approach was ineffective in dealing with the Race Laws, which were formally valid and required little if any judicial creativity in order to be effective. In the post-war era Piero Calamandrei and other scholars began to question the idea of judges as simple mouthpieces of the law (*bocca della legge*), and called for a new kind of interpretation that advanced democratic ideals of justice and fidelity to the overall legal system, rather than merely the statute at issue.[21] These ideas, of course, reflected the general democratisation of culture in post-war Italy and strong foreign (especially Anglo-American) intellectual influence;[22] nonetheless the experience of the Race Laws and of Fascism generally appears also to have weighed upon them.

---

[19] On the issue of Roman law see O De Napoli, 'Razzismo e diritto romano: una polemica degli anni Trenta' (2006) *Contemporanea: Rivista di storia dell'800 e del '900* 35–63. Among the most useful works on judicial interpretation of the Race Laws are Fubini, *La condizione giuridica dell'ebraismo italiano* and G Speciale, *Giudici e razza nell'Italia fascista* (Turin, Giappichelli, 2007); see also Livingston, *The Fascists and the Jews of Italy*.

[20] *Rosso c Artom* 64 Foro Italiano 915 (Corte d'Appello di Torino 1939); *Falco c Banco di Napoli* 66 Foro Italiano III 249 (Consiglio di Stato 1941).

[21] Cappelletti, Merryman and Perillo, *The Italian Legal System* ch 7. This issue will be discussed further in the following section. Calamandrei was involved in a number of Race Laws cases, although his behaviour before 1943 has been questioned by at least one source: see for example Cerri (ed), *Le leggi razziali e gli avvocati italiani* 26.

[22] For example, the works of American interpretation scholars like Ronald Dworkin and William Eskridge, Jr – not to mention Hart, Kelsen, and other European scholars – are now regularly cited by Italian interpretation scholars, together with the usual Italian sources. For a reasonably up-to-date source, see F Modugno, *Interpretazione Giuridica* (Padova, CEDAM, 2009).

To some extent, the debate in Italy parallels those in Germany, France, and other countries. Thus, scholars like Ingo Muller in Germany and Richard Weisberg in France have pointed out the complicity of those countries' legal establishments in their respective antisemitic campaigns, in Weisberg's case finding that many French laws were actually more severe than their German equivalents. On a more abstract level, David Fraser has questioned the entire concept of a discontinuity between the pre- and post-Holocaust legal worlds in Europe and elsewhere, noting that Auschwitz itself was the culmination of a process that appeared legal if not moral both to the participants and outside observers at the time.[23] Scholars have likewise noticed the uncomfortable parallels between the treatment of Jews in the 1930s-40s and that of immigrant (particularly Muslim) groups in contemporary Europe.[24] The Anglo-Saxon countries, with their selective amnesia regarding the history of slavery deportations or Japanese-Americans and so forth, are not immune to this phenomenon. The issue of racism and antisemitism is to some degree unique or at the very least different from ordinary civil or criminal law, which display a greater degree of continuity as well as greater influence on the average citizen's day-to-day life in the relevant countries. Nevertheless the Race Laws suggest a phenomenon of legal amnesia or, perhaps, selective memory, which also manifests itself in other, less extreme areas.

The Impact on Post-war Jurisprudence

As suggested above there was a higher degree of continuity between the Fascist and post-Fascist legal systems – not to say the overall political and economic order – than many or most Italians would like to admit. Part of this is simply a continuity of law and institutions. While initially an *epurazione* or purge of legal and other personnel was supposed to occur, in practice few people lost their jobs, and relatively few of those displaced by Fascism, including Jews, Communists, and others, returned to their posts.

The end of the war, and the coming of the Italian Republic in 1946, did occasion substantial reflection on the meaning of democracy and (what was closely related) on the failures of the legal system during the Fascist era. As suggested above, one important area of reflection concerned the role of courts and judges in creating and interpreting law. Historically, the role of judges, as opposed to professors and other experts – of *giurisprudenza* as opposed to *dottrina*, to use the typical civil law terms – was limited in an Italian context, with many observers

---

[23] I Muller, *Hitler's Justice: The Courts of the Third Reich* (Cambridge MA, Harvard University Press, 1992); R Weisberg, *Vichy Law and the Holocaust in France* (New York, Routledge Press, 1998); D Fraser, *Law After Auschwitz: Toward A Jurisprudence of the Holocaust* (Durham NC, Carolina Academic Press, 2005).

[24] Compare Joerges and Ghaleigh (eds), *Darker Legacies of Law in Europe* Pt IV (discussing contemporary responses to Fascist-era legal theory).

denying that judges had any law-making role at all. In the post-war era the ideas of scholars like Betti, Ascarelli, and especially Calamandrei, who argued for an expanded judicial role in advancing democracy and protecting the values of the overall legal system, became more popular. Calamandrei expressly founded his theories on political changes and the appropriate role of judges in a democratic system, making explicit reference to the Race Laws:

> Now I think that this conspicuous immobility of the judges – who, in response to the neglect of the legislators, almost seem to enjoy applying to the very letter decrepit old laws that no longer correspond to the changed needs of society – is incompatible with the useful and trustful cooperation that should exist between powers in a democratic regime.
>
> I understand that in an authoritarian regime . . . the judges . . . might think themselves limited to applying the statutes as dictated, without adding or taking away anything, in order to leave all the responsibility to [the legislator], especially when infamous laws, like those of racial persecution, are involved. But in a free regime, in the presence of a constitution in which the judiciary is a power placed on the same plane as the legislative, this agnostic jurisprudential attitude, this great pleasure taken in pointing out the inadequacy of the statutes and of making all the blame fall on the inertia of the legislature, is no longer consistent with the constitutional duties of the judiciary.[25]

The requirements of a democratic system, and the perceived failures of Fascism, also affected Italian legal education and legal scholarship. Writing in the 1960s, Cappelletti, Merryman and Perillo found that Italian legal scholarship remained highly insulated and largely untouched by the social sciences, although (as they noted) the situation was already changing at that time.[26] Forty-five years later, economics and other social sciences have clearly gained significant influence, although not always in the progressive direction that earlier scholars might have expected. Partly this situation results from the influence of American and Northern European scholars, translated versions of whose work may be found alongside the Italian classics at any good legal bookstore. Yet much of the work is local in origin: Italian scholars now regularly take both traditional social science and contemporary movements like feminism and environmentalism into account in evaluating legal developments, as is the case in any advanced democracy. Like the changes in interpretative theory, this too is a reflection of the country's maturity and the increasing distance from the conformity of the Fascist era.

Institutional changes reflect a similar pattern. The introduction of the Constitutional Court, the efforts to protect the independence of judges, and the adherence of Italy to European Economic Community and later European Union (EU) norms were part of a broader process of democratisation/integration in the post-war period. Yet they also marked an implicit recognition of the subversion of democratic norms in the Fascist era and a desire to prevent future subversion.

---

[25] Cappelletti, Merryman and Perillo, *The Italian Legal System* 267–68, quoting Piero Calamandrei, 'La funzione della giurizprudenza nel tempo present' (1957) 6 *Studi sul processo civile* 89.
[26] Ibid 195–97.

Notwithstanding the fashionable scepticism about Italian democracy, they have to a large degree achieved their goals.

The changes above have also had an impact on the area we began with, criminal law. While the Penal Code has never been completely redrafted, it has been amended on numerous occasions, at least sometimes in an effort to correct the excessive harshness and pro-government orientation of the Rocco Code. Among the more notable changes are the elimination of the death penalty, recognition of the right to strike, and numerous other changes in the definition of specific crimes. It should also be noted that the Code of Penal Procedure, which may have a greater influence on an average criminal defendant, has been completely redrafted and subsequently amended, to the extent that many believe that Italy is no longer a civil law jurisdiction for criminal purposes, but a hybrid jurisdiction reflecting many common law characteristics. Among the changes introduced by the revised code are a partial reallocation of fact-finding from the pre-trial investigation to the trial phase, and an increased opportunity for defendants to challenge prosecution witnesses in open court. Italy has also experimented with juries in some cases, and modified various aspects of the appeals process. This is in addition to the ability of defendants to make constitutional challenges both within Italy and (in some cases) to the European Court of Justice. The combined weight of these changes has convinced some observers that the 'adversarial' aspects of the Italian system now balance or even outnumber the traditional 'inquisitorial' features that are typical of civil law systems.[27]

Together with these developments, the experience of the Race Laws has led to an enhanced, if difficult to quantify, sensitivity to issues of human and especially minority rights. This issue is particularly salient with regards to the growing Islamic community in Italy, which is subjected to fears and pressures at times reminiscent of the Jews in an earlier era.[28] While Italy's record is hardly perfect in this area, it seems clear that the kind of open prejudice which existed in the Fascist era would now be both legally and culturally unacceptable in an Italian context. This too is at least indirectly a legacy of the Race Laws, and forms part of the national consensus moving forward into a new century.

Like the Race Laws themselves, the post-war influence of the laws – and Fascism generally – has been the topic of much debate. This is particularly true since the post-war changes in Italian law reflected many factors – Anglo-American influence, the Republican Constitution, the rise of the EU – and not exclusively the triumph of democracy and the waning of Fascist influence. The concept of legal transplants, and (more recently) of globalisation and the convergence of legal

---

[27] See M-A Glendon, PG Carozza and CB Picker (eds), *Comparative Legal Traditions: Texts, Materials and Cases on Western Law*, 3rd edn (St Paul MN, Thomson West, 2007) Pt V (hybrid legal traditions). On changes in Italian and European legal theory since World War II, see generally G Fassò, *Storia della filosofia del diritto, Vol 3: Ottocento e Novecento* (Rome-Bari, Laterza, 2006).

[28] On the similarities and differences between these phenomena, see M Bunzl, *Anti-Semitism and Islamophobia: Hatreds Old and New in Europe* (Chicago IL, Prickly Paradigm Press, 1997).

systems, are especially relevant here.[29] Yet while it is misleading to overstate the influence of the Fascist era, it is equally misleading to underestimate it. Even where Italy has undergone changes similar to other countries, the changes have been coloured by the Fascist inheritance and the desire (conscious or not) to distance the country from it. It has been said, in an individual context, that people often relive family traumas even without completely realising that they are doing so. So Italy continues to be affected by the Fascist experience 70 years after it formally ended, even if Italians themselves are not always wholly aware of this influence.

Concluding Thoughts

The issue of how to respond to painful episodes in a nation's past and their effect on contemporary jurisprudence is not limited to Italy. Similar questions arise in Germany, France, and other European countries as well as the United States, South Africa, and other places that maintained (and some would argue still maintain) discriminatory legal structures. For example, there is a tendency in the American legal academy to adopt a celebratory view of the civil rights movements which emphasises the relatively brief period of progress after 1954 and ignores or glosses over the much longer period of slavery and Jim Crow, which were largely upheld and in many cases reinforced by the legal system. The enduringly positive image of colonialism in the United Kingdom and other European countries, however improbable on the facts, is a further example of this phenomenon.

The strategies observed in Italy, including an effort to cordon off or minimise the impact of the past and an arguably more constructive effort to learn from its lessons, are also typical of many countries. Nevertheless Italy presents a special case because such a large proportion of its legal inheritance, at least with regard to statutory law, derives from the Fascist era and because there is remarkable continuity in the interpretation and application of that law. To argue that the Fascist period constitutes an aberration or a 'parenthesis' is accordingly harder in the legal than in some other fields, and the distortions that must be made in order to advance this argument correspondingly greater. Both the Penal Code and the Race Laws are examples of this ongoing process.

While Italians (and others) are often unwilling to confront their past in explicit terms, the implicit efforts to do so leave a somewhat more positive impression. The acceptance and even enthusiasm of Italian scholars for changes in interpretative theory and other scholarly methods, if not officially characterised as responses to the Fascist experience, are heavily influenced by that experience and the determination not to repeat it. Institutional changes, like the introduction of the

---

[29] See generally A Watson, *Legal Transplants: An Approach to Comparative Law*, 2nd edn (Athens GA, University of Georgia Press, 1993).

Constitutional Court and the adherence to EU norms, similarly reflect a readiness, if not necessarily to confront the Fascist past, then at least to internalise its lessons. The post-war changes in criminal law and criminal procedure – changes which undermine at least a portion of Fascist ideology, even if they take place in an atmosphere of formal continuity – are part of this broader pattern. In this sense the concept of Fascist-era enactments as 'tainted law' – not per se invalid but requiring special and continuous scrutiny in order to test and refine their consistency with modern democratic norms – has been implicitly if not explicitly accepted in an Italian context.

It may be that a more realistic view of the impact of Fascism on Italian law must await a more realistic view of the *ventennio* (the roughly 20-year period of Fascist rule) in general. As Ruth Ben-Ghiat and others have argued, Fascism was not merely reactionary, but considered itself highly modern and even avant-garde in its actions and sensibilities.[30] There is a greater deal of continuity between that era and our own with regard to numerous areas – science and technology, eugenics, leisure activities, the organisation of political and social life – than we frequently wish to acknowledge. The Italian Penal and Civil Codes, with their mixture of 'regressive' anti-individualism and 'progressive' concern for social welfare – a mix that seems contradictory to us but appeared rather less so at the time – are but one example of this phenomenon. It may be that it is still too soon after the destruction wrought by Fascism to attempt an honest accounting of its impact in law or elsewhere. Perhaps, as David Fraser has suggested, the language of law is inadequate to the evaluation and correction of a disaster which law itself contributed so mightily toward creating. But it is worth the effort to try.

---

[30] See generally, R Ben-Ghiat, *Fascist Modernities: Italy 1922–1945* (Berkeley CA, University of California Press, 2004); compare V De Grazia, *How Fascism Ruled Women: Italy 1922–1945* (Berkeley CA, University of California Press, 1993). The idea of Fascism as a 'parenthesis' is, of course, partially a factor of our own lack of historical perspective. As the Chinese leader, Zhou Enlai is reported to have said when asked to comment on the legacy of the French Revolution, 'It's too early to tell' (but it has been suggested that Zhou may actually have been speaking of 1968 rather than 1789: see http://media-mythalert.wordpress.com/2011/06/14/too-early-to-say-zhou-was-speaking-about-1968-not-1789/).

II

Criminal Law, Fascism and Authoritarianism in Romania, Spain, Brazil and Japan

5

The Enemy Within: Criminal Law and Ideology in Interwar Romania

COSMIN S CERCEL*

In 1930, an imprisoned Antonio Gramsci wrote with regard to the 'crisis of authority' which befell European polities at the end of World War I: 'The crisis consists precisely in the fact that the old is dying and the new cannot be born; in this interregnum a great variety of morbid symptoms appear.'[1] In these lines, one can easily perceive a fundamental self-reflection of the troubled times following the Great War. If nowadays this epoch is generally considered under the aegis of upheaval, emergency and radical shifts in the ways of understanding politics and society, it is also imagined as being marked by the two cataclysms which chronologically limit it. Thus, this age is now retrospectively conceived as being the *interbellum* to such an extent that the fundamental distinctive trait one associates with this time is the experience of war.

However, for Gramsci, the question at stake in the European crisis is that of authority, which is somehow suspended between the old and the new. The interwar period was understood by contemporaries as an *interregnum*, as a space and time between two distinct regimes of power. Moreover, according to his reading, it is this very transition which conjures strange political forms and phenomena in the life of power. As Roger Griffin observes, the interwar period is marked by

> the general belief . . . that Western history was itself at a turning point from which it could either collapse into terminal barbarism and anarchy amidst social breakdown and war, or give birth to a new type of society beyond the current age of chaos and decadence.[2]

---

* Unless otherwise indicated, all translations are my own.
[1] A Gramsci, '"Wave of Materialism" and "Crisis of Authority"' in Q Hoare and G Nowell Smith (eds and trans), *Selections from the Prison Notebooks* (New York, International Publishers, 1971) 276.
[2] R Griffin, 'Political Modernism and the Cultural Production of "Personalities of the Right" in Inter-war Europe', in R Haynes and M Rady (eds), *In the Shadow of Hitler: Personalities of the Right in Central and Eastern Europe* (London, Tauris, 2011) 20–37, 23.

The interwar period is caught by an 'ethos of crisis',[3] it calls for 'palingenetic rebirth'.[4] It wants both to accelerate time and to suspend it. It disdains history and still wants to engage in historical endeavours. It enacts both fantasies of radical change and returns to embellished forms of the past. In this way it exposes the divisions and paradoxes of modernity itself. For inasmuch as modernity brings to the fore the question of anomie and alienation, it also tries to create its own 'panacea'.[5]

Yet the concept of 'interwar' is also an expression of a legal crisis, or of a crisis of legal thought in itself, in that law is marked by the uncertainties and ambiguities reigning in the realm of culture and politics. The epitome of this crisis is the state of exception, or the suspension of the law. Indeed, after World War I, forms of the suspension of law, either under the guise of suspension of constitutional guarantees or of the whole legal framework, emerge and multiply prolifically. On the authoritarian side of the political spectrum, such recourses to the unbridled force of the state are celebrated as a regenerative turn able to cure what was perceived as a decadent legality devoid of political pathos. In Carl Schmitt's words, '[i]n the exception the power of real life breaks through the crust of a mechanism that became torpid by repetition.'[6] Thus the law is redeemed of its lifeless normative existence, inasmuch as 'the exception reveals most clearly the essence of the State's authority.'[7] Yet the status of legality during the interwar period is not contested only by the emerging 'autocracies'[8] and their supporters. In a paradoxical move, the militant democracies of the time also call for a suspension of the law. As '[a] virtual state of siege confronts European democracies', democratic polities renounce their basic foundations, as long as the '[s]tate of siege means, even under democratic constitutions, concentration of powers in the hands of the government and suspension of fundamental rights'.[9]

According to Giorgio Agamben, 'World War One (and the years following it) appear as a laboratory for testing and honing the functional mechanisms and apparatuses of the state of exception as a paradigm of government'.[10] The results of these practices would prove themselves disastrous, for what is questioned through the state of exception is the very possibility of law to articulate itself and to be distinguishable from mere assertions of power. In this sense, the state of

---

[3] Ibid.

[4] Ibid. See also R Griffin, *The Nature of Fascism* (London, Routledge, 1991) 32–36.

[5] As Griffin writes with regard to fascism, '[u]ltra-nationalism offers its believers a solution to the modern crisis of identity, an instant "grand narrative" within which to locate the trajectory of the self, a panacea to anomie': R Griffin, 'Modernity Under the New Order: The Fascist Project for Managing the Future', in M Feldman (ed), *A Fascist Century* (Basingstoke, Palgrave Macmillan, 2008) 24–45 at 44.

[6] C Schmitt, *Political Theology* (George Schwab trans) (Cambridge MA, MIT Press, 1985 [1933]) 15.

[7] Ibid 13.

[8] K Loewenstein, 'Autocracy Versus Democracy in Contemporary Europe I' (1935) 29 *American Political Science Review* 571–93.

[9] K Loewenstein, 'Militant Democracy and Fundamental Rights I' (1937) 31 *American Political Science Review* 417–32, 432.

[10] G Agamben, *State of Exception* (K Attell trans) (Chicago IL, University of Chicago Press, 2005 [2003]) 7.

exception appears as a return of anomie in the very mechanism of the law: '[s]ince "there is no rule that is applicable to chaos", chaos must first be included in the juridical order through the creation of a zone of indistinction between outside and inside, chaos and the normal situation – the state of exception'.[11]

Exploring the politico-legal nosology of the interwar period – of which fascism is a central experience – calls thus for an investigation of the dissolution of legality and of the intellectual, social and cultural mechanisms at work in this process. The aim of this chapter is therefore to construct a critical analysis of the uses of criminal law in the context of the royal dictatorship and the rise of fascism in Romania during the 1930s. It explores the effacement of traditional categories of legality entailed by the emergence of the Criminal Code of 1936, by focusing on the notion of crimes against the constitutional order and its intricate relation to the socio-political context of the time. In this sense this chapter investigates critically and historically the relation between criminal law, constitutional law and the rise of fascism in Romania while stressing three crucial and overlooked elements: the ideological tenets of the Code present both in its substantial and formal structure, the politico-legal significance of the Code in the historical moment of its enactment, and the erosion of classical forms of legality determined by the Code's ideological appropriation. Moreover, it tackles the question of continuity between democratic legislation and authoritarian law.

As a traditional repository of states' internal sovereignty and the most perceptible site of states' repressive powers, criminal law played a central role in the reconstruction of state power in its dialectics of reception and opposition to fascist ideology. Given that at the level of criminal legislation one can grasp the values founding the normative order that it aims to protect, I seek to bring to light the ambiguities at the core of the conservative authoritarian project of containing fascism through legal means, which were already impregnated by this ideology.

In order to analyse this issue, I will try to approach the relation between text and context, while drawing on the Foucaultian concept of archaeology as an attempt at linking the semiotic to the semantic.[12] Following this line of argument, my aim is to examine some of the basic discursive formations of the Romanian legal order of the time, which were at the core of the process of dissolution of legality, namely the category of crimes against the constitutional form of the state. Accordingly, I attempt to respond to the Foucaultian call 'to grasp the statement in its exact specificity of its occurrence; determine its conditions of existence, fix ... its limits, establish its correlations which other statements it may be connected with'.[13] In short, my main focus is to examine forms of thought embedded in the

---

[11] G Agamben, *Homo Sacer: Sovereign Power and Bare Life* (D Heller-Roazen trans) (Stanford CT, Stanford University Press, 1998 [1995]) 19.

[12] '[A]rchaeology ... does not imply the search for a beginning; it does not relate analysis to geological excavation. It designates the general theme of a description that questions the already-said at the level of its existence: of the enunciative function that operates within it, of the discursive formation ... to which it belongs': M Foucault, *Archaeology of Knowledge*, (AM Sheridan-Smith trans) (London, Routledge, 2002 [1969]) 148.

[13] Ibid 30.

criminal and constitutional legal framework, responding to their respective discursive constraints, but still considering them as parts of a wider socio-political
context.

In the first section I shall engage with a reading of the Romanian historical context in order to situate the conditions of possibility of these discursive formations.
At this stage, my main focus is represented by the radical change befalling sovereignty in the context of the interwar period as well as by the rise of fascism.
Moving toward the legal provisions of the Code, I shall insist on the textual, doctrinal and strictly legal dimensions of the subject matter I address. In doing so, I
intend to undertake a first level of contextualisation by insisting on the specificities of Romanian legal discourse and legal thought of the time. In the last section,
I shall formulate a critical interpretation of the historical context, in order to
examine the hidden utterances of legal discourse and the historical significance of
the politics of suppressing dissent through criminal law.

The Romanian Interregnum:
State, Politics and the Rise of Fascism

Two major historical dynamics extend beyond what we traditionally understand
as the legal discourse of the time and determine its inner structure. First of all,
there was the radical territorial and demographic change in Romanian state mor-
phology as a consequence of World War I. Unlike Hungary, Austria or Germany,
and even Italy, Romania was 'easily the biggest winner'[14] of the Paris Peace
Conference in terms of territorial gains. Not only did the surprising collapse of
the German Western Front open the possibility for Romania to mobilise again
and circumvent the dire provisions of the Peace with the Central Powers[15], but
also Romania's participation in the diplomatic negotiations seemed to have been
fruitful.[16] Ultimately, much to the surprise of many, the once small kingdom in

---

[14] M Mann, *Fascists* (Cambridge, Cambridge University Press, 2004) 238.

[15] According to the provisions of the Treaty Romania had to demobilise the bulk of its army and
hand its equipment to the victors (Articles 4–6). In terms of territorial changes, Romania was required
to cede to the Austro-Hungarian Empire territories across the Northern border including strategic
passes through the Carpathian mountains (Article 11), to transfer to Bulgaria the *Cadrilater*, a territory situated in Southern Dobruja and part of Romania since the end of the Second Balkan War of
1913 (Article 10 a). Northern Dobruja up to the Danube Delta was to be administered jointly by the
Central Powers (Article 10 b). Furthermore, the occupation over Wallachia was to continue to a later
unspecified date (Article 14). According to the subsequent economic agreements, Germany acquired
monopoly over Romanian oil exploitation for 90 years and assumed the control of navigation on the
Danube and Romanian ports: See 'Treaty of Peace Between Roumania and the Central Powers',
Department of State, *Texts of the Roumanian 'Peace'* (Washington, DC, United States Government
Printing Office, 1918) 5–28 and K Hitchins, *Rumania 1866–1947* (Oxford, Oxford University Press,
1994) 274–75.

[16] Defending the Romanian position within the Peace Conference in Paris was anything but an easy
task for the diplomats entrusted with this mission, due mainly to Romania's poor performance during

south-eastern Europe found its territory and its population doubled. As a result, Greater Romania encompassed 296,000 square kilometres and counted more than 16 million inhabitants.[17] Despite the national enthusiasm accompanying it, such a territorial and demographic shift was at the origins of major political struggles, administrative convolutions and legal debates following the war. It arguably entailed the dissolution of the old political consensus, and thus opened the way to various forms of populism and authoritarianism.[18]

Secondly, the experience of the world war as well as the Russian Revolution and the European civil war,[19] also left significant traces on Romanian politico-legal practice. Actively taking part in the regime change in Hungary after the unfortunate adventure of the short-lived Hungarian Soviet Republic,[20] the renewed state symbolically placed itself as a defender of the national and regional status quo. Such a position substantially fuelled nationalist ideology and contributed to the creation of an important myth of a state under constant siege, which was to recur during the interwar period.[21] Incidents such as the Senate plot of 1920[22] or the Tatar Bunary uprising of 1924[23] in the newly acquired Bessarabia, did not fail to exaggerate the perception of the external and internal threat of Bolshevism. As Romanian authorities recalled with regard to this issue,

> [Bolsheviks] treated our country and especially Bessarabia with the utmost attention. There they made strong efforts to provoke the revolt of the population against the Romanian regime, taking advantage of all the animosities, of all the asperities and of all the conflicts of the first years of transition following the union.[24]

the first stages of its participation in the war, the Romanian Armistice with the Central Powers signed in early 1918, and Romanian intervention in Hungary in 1919. See C Upson Clark, *United Roumania* (New York, Dodd, Mead and Co, 1932) 221–50. On the legal and political ambiguities entailed by Romania's status on the diplomatic front, see GE Torrey, 'Romania in the First World War: The Years of Engagement, 1916–1918', (1992) 14 *The International History Review* 462–79.

[17] As opposed to approximately 140,000 square kilometres and eight million inhabitants before the war: V Georgescu, *Romanians: A History* (A Bley-Vorman trans) (Columbus OH, Ohio State University Press, 1991) 189–91 and Hitchins, *Rumania 1866–1947* 290.

[18] Hitchins, *Rumania 1866–1947* 379–425; Georgescu, *Romanians: A History* 192–98. See also Z Ornea, *The Nineteen Thirties: The Romanian Extreme Right* (Boulder CO, East European Monographs, 1999) 41–58.

[19] The term was coined by Nolte's controversial statement on understanding fascism as a reaction to Bolshevism: Ernst Nolte, *Der europäische Bürgerkrieg, 1917–1945* (Frankfurt, Herbig Verlag, 1989).

[20] Hitchins, *Rumania 1866–1947* 281–88. See also, D Dinet, *Cataclysms: A History of the Twentieth Century from Europe's Edge* (W Templer and J Golb trans) (Madison WI, University of Winsconsin Press, 2008) 77–85.

[21] This became one of the foundational myths of Romanian fascism. See for example Ornea, *The Nineteen Thirties* 280–81; R Ioanid, *The Sword of the Archangel: Fascist Ideology in Romania* (P Heinegg trans) (Boulder CO, East European Monographs, 1990) 98–100.

[22] R Haynes, 'Corneliu Zelea Codreanu: The Romanian "New Man"', in R Haynes and M Rady (eds), *In the Shadow of Hitler: Personalities of the Right in Central and Eastern Europe* (London, Tauris, 2011) 169–87 at 171.

[23] See C Upson Clark, *Bessarabia, Russia and Roumania on the Black Sea* (New York, Dodd, Mead and Co, 1927) 223–31.

[24] ZI Husărescu, *Mişcarea subversivă în Basarabia* (Chişinău, Atelierele Imprimeriei Statului, 1925) 24.

These major dynamics significantly affected the life of the polity, making the interwar period perhaps one of the most politically charged periods in modern Romanian history. Accordingly, the 1930s represent the culmination of a series of social, economic and cultural shifts, which slowly undermined the democratic promises of the project of rebirth steered by the state since the outcome of the Great War. Indeed, the introduction of universal male suffrage in late 1918,[25] the land reform of 1921,[26] as well as the constitutional reform of 1923,[27] could all be read as signs attesting to at least a formal commitment to the tenets of parliamentary democracy and modern constitutionalism. Moreover, the socio-economic reconstruction, including a relative increase in industrialisation and the overall modernisation of the country, also contributed to building a sense of a new beginning which was eventually stalled only by the crisis of 1929.[28]

However, whereas this movement toward a new Greater Romania was a definitive trope of the time, continuities with the problematic constitutional practices at work before the war, as well as the emergence of new political trends, limited the scope of these democratic endeavours. Not unlike its pre-war predecessor, the new Romanian State was a constitutional monarchy in which the King retained significant royal privileges relating to both the legislative process and the implementation of the rule of law. Primarily, the Constitution of 1923 granted the King extensive legislative powers amounting to a right to veto, which could be exercised discretionarily.[29] The King was also granted the prerogative to issue regulations (*regulamente*) necessary for the enforcement of laws,[30] which entitled him to be an interpreter of the law and to hold a pre-eminence over the executive.

Moreover, the practice of switching parties in power – largely used under the constitution of 1866 – continued to be common currency until the establishment of the dictatorship in 1938 and its suppression of pluralism. By the right conferred on the King to name the prime minister, the rotation in office was assured as the party chosen by the King to form the new government had the advantage of organising elections and thus indirectly influencing the results through illegal means.[31] As Hitchins points out, 'unlike parliamentarism in Western Europe, where the government was a creation of legislature, in Rumania the parliament continued to be an extension of the government'.[32]

---

[25] Art 1 Decree Law for the election of deputies and senators through universal, mandatory, equal, direct and secret vote under proportional representation, *M Of.*, 16 November 1918.

[26] Statute of 17 July concerning land reform, *M Of.*, 17 July 1921.

[27] The Constitution of Romania, *M Of.*, 29 March 1923.

[28] Georgescu, *Romanians: A History* 198–99. On Romania's reconstruction after the war, see J Aulneau, *Histoire de l'Europe Centrale* (Paris, Payot, 1926) 524–32.

[29] Art 34 of the Constitution of Romania 1923.

[30] Art 88 ibid.

[31] CD Booth, 'The Political Situation in Southern-Eastern Europe II: Romania and Bulgaria' (1929) 8 *Journal of the Royal Institute of International Affairs* 445–47, 446, where the author notes: 'The never-failing assistance of the *gendarmerie*, the ingenuity of the functionaries entrusted with counting votes . . . resulted as a rule in a majority of votes being given to the government in power.'

[32] Hitchins, *Rumania 1866–1947* 379.

The degree of political fragmentation and the limits of parliamentary representation should also not be neglected when analysing interwar Romania. Long-standing political forces such as the landed aristocracy, represented by the Conservative Party, disappeared in the new political landscape as a result of the shift in the electoral basis, the land reform and arguably due to their Pro-German stance during the war.[33] A fragile Left, fragmented over the question of the communist revolution and the imperialist foundations of Greater Romania, as a consequence of the establishment of the Communist International,[34] was merely surviving state repression. Indeed, the Social Democratic Party, banned during the war due to its pacifist politics, reorganised itself in 1918 and prepared to join the Comintern as early as 1921. However, even by 1920 a strong division was apparent inside the Party between the moderates, who were defending a gradual approach to transition towards socialism, and the radicals, who followed Moscow's revolutionary line. As a result of this internal conflict, the radical faction withdrew in 1921 and founded the Communist Party of Romania, which was banned in 1924 but continued to operate underground until 1944.[35] The moderate faction reorganised itself only in 1927 as the Social Democratic Party, uniting all non-revolutionary socialist movements in Greater Romania under the leadership of Constantin Titel Petrescu, and acted within the confines of the parliamentary system, before being outlawed in 1938.[36]

New authoritarian-leaning movements such as Marshal Averescu's People's Party were also organising themselves, based on the ideological creed of 'honest and efficient government, to be achieved by strict adherence to the Constitution.'[37] They ended up by securing an important role in the established political sphere as Averescu came to power twice, in 1920 and 1926, and was one of the artisans of land reform as well as the initiator of Romania's renewal of diplomatic relations with Fascist Italy.[38] One of the supporters of nascent fascism in the guise of the Guard of National Awareness and head of government during the crackdown on the Socialist strike of October 1920, the 'hero of Mărăşti',[39] Averescu was arguably also one of the first saviour figures in modern mass politics in Romania. As Lucian Boia notes, 'Averescu appeared as the potential reformer of Romanian society, the only one capable of setting the country on a new historical course'.[40]

For their part, the new democratic forces gathered around the National Peasants' Party (NPP) were nonetheless hoping that 'on the ruins of capitalism a

---

[33] Ibid 398–400.

[34] Georgescu, *Romanians: A History* 193.

[35] Hitchins, *Rumania 1866–1947* 400.

[36] Ibid 401–02.

[37] Ibid 396.

[38] JS Rouček, 'The Political Evolution of Roumania' (1932) 10 *Slavonic and East European Review* 602–15, 610.

[39] As a general leading the Second Army in defence of Moldavia in 1917, Averescu stopped the Austro-German advance in the battle of Mărăşti. He was thereafter praised during the interwar period as a war hero of mythical proportions: L Boia, *Myth and History in Romanian Consciousness* (JC Brown trans) (Budapest, Central University Press, 2001) 210–12.

[40] Ibid 210.

new form of State shall be built in the image and according to the likeness of the Romanian worker, who is the peasant'.[41] A result of the fusion in 1926 between the Peasants' Party from the Old Kingdom and the National Party in Transylvania, the new political organisation struggled in the first place to mitigate the divisive lines of two distinct ideological standpoints and constituencies. On the one hand, the Peasant's Party occupied during the early 1920s a rather radical position, inasmuch as it embraced a non-Marxist conception of class struggle inspired by the Narodnik movement in Russia.[42] The Peasant's Party relied mainly on peasantry and rural intellectuals, and was committed to social reform and the enlargement of political rights.[43] On the other hand, the National Party had previously acted as a promoter of Romanian communities' interests in the Austro-Hungarian Empire, relying especially on the middle classes and the Romanian bourgeoisie in Transylvania, and its ideological stand was infused with late nineteenth-century nationalism.[44]

An unlikely fusion for many a contemporary, the NPP came to dominate political life only two years after its establishment, in an attempt to confine the growing authoritarian practices fostered by the National Liberal Party (NLP).[45] The latter, an heir of nineteenth-century Romanian politics, continued to be the most prominent political force during the interwar period, problematically mitigating liberal ideological creeds through political practice. As such,

> the liberalism practised by the Liberal Party differed substantially from that in the West. In politics the Liberals used whatever means they had to in order to assure victory at the polls: they mobilized the police, the civil service and the all-powerful prefects in order to further their ends.[46]

In short, Romanian political life during the 1920s and early 1930s was characteristic of a 'semi-authoritarian regime',[47] that is, of a polity which 'tried to hold on to late nineteenth-century methods of rule'.[48] In Mann's words, such a regime was 'essentially a "dual state" in which an elected legislature and a nonelected executive both wielded considerable powers'[49] and where 'pressure from below was deflected by manipulating elections'.[50] However, this state of affairs was already caught by the ethos of crisis, as most of the political forces were dramatically marked by the radical territorial, demographic and cultural changes entailed

---

[41] I Scurtu, *Istoria României între anii 1918–1944* (Bucharest, Editura didactică şi pedagogică, 1994) 7.

[42] For an account of the work of one of the initial ideologists of the Peasant's Party, Constantin Stere, see M Kitch, 'Constantin Stere and Romanian Populism' (1975) 53 *Slavonic and Eastern European Review* 248–71.

[43] Hitchins, *Rumania 1866–1947* 391.

[44] Ibid.

[45] RA Haynes, 'Reluctant Allies? Iuliu Maniu and Corneliu Zelea Codreanu Against King Carol II of Romania' (2007) 85 *Slavonic and East European Review* 105–34, 107.

[46] Hitchins, *Rumania 1866–1947* 390.

[47] Mann *Fascists* 44.

[48] Ibid.

[49] Ibid.

[50] Ibid.

by the war. One could thus conclude, following Stanley Payne, that the post-World War I political landscape showed troubling signs:

> the basic habits of politics were altered, as the secular trend toward liberal democracy and greater representative government was challenged and in some areas reversed. The consequence was a brutalization of political life which made the recourse to political violence seem natural and even normal.[51]

Political uncertainty was furthered by a series of public scandals related to Prince Carol's estrangement from his wife. As a result, the royal heir was forced to sign his abdication in early 1926 at the insistence of the leader of the NLP, Ion IC Brătianu. The death of King Ferdinand, followed by that of Brătianu himself in 1927, brought a new wave of political instability which the NPP government was not able to appease.[52] The return of Prince Carol in June 1930, with the initial support of Iuliu Maniu,[53] at that time president of the NPP and prime minister of the country, ended up with Parliament annulling the edict issued by the Crown Council with regard to the Prince's renunciation of the throne.[54] Following his return to the throne, King Carol II did not fail to express his disdain for democratic institutions, and the practice of appointing governments of national union became the norm rather than the exception.[55]

Historians of the interwar period seem to agree on Carol's malignant influence over political life in Romania. As such, Payne paints Carol II in rather stark colours as 'the most cynical, corrupt, and power-hungry monarch who ever disgraced a throne anywhere in twentieth-century Europe,'[56] while Romanian historian Lucian Boia notes that 'even in the monarchist discourse of the present day his personality is passed over quickly.'[57] Whilst the accrual of authoritarian tendencies in Romanian politics could already be observed during the first years of Carol's rule, the ambivalence of his reign should also be noted, as economically the fourth decade of the twentieth century was one of growth, both in terms of employment and industrialisation. Furthermore, in his attempt to attain hegemony under the guise of the new style of authoritarianism already rampant in Europe, he nonetheless encountered the opposition of Romanian fascism, which had already been striving for at least a decade to gain dominance in the authoritarian nationalist milieu.

Described as 'the most unusual mass movement of interwar Europe,'[58] Romanian ultranationalism, embodied by the Legion of Archangel Michael – later

---

[51] Payne, *A History of Fascism* 71.

[52] Georgescu, *Romanians: A History* 192.

[53] Maniu favoured Carol II's rule over the reign of the Regency Council. However he made the Princes's return conditional on reconciliation with Princess Helen of Greece, which the latter refused: Haynes, 'Reluctant Allies? Iuliu Maniu and Corneliu Zelea Codreanu Against King Carol II of Romania' 108.

[54] Clark, *United Roumania* 323–30.

[55] Georgescu, *Romanians: A History* 196. See also Mann, *Fascists* 264.

[56] Payne, *A History of Fascism, 1914–45* 278.

[57] Boia, *Myth and History in Romanian Consciousness* 205.

[58] Payne, *A History of Fascism, 1914–45* 279–80.

known as the Iron Guard – still continues to puzzle historians and political scientists alike. Payne considers the Legion as belonging to one of the 'four major variants of fascism'[59] and notes that in Romania, 'fascist-type movements came to play an important role'.[60] While stressing its particularities – such as the insistence on religious tropes in the discourse it promoted – other historians have understood the Legion's ideology as a form of 'clerical fascism'.[61] The undeniable religious thrust of the legionary ideology prompted the historian Eugen Weber to describe this movement as essentially a reaction to modernity specific to a backward society.[62] On closer analysis, 'the only "fascist" movement outside Italy and Germany to come to power without foreign aid'[63] appears as professing a form of sacralisation of politics pertaining to a Romanian version of modern palingenesis,[64] which glorified the nation and its past, and identified the Jewish population as the agent of the dissolution of society.[65]

As a 'distinct sub-type'[66] of fascism entangled in the ambiguities of counter-revolution, Romanian ultranationalism affirmed itself as a political force as early as the beginning of the 1920s, in the context of social and political unrest marked by strikes and authoritarian responses to social conflicts.[67] Arguably a product of the reactionary politics of suppressing dissent already employed by state authorities in the early 1920s, the movement organised and asserted itself to the point of openly contesting the state's sovereignty. Built around Corneliu Zelea Codreanu, a charismatic leader[68] with strong ties in the ultranationalist milieu,[69] the fascist movement initially took the form of a nationalist, trade-union-based, ephemeral organisation known as the Guard of National Awareness.[70] During that time it participated in quelling strikes during 1919 and 1920 in Moldavia, affirming itself as primarily an anti-communist movement. After a period of activism within universities against the provisions of the new Constitution, which recognised full

---

[59] Ibid 245.

[60] Ibid.

[61] R Eatwell, 'Reflections on Fascism and Religion' (2003) 4 *Totalitarian Movements and Political Religions* 146–66.

[62] E Weber, 'Romania' in H Rogger and E Weber (eds), *The European Right: A Historical Profile* (London, Weidenfeld and Nicholson, 1965) 96–105 at 96. See also E Weber, 'Men of the Archangel' (1966) 1 *Journal of Contemporary History* 101–26 at 103.

[63] Weber, 'Men of the Archangel' 103.

[64] C Iordachi, 'God's Chosen Warriors: Romantic Palingenesis' in C Iordachi (ed), *Comparative Fascist Studies: New Perspectives* (London, Routledge, 2010) 316–57, 320.

[65] P Morgan, *Fascism in Europe 1919–1945* (London, Routledge, 2003) 45.

[66] S Payne 'The NDH State in Comparative Perspective' (2006) 7 *Totalitarian Movements and Political Religions* 409–15, 411.

[67] Haynes, 'Corneliu Zelea Codreanu: The Romanian "New Man"' 171.

[68] C Iordachi, 'Charisma Religion and Ideology: Romania's Interwar Legion of the Archangel Michael' in JR Lampe and M Mazower (eds), *Ideologies and National Identities* (Budapest, Central European University Press, 2004) 19–53.

[69] Codreanu's father was already a member of the National Democratic Party in 1920 and a close friend to AC Cuza, at that time the informal leader of the ultranationalist movement: Ornea, *The Romanian Extreme Right* 265.

[70] Ornea, *The Romanian Extreme Right* 265; CZ Codreanu, *Pentru legionari* (Sibiu, Totul Pentru Ţară, 1936) 9.

citizenship rights for minorities,[71] Codreanu joined his mentor AC Cuza in founding the *Liga Apărării Național-Creștine* (LANC, or League for National Christian
Defence).[72] Within its structure he established a network of radical groups named
the Brotherhoods of the Cross.[73] In the subsequent period, the militancy of the
ultranationalist group took the form of social activism devised to build a direct
relationship with its potential constituency.[74]

The paramilitary style and radical stand of the nascent movement did not pass
unnoticed by the state's authorities. A series of conflicts with the state thus ensued,
with the ultranationalists shifting from a vigilante organisation operating against
international communism, to an insurrectional group aiming for a political takeover. As early as 1923, the core members of the future Legion were arrested on
suspicion of plotting the assassination of NLP members of government. However,
they were acquitted on the ground that the legislation of the time did not criminalise preparatory acts to a crime, but only attempts.[75] Also, during the proceedings one of the leaders, Ion Moța, shot his former fellow, Ion Vernichescu, who
had been exposed as an informant, but Moța was acquitted for having acted in
self-defence.[76]

The movement's political activism took the peculiar populist form of organising work camps and thus allegedly addressing in a non-mediated manner people's
'authentic' problems. One such work camp was banned by the chief of police of
Iași in 1924, resulting in clashes between students and the police. Acting as a lawyer in the trial opposing the students to the state authorities, Codreanu shot dead
the chief of police in the Magistrate's Court, but was acquitted in 1925 on the
same ground of having acted in self-defence.[77]

A celebrated hero in ultranationalist circles, and having finished his doctoral
studies in Grenoble, Codreanu founded the Legion of Archangel Michael in 1927
by reuniting the radical factions inside the LANC.[78] A constant instigator and perpetrator of anti-Semitic violence during the first years of the next decade, the fascist movement took advantage of the political division caused inside the democratic
camp by the return of Carol II. In 1931, notwithstanding the party's prohibition,[79]
Codreanu was elected as a member of Parliament, which paved the way for a full-
scale conflict with the state institutions.[80] By the end of the 1930s the movement,
having changed its name and organisation several times, ended up by gaining third
place with 15 per cent of the votes in the parliamentary elections of 1937 (after the
NLP and NPP), thus posing a real threat to the political system itself.

---

[71] Ornea, *The Romanian Extreme Right* 266.
[72] Ibid.
[73] Mann, *Fascists* 265.
[74] Haynes, 'Corneliu Zelea Codreanu: The Romanian "New Man"' 176.
[75] Ornea, *The Romanian Extreme Right* 266.
[76] Ibid.
[77] Ibid 267.
[78] Ibid 268.
[79] As a result of a failed attempt by a member of the Iron Guard to assassinate the Secretary of State
of the Ministry of the Interior: ibid 273–74.
[80] Payne, *A History of Fascism* 282.

In response to the fascists' rise to power, and after an abortive attempt to gain control over it, King Carol II tried to suppress the Legion completely. However, this move was directed more by *realpolitik* interests than by ideological principles. As Haynes rightly observes, the Legion was at its origins 'a pro-monarchist organisation',[81] and King Carol sought to 'gain advantage of the Legion's growing influence over the country's nationalist youth'[82] as much as he wished to cooperate with the Legion. It was only stark opposition to the King's camarilla and the consequent anti-Carolist position of the fascist movement which determined its repression. In a last attempt to mitigate the rise to power of fascist groups, King Carol II appointed a government from one of the wings of the ultranationalist movement, namely the National Christian Party led by Octavian Goga, a noted Romanian nationalist poet and politician from Transylvania.[83] As the Goga Government failed to provide the desired appeasement, the King decreed a dictatorship.

Significantly for the purpose of this investigation, the establishment of dictatorship in 1938 was preceded by the adoption of the new Criminal Code in 1936 and the drafting of the new authoritarian constitution. In devising their reaction, not only did the defenders of the status quo employ tactics and ideological tropes present in the Legion's ideology, but they also built a new regime of legality for state-sanctioned violence. It is these legal and historical dynamics that I wish to explore further in relation to the enactment of the 1936 Criminal Code.

Defending the State:
Criminal Law, Legal Theory and Ideology

The Criminal Code of 1936, also known as the Carol II Criminal Code,[84] was in force until 1969[85] and is considered by the Romanian interpretative community as having laid the foundations for subsequent criminal legislation.[86] The project of

---

[81] Haynes, 'Reluctant Allies?' 110.

[82] Ibid.

[83] Hitchins, *Rumania 1866–1947* 419–20.

[84] By virtue of the Statute on naming the Codes for unifying legislation. See Statute no 577, *M Of*., 27 March 1936.

[85] The Criminal Code of the Socialist Republic of Romania entered into force on 1 January 1969: see the Criminal Code of the Socialist Republic of Romania, *B.Of*., 21 June 1968, art 363. After the regime change in 1947, the Code was modified in 1948 by a statute whose aim was to align the Code to the new constitutional context, without changing its structure and substance: see Statute no 5 modifying certain provisions of the Criminal Code, *M.Of*., 19 January 1948.

[86] The Statement of purpose opening the draft of the New Criminal Code which came into force on 1 January 2014 affirms that 'in valuing the tradition of our criminal legislation, it [the legislative drafting] has started from the provisions of the Criminal Code of 1936, most of them already maintained in the Code in force': Ministry of Justice of Romania, *Statement of purpose of the legislative draft of the Criminal Code*: www.just.ro/Sections/PrimaPagina_MeniuDreapta/noulcodpenal/tabid/940/Default.aspx.

drafting a new Code started as early as 1920 with the appointment of a Commission within the Ministry of Justice. A first version of the Code was rejected by the Legislative Council on the grounds of not differing significantly from the Code already in force. The work on a completely revised version started in 1921 and it involved a constant and often uneasy collaboration between the Ministry of Justice and the Legislative Council.[87] The text was thus a collective enterprise, which was influenced by leading figures in the legal world of the time, such as Vespasian V Pella, an international criminal law specialist, and Ion Ionescu-Dolj, the president of the Legislative Council and a professor of criminal law.[88] However, the highly collaborative dimension and the constant political intricacies in which the drafting was entangled, meant at the same time the Code was strongly embedded in the legal milieu of the interwar period. A first draft was submitted to Parliament in 1928 and a second one in 1933, both of them being withdrawn by the following government as a result of the political division between the NPP and the NLP.[89] Only a third draft succeeded, being approved by the two Chambers of Parliament in 1936. King Carol's support for the draft did not pass unnoticed, in so far as 'the word of His Majesty . . . put an end to certain enmities which could have become damaging.'[90]

The Code's explicit aim was to achieve the legal unification of the various regions of Romania, by replacing the Romanian Criminal Code of 1864[91] as well as Austrian, Hungarian and Russian criminal legislation in force, respectively, in Transylvania, Bukovina and Bessarabia,[92] Romania's recently acquired provinces. It thus placed itself in a line of state-steered policies of unification with strong nationalistic undertones. As one of the members of the Romanian Academy claimed, 'the legal unification is necessary . . . for achieving the spiritual unity of the nation, for strengthening further national consciousness.'[93] The Code was thus intended to be part of 'a uniform legislation devoted to the spiritual unification of the masses.'[94] Furthermore, the Code was deemed to accomplish another less explicit political project, that is, to align repression in Romania to that existing in 'all the states which aspire to calm, order and constructive work inside their boundaries.'[95]

Inspired by the 1930 Italian Rocco Penal Code, as well as by French criminal law, the Romanian Code does not strike the reader prima facie as an authoritarian legal mechanism, despite the fact that it continued to be in force during one of the most troubled periods in modern Romanian history. Thus, it reiterates the

---

[87] J Radulesco, 'Le Projet de Code pénal roumain' in (1928) 1–3 *Bulletin mensuel de la Société de législation comparée* 543–44.
[88] Ibid 545.
[89] V Pop, 'Prefață', in C Rătescu et al, *Codul Penal Carol al II lea adnotat*, vol 1 (Bucharest, Editura Librăriei Socec, 1937) vii–xiii, ix.
[90] Ibid.
[91] See Criminal Code (of the United Principalities), *M Of.*, 30 October 1864.
[92] Pop, 'Prefață' vii.
[93] A Rădulescu, *Unificarea legislativă* (Bucharest, Cultura Națională, 1927) 6.
[94] Ibid.
[95] Pop, 'Prefață' above xi.

principle of legality of punishment and of security measures,[96] it introduces a
fairly developed system of individualisation of punishment,[97] as well as a strong
distinction between crimes, felonies and misdemeanours.[98] Moreover the Code,
in its original form, makes no reference to the death penalty. In this sense, it follows the constitutional provisions of the time, which stated that the 'death penalty
shall not be reinstated except for the cases provided by the Military Code of
Criminal Justice in time of war.'[99] The death penalty appears as an exceptional
measure, one which is instituted outside the regime of the Criminal Code. In this
respect, it seems that the Code did not in itself introduce any radical break from
the fundamental principles of instituting and regulating repression existent prior
to its entry into force. However, on closer inspection, based on an exercise of close
reading, combined with a systemic interpretation of the Code and the criminal
legislation of the time, both the Code's content and its function appear to be more
problematic.

In what follows, my focus will be on the offences punished under Title I,
Chapter 2, Sections I and II, Articles 207–11, namely crimes and felonies against
'the person of the King, the royal family and the constitutional form of the state'[100]
and 'against the internal security of the state.'[101] My interest in these legal provisions, which sought to punish acts directed either against the constitutional form
of the state or against internal security, is underpinned by the hypothesis that it is
at this level that authoritarian ideology was linked to the legal structure of the
state. My assumption is that the discursive formations sustaining this form of
repression open the possibility of grasping the dialectics between fascist and conservative-authoritarian ideological stances.

Article 207 punishes the crime of undermining the constitutional order, which
consists in 'violent acts with the aim of changing the constitutional form of the
State, the lawful succession to the throne . . . incit[ing] the inhabitants to rise
against the King's authority or against the constitutional powers of the State.'[102]
Article 208 institutes punishments for preparing such acts. Of paramount importance for this investigation appears to be article 209, defining as a felony of 'conspiring against the social order'[103] six types of actions consisting in: '1. carrying
propaganda in favour of instituting, through violence, the dictatorship of a class
over another, or in favour of suppression, through violence, of a social class, or,
generally, in favour of overthrowing, in a violent manner, the social order existing
inside the State';[104] '2. founding or organising secret associations . . . regardless of

---

[96] The Romanian Criminal Code, *M Of.* no 65, 18 March 1936, art 1.
[97] Concerning punishments see ibid arts 22–27 and on security measures see ibid arts 71–85.
[98] Ibid art 95.
[99] See the Constitution of Romania, *M Of.*, 29 March, 1923, art 16.
[100] The Romanian Criminal Code Part 2, Title 1, c 2, § 1.
[101] Ibid Pt 2, Title 1, c 2, § 2.
[102] Ibid art 207.
[103] Ibid art 209.
[104] Ibid.

their international nature;[105] 3. 'acting, through *violent* means, in order to produce terror, fear or public disorder, with the aim of changing the economic and social order in Romania';[106] 4. 'contacting a person or an association with international character abroad or within the country with the aim of receiving instructions or any form of help for preparing a *social revolution*';[107] 5. 'helping by any means, an association from abroad or from within the country which would have as a goal to fight, through the means described at point 1 and 3, against the economic and social order in Romania';[108] and 6. 'affiliating oneself with, or becoming a member of one of the associations described above at points 2 and 3.'[109] Article 210 defines and represses the crime of rebellion, consisting in 'arm[ing] the inhabitants or incit[ing] them to arm themselves one against another, or to commit assaults and murders'[110] in order 'to provoke civil war'.[111] Lastly, article 211 punishes 'armed insurrection',[112] which consisted in 'organis[ing] or determin[ing] the organisation of armed forces, or procur[ing] for them or aid[ing] the procurement of weapons or munitions.'[113]

At first glance, these articles appear to be closely linked not only through their mere proximity in the Code's structure, but moreover in the way they build the symbolic core of the State that is to be protected. One cannot fail to grasp the emphasis put by the authors of the Code on the need to protect the constitutional order in its monarchical guise as well as in its statism. The text also appears to be devised as a response to social dissent, which the framers originally understood as being provoked mainly by communist and socialist agitation. Furthermore, following a classical distinction between the formal constitution and the material structure of the state, the Code stands for the defence of the overall social status quo, in both its economic and purely social form, to which article 209 bears witness. Accordingly, these articles tend to protect the constitution in its totality and distinguish themselves as a strategy of repression aimed at preventing radical political upheaval. By repressing different forms of organisation of armed forces, the Code reasserts the traditional form of the state as the 'monopoly of the legitimate use of force.'[114] In this sense, articles 207–11 seem to play a key role not only in devising the state's defences against radical politics, but also in articulating an ideological narrative on the values to be protected. Here one could easily retrieve echoes of the classic *topoi* of the conservative-authoritarian discourse specific to

---

[105] Ibid (emphasis added).
[106] Ibid.
[107] Ibid (emphasis added).
[108] Ibid.
[109] Ibid.
[110] Ibid art 210.
[111] Ibid.
[112] Ibid art 211.
[113] Ibid.
[114] 'A compulsory political organization with continuous operations will be called a "state" insofar as its administrative staff successfully upholds the claim to the *monopoly* of the *legitimate* use of physical force in the enforcement of its order': M Weber, *Economy and Society*, G Roth and C Wittich (eds) (Berkeley CA, University of California Press, 1978 [1922]) 54 (original emphasis).

the Eastern-European interwar period: king, state, order, and society, which are all to be defended with the full power of the state.[115]

Not least, at a formal level, articles 207–11 bear as a specific imprint the recurrence of indeterminate, *open-textured* concepts such as 'violence', 'social order', 'economic order', 'civil war' and 'social revolution'. These terms, inscribed with a high degree of indeterminacy and rhetorical power, seem to blur the otherwise coherent legal narrative the Code offers. Indeed, the meaning of violence, as in 'violent act', or 'through violence', not only makes the difference between crime and lawful action, but also between politically significant action and anti-constitutional offence. Against the background of an interpretative community traditionally relying on state-sanctioned authoritative definitions of legal terms,[116] such open-ended notions seem to leave a wide discretion to the interpreter, who is called to decide upon the meaning with very little discursive constraint. Moreover, given the matter at stake in such an interpretation, the interpreter is called to act as a very defender of the constitution.

For the legal historian, these concepts appear as the crack in law's symbolic framework through which historical context permeates the legal discourse, thus linking the textual structure to manifold social phenomena and the movements of history. Indeed, such statements bring before us the question of the relation between law and context to the extent that they refer to a reality which appears to be structurally outside the Code's normative scope. By their presence in the text of the Code, indeterminate concepts like violence, social and economic order, or social revolution, signal the presence of an outside which is yet to be explored. In a topology of law and violence, they represent their point of juncture as well as the paradoxical trait of being both inside and outside the sphere of the law. Accordingly, in order to trace their latent meaning and to approach the overall strategy of organising repression through punishing sedition in the context of Romania's interwar period, one should take into account their immediate conceptual environment.

A starting point for my exploration could be set up in the legal treatment of the offences defined and repressed through articles 207–11 offered by the 1936 Code itself. Following this enquiry, it is perhaps striking to note that, in spite of the overt political content these offences point to, they do not fall a priori in the category of 'political crime'.[117] Accordingly, by virtue of article 27 of the same Code, offences 'which aim at either changing the foundations of any social organisation or only Romania's foundations of social organisation'[118] shall not be considered 'political.'[119] From this vantage point, it seems that the Romanian legislator's

---

[115] See R Haynes, 'Introduction', in Haynes and Rady (eds), *In the Shadow of Hitler* 1–20 at 4.
[116] As Pierre Legrand would note with regard to the civilian tradition, to which Romanian law belongs, '[t]he civil law is a law of the Text': P Legrand, 'Antiqui Juris Civilis Fabulas', (1995) 45 *University of Toronto Law Journal* 311–62, 317.
[117] The Romanian Criminal Code art 27.
[118] Ibid.
[119] Ibid.

choice was to exempt from the political sphere actions that could have endangered the normative and material constitutional core of the state.

At this juncture, it is also worth noting that in other Codes of the time, the political character of offences could have acted either as an aggravating circumstance per se – as in the case of the Russian Soviet Federative Socialist Republic (RSFSR) Criminal Code[120] – or as a mitigating circumstance, as in the case of France.[121] The Romanian Code's position is rather equivocal with regard to this question, as the political character of a crime is a matter related to the individualisation of punishment, which does not touch either the *actus reus* or the *mens rea* of the offence, but is to be determined by the judge in the process of deciding a punishment.

As the commentary on the article attests, the origins of this legal treatment are to be found in the so-called 'Belgian clause'[122] – a concept borrowed from the international criminal law of the time – which treated as a common crime assassination attempts directed against heads of state.[123] However, as the same commentators point out, the concept of 'political crime' tends to be theoretically uncertain,[124] hence the decision by the legislator to define by negation its conceptual core. Thus, by an exclusion of the 'political' signification of such acts with respect to the constitutional order, the limits of the political sphere itself are constructed.

What one witnesses here is not only a form of raising statist defences against political competitors who risk undermining the state apparatus, but also an inscription of politics in the sphere of the law. Politics is henceforth a dimension which can be subjected to regulations and can be understood as a domain of application or of investment for various repressive strategies. In order to grasp the ambiguity of the signifier 'political' in the framework of the criminal legislation of the time, it should be noted that other crimes, such as electoral offences and some press offences, may benefit from the alleviated legal treatment determined by their political character. In this sense, political agency as well as political subjectivity is to be recognised as a determinant factor in perpetrating a crime, inasmuch as it does not aim to destabilise and counter the constitutional discourse itself.

[120] Such is the case of arts 46 and 58 of the RSFSR Criminal Code of 1926, defining counter-revolutionary crimes: HJ Berman and JV Spindler, *Soviet Criminal Law and Procedure* (Cambridge MA, Harvard University Press, 1966) 22–23.

[121] The French Criminal Code of 1810 in force at that time did not expressly state the political character of a crime as a mitigating circumstance in its art 463. However, it was widely accepted that the political nature of an offence could so operate should the judge consider it appropriate to take it into account. See R Garraud and P Garraud, *Précis de droit criminel*, 14th edn (Paris, Sirey, 1926) 226.

[122] '[T]he last paragraph is only a textual consecration of the . . . Belgian Clause': I Ionescu-Dolj, 'Origina textului', in Rațescu et al, *Codul Penal Carol al II lea adnotat* 83.

[123] Following an assassination attempt directed against Emperor Napoleon III, the Belgian kingdom introduced in 1856 an amendment to the Belgian extradition law 'stipulating that murder of the head of a foreign Government or of a member of his family, should not be considered a political crime': L Oppenheim, *International Law: A Treatise*, RF Roxburgh (ed) (Clark, Lawbook Exchange, 2005 [1920]) 517.

[124] For example Ionescu-Dolj considers the definition of political crimes to be 'so uncertain in scientific terms' in 'Origina textului' 83.

If article 207 – labelled 'undermining the constitutional order' – reiterates to some extent article 78 from the 1864 Code, it also tries to individualise the object of the offence (constitutional foundations, order of succession, etc). Moreover, it introduces a qualification for the material element of the offence, which is the perpetration of acts 'through violence'. As the authoritative commentator on the article states, the introduction of this clause was needed in order to 'defend the State . . . in response to new movements in which *violence* has become the weapon of struggle for many a party, faction or political group.'[125] At this juncture, it should also be noted that the trend had already been set by the Statute for the Defence of State Order dating from 7 April 1934. This latter text was devised to dissolve

> all political factions . . . which in their ideological propaganda or in the accomplishment of their programme will prepare or carry out acts of organised *violence* . . . or will preach the *violent* destruction of the State's political order or of the social order.[126]

Even more ambiguous is article 209 repressing the felony of 'conspiring against the social order'. The legal precedent for this offence had been established by article 11 of the Statute for the repression of new offences against public order of 18 December 1924.[127] At the time of its drafting, the latter did not fail to spark controversy, in that it also punished preparatory measures to these actions. It introduced a break with the interpretative doctrine set up by the 1864 Code, which criminalised only actual attempts and acts. Thus, the act of conspiring against the social order had been termed as being an 'exceptional felony',[128] which was enforced in consideration of the 'higher interest of the State'.[129] While in both forms the statement appears neutral, being directed against any political faction, the preliminary works from the drafting stage could not be more specific about the enemy to be repressed. That is, the legal prescription was to serve as a defence against 'revolutionary communism', which 'represents nowadays the most serious threat to international public order'.[130]

For their part, articles 210–11, directed at rebellion and armed insurrection, are mere reiterations of articles 81 and 82 of the Criminal Code of 1864 reinforcing state protection against either civil war or armed resistance. They appear as classical repressive mechanisms against major social upheaval, which would undermine the state's basic functions through the use of force as well as through the organisation of paramilitary forces directed against state authority.

To sum up, articles 207–11 present the paradox of repressing ordinary crimes through overt exceptional means. Their presence in the Code's framework

[125] Ion Ionescu-Dolj 'Comentare' in Rătescu et al, *Codul Penal Carol al II lea adnotat*, Vol II (Bucharest, Editura Librăriei Socec, 1937) 54–55 at 54.
[126] Art 1 of the Statute for the Defence of State Order, *M Of.*, 7 April 1934 (emphasis added).
[127] Statute for the repression of new offences against public order, *M Of.*, 19 December 1924, art 11.
[128] See IG Perieţeanu and A Fulga, 'Comentariul la articolul 1 din l[egea] l[iniştii] p[ublice]', in Rătescu et al, *Codul Penal Carol al II lea adnotat*, vol II, 272–315, 289.
[129] Ibid.
[130] Ibid 277.

responds both to a time-honoured logic of repressing any assertion of sovereignty competing with the established authority of the state, as well as to a newer conception of containing violent dissent. Their distinctive mark resides in the recurrent use of indeterminate concepts as well as their appeal to higher values, such as the protection of the state or of the Constitution.

The interpretation of these legal provisions took place in a specific legal culture and inside a more encompassing legal framework, which determined the ways in which meaning could be stabilised. As such, it is important to stress that modern law operates through a process of reducing complexity and thus limiting the floating of signification.[131] In Luhmann's words 'law needs to be as predictable as possible or an instrument whose effects should be calculated in advance'.[132] In our case, whereas criminal law-specific doctrines of interpretation and commentaries on the Criminal Code offer a limit to the plurality of meanings, this formal limitation is not all-encompassing. Core concepts such as state and constitutional organisation are to be sought at the level of legal theory or state theory, which offer the rational façade of legal interpretation as well as the ideological justifications for the interpreters' choices. This is the reason why, before critically engaging with the statements enclosed in articles 207–11, in an attempt to render them meaningful for a thorough analysis of law and fascism, it is important to take into account the specific characteristics of Romanian legal thought of the time.

In 1930 in a *Treatise of General Theory of Law,* one of the most influential Romanian legal theorists of the time, M Djuvara, Professor of Legal Theory at the University of Bucharest and one of the authors of the Code, found no theoretical impediment whatsoever in writing that the law 'seeks to find preventive measures in order to eliminate evil through special measures of social hygiene'.[133] Such utterances, as strange as they may sound today coming from a celebrated neo-Kantian philosopher and member of the NLP of the time, do indeed echo the pre-eminence granted to the state, the social collective and biopolitics in Romanian legal thought of that period. Indeed, as the same author ventures to decree: 'Society . . . and thus the State . . . constitutes the material from which the fundamental reality of each of us is woven into our soul.'[134] Moreover, according to this collectivist view, 'there is no opposition between State and individual, but a link which melts them together',[135] these two elements being nothing less than 'two . . . faces of the same reality.'[136]

These arguments should not be treated as simple ideological assertions or purely theoretical speculations devoid of consequence. First, because the way in which the state was theorised would have tremendous practical consequences in the administration of criminal justice, as in the Romanian legal tradition the state

---

[131] N Luhmann, 'Le droit comme système social' (1994) 11–12 *Droit et Société* 60–61.
[132] N Luhmann, *Law as a Social System* (KA Ziegert trans) (Oxford, Oxford University Press, 2004 [1993]) 61.
[133] M Djuvara, *Teoria generală a dreptului* (Bucharest, All Beck, 1999 [1930]) 106.
[134] Ibid 73.
[135] Ibid 83.
[136] Ibid.

is always thought to be the derivative object of any offence. As such, a certain conception of the state would follow the interpreter of the law each time he applies the legal text. Secondly, these statements are not only translations of a fascination with organicist conceptions of state and nationhood grounded in politico-legal culture, but also epistemic standpoints. As Djuvara would note later in his work, law is not to be sought only in texts, for 'the effectively practised law is ... something different from the law formulated through written legislation'[137]. Moreover, 'the real constitutional law of a State is not the law solemnly inscribed on paper, but the law that recognised political organs practise effectively in their efforts to order and supervise the interests of a given society'.[138]

To be sure, according to his view, the law is the monopoly of the interpretative community, as 'jurisprudential law is the real law, the living law'.[139] In this sense, legal interpretation is self-referential and is the product of a community whose boundaries with the state itself are blurred. The jurist called to apply the Code has to rely on the written text, but also on the existing practice and the overall functioning of the state. His decision will be an 'individual'[140] one, 'independent of the sources of the law,'[141] but has to be given 'always in the name of a rational and superior principle'.[142] Accordingly, legal interpretation is a 'creative act',[143] one which is only relatively bound by the existing law and legal precedent. If the use of analogy is implicitly forbidden by the principle of legality of punishment (ie its legal certainty), the interpreter of the Code is called to act creatively in defending the higher interest of the state, which is understood as a 'legal reality ... floating above us and dominating us.'[144]

Defending the state and its structure through the means of criminal law appears to have been an extremely important and urgent matter, considering the various real or imagined threats which seemed to undermine the polity during the interwar period. It would thus be a comfortable and a historically accurate position to construe the legal treatment of crimes against the state as a *reaction* to what appeared as violent social unrest. Indeed, article 209 (and the Act dating from 1924) could easily be read as a legal response to communist ferment and part of a whole series of measures through which the state sought to contain the threat raised by the Third International and by perceived Soviet irredentism. In this sense, it is worth noting that its origins can be traced back to the constant recourse to the state of siege between 1918 and 1928.[145] The 1934 Law and other articles

---

[137] M Djuvara, 'Drept rațional, izvoare și drept pozitiv', in Djuvara, *Teoria generală a dreptului* 455–595, 548.
[138] Ibid 549.
[139] Ibid 551.
[140] Ibid 553.
[141] Ibid.
[142] Ibid.
[143] Ibid 555.
[144] Ibid 73.
[145] Between 1918 and 1928 no fewer than 12 decrees were issued, instituting or upholding the partial or general state of siege: V Pantelimonescu, *Starea de asediu: doctrină, jurisprudență și legislație* (Bucharest, Cartea Românească, 1939) 32–45.

from the Code could be read as a warning against strike action and fascist agitation, inasmuch as they place themselves in the continuity of the decrees instituting the state of siege during 1933 and the years that followed.[146] These decrees were aimed at offering legal grounds for military intervention against the railway workers at the Grivița workshops in Bucharest in February 1933 and for dissolving the Legion later that year as a consequence of the assassination of the NLP prime minister, IG Duca.[147] In this light, the Code's defence of the constitutional order can be seen as a variation on the politico-legal theme of the state under siege. Such a reading, however, would not only place us in the ideological framework of the state terror that was soon to be unleashed, but also misses one essential point, namely the way in which law itself is changed by responding to external violence. Therefore, in order to understand the legal, political and ultimately historical significance of the change which befell legal discourse at this time, it is necessary to focus on the manifold ways in which it related to the context of its emergence.

The Return of the Sovereign

In this section, I aim to address the question of the place occupied by the legal framing of crimes against the state in the authoritarian turn in Romanian politics. Following Gramsci's dictum opening this inquiry, these legal provisions are to be considered as *symptoms*, that is, socio-linguistic structures which bear the traces of a tension and a continuous semantic commerce with the material and intellectual history of the interwar period. In this sense, these excerpts from the Code will be read as being inscribed in the very interregnum separating the old liberal-conservative consensus and the brave new authoritarian world yet to be born. It is in this way that we can better apprehend their meaning in the politics of knowledge of the time.

From this vantage point, it seems worth noting that European legal discourse in the interwar period found itself both practically and intellectually at the crossroads between the classic formalist paradigm and new realisms. It also stood at the threshold separating constitutionalism and dictatorship. The emergence of dictatorial regimes – either as a consequence of revolutions such as in the case of the USSR, or as a consequence of political unrest, such as in Bulgaria, Poland, Yugoslavia and Greece, or as a consequence of conservative authoritarian or fascist takeover, as in Italy, Spain, Portugal and ultimately in Germany – is not only a political phenomenon, but also a legal one. Not only had jurists to legitimise new structures of power, but they also had first to conceptualise them. In this

---

[146] The new series of decrees instituting at various moments the partial state of siege started in 1933 and ended in 1938, when a general state of siege was instituted: D Popescu, *Regimul juridic al stării de asediu* (Iași, Institutul de Arte Grafice Alexandru Terek, 1942) 47–67.

[147] Ibid 40–47.

sense, works such as Carl Schmitt's *On Dictatorship*[148] or *Political Theology*,[149] or Pashukanis's *Legal Theory and Marxism*[150] are the landmarks of new uses of legal discourse.

In this period, law entered into the logic of excess, being caught by the crisis of modernity. Legal categories specific to classical legality, such as individual rights and constitutional guarantees, withered away in the face of the new foundations of the normative order, which lay within the sphere of the social collective and in the presupposed reality of the state. In the Romanian case the process, however, was ambiguous as the law entered the age of excess by trying to stop time before the coming maelstrom. If the fascist forces of palingenetic rebirth opposed the rigidity of the legal framework and overtly challenged it, the response of the state was also one which dissolved the very structure of the legal framework.

In order to understand fully the place and the symbolic function of the Code's provisions aiming to protect the constitutional order in the dialectical relation between conservative authoritarianism and fascism, it is crucial to explore the politico-legal dynamics that followed shortly after its entry into force. The legal mechanism at the core of the institution of the royal dictatorship was, undoubtedly, the Constitution of 1938. Decreed by the King and brought to the 'good knowledge and consent'[151] of the Nation, the new fundamental legal text asserted the supremacy of the executive over the legislative and also secured a prominent role for the King in the politico-legal framework. Accordingly, the 'King is the Head of the State'[152] and – 'during the time while the Legislative Assemblies are dissolved and between the sessions'[153] – he can issue 'Decrees vested with force of law in every matter'.[154] For their part, the civil and political rights of citizens are matched by 'duties',[155] a section which opened the second title of the Constitution. As such, Romanians 'have the duty to consider their Fatherland as the foremost foundation of their reason to live'[156] as well as 'to sacrifice themselves for the defence of its integrity, independence and dignity.'[157] Apart from these rather dramatic injunctions creating peculiar legal obligations for citizens, the Constitution also contains a series of provisions which link directly to the subject matter investigated here. As such, article 15 opens the possibility for the Council of Ministries to apply capital punishment

> also in time of peace for plots against the Sovereign, Members of the Royal Family, foreign Heads of State and State dignitaries for motives related to the exercise of the func-

---

[148] C Schmitt, *Die Diktatur* (Berlin, Duncker & Humblot, 1994 [1921]).

[149] C Schmitt, *Political Theology* (G Schwab trans) (Cambridge MA, MIT Press, 1985 [1933]).

[150] E Pashukanis, 'The General Theory of Law and Marxism', in P Beirne and R Shalet (eds), *Selected Writings on Marxism and Law* (PB Mags and JN Hazard trans) (London, Academic Press, 1980 [1924]) 37–132.

[151] The Romanian Constitution of 1938, *M Of.*, 27 February 1938 art 100.

[152] Ibid art 30.

[153] Ibid art 46.

[154] Ibid.

[155] Ibid Title II.

[156] Ibid art 4.

[157] Ibid.

tions with which they have been entrusted, as well as for cases of *political assault and political assassination.*[158]

It thus appears quite clear to which extent the ways in which the formulation and the strategy of repressing political dissent played a role in devising the emergence of the authoritarian state. The criminal legislation not only appears as being reactive to a political reality marked by violence and instability, but also prepares the ground for the full assertion of the power of the King. From this vantage point, articles 207–11 are equally attempting to contain both communist and fascist activism and to affirm the full authority of the Sovereign who will ultimately suspend all traditional legal protections.

To be sure, the pre-eminence of the executive, as well as the practice of governing by decree, were not new forms in the exercise of power in Romanian politics, as the appeal to the 'higher interest of the State', and the recourse to emergency and exceptional measures, were marks of legal life all through the interwar period. As a prominent Romanian constitutionalist of the time noted with regard to the major changes in the uses of law, 'more important, more intense has been the influence of the world war which started in 1914 on Romanian public law.'[159] In his view, to these war-time measures one could trace back

> the evolution of the authority of the government by conferred right to declare the partial or general state of siege, the transfer of certain judicial attributions from the judiciary to martial courts, the extension of Military Authorities [as well as] of the law of the state of necessity, owing to which the government could suspend, abrogate or create laws by decree.[160]

To these practices of various forms of suspending or circumventing the traditional forms of legality, understood as an expression of the general will represented through constitutionally limited bodies, one could also add a constant presence of the military in public life. Once again, the recourse to martial measures can be traced back to the Romanian authorities' responses in early 1918 to the Russian Revolution.[161]

The use of the state of siege in quelling strikes or rebellions, or simply as a deterrent to any attempt to undermine the social order, should also be noted in this respect, as the state of siege creates a militarisation of the judiciary and blurs the fundamental normative categories of war and peace. Now, what we are witnessing in these manifold forms of responding to real or constructed threats is the 'possibility of suspending the law',[162] with its 'dire consequence . . . which is the change of meaning of . . . legality'.[163]

---

[158] Ibid art 15, emphasis added.
[159] C Dissesco, 'L'évolution du droit public roumain', in *Les transformations du droit dans les principaux pays depuis cinquante ans: livre du cinquantenaire de la Société de législation comparée* (Paris, LGDJ, 1922) 297–305, 301.
[160] Ibid.
[161] Clark, *United Roumania* 173.
[162] Dissesco, 'L'évolution du droit public roumain' 301.
[163] Ibid.

The Code of 1936 was thus a mechanism devised to police dissent, but at the same time it responded to a certain logic which went beyond its implicit or explicit goals. As such, it was a by-product of a moment in legal history in which the force underlying legal discourse was in the process of being de-structured, and the symbolic articulation of the law was pushed to its limits. As part of the legal framework of the dictatorship, as an embodiment of the exception, it called into question the basic relation between fact and norm. Its recourse to open-ended concepts should thus be read as a structural feature derived from the very impossibility of legal language to articulate historical facts. Indeed, the Code's strategy of limiting political subjectivities to a rigid position, its prohibition of revolutionary movements and radical politics were, in the precise historical moment of its framing, nothing short of an attempt to stop time. The articles devised to protect the constitutional order appear as a reaction to the ideology of rebirth and regeneration professed by the Legionary fascists. Those articles were thus a form of protecting the status quo, which was already crumbling from various attacks. To the extent that fascism is connected to

> a sense of 'metastasis', or rebirth, subjectively experienced as moving from a mere 'existence' of anomie and isolation into a qualitatively different time in which individual life and death itself is transcended by becoming merged with the eternity of the nation and race[164]

the royal dictatorship can be seen as a traditional legal defence, which aimed at suspending the constitution in order to preserve it.[165] In this sense, what we are facing both in legal and in political terms is the process of repressing a potentially revolutionary situation. This position could also be confirmed by the ways in which the fascist movement portrayed itself as a revolutionary force,[166] situated on the left of the political spectrum, preaching an anti-oligarchical and anti-conservative rebirth of the Nation. Accordingly, the legal framework was intended to protect the constitutional order against a radical upheaval. Yet this perspective obscures the change in the structure of the legal framework itself. The law was not only politicised by its complicity with the structure of power, but was also made secondary to the interplay between *raison d'état*-driven politics and ideology. In this sense the Code, understood in its political situation in the framework of the royal dictatorship, occupied a place on the threshold between classic repression and new forms of (bio)political and ideological investment. Moreover, seen through these lenses, the royal dictatorship appears once again as a symptomatic last attempt to reassert the classical tenets of state sovereignty. The emergence of the Code in a time of political, cultural and symbolic uncertainty, as well as its peculiar logic in criminalising dissent, point towards a change of law's status in

---

[164] R Griffin, '"I Am No Longer A Human. I Am A Titan. A God!": The Fascist Quest to Regenerate Time', in Feldman (ed), *A Fascist Century* 3–23 at 15–16.

[165] Schmitt, *Die Diktatur* 170–73.

[166] M Platon, 'The Iron Guard and the Modern State. Iron Guard Leaders Vasile Marin and Ion I Moţa and the "European New Order"' (2012) 1 *Fascism* 65–90 at 69.

society. The theoretical framework already permeated by concepts with strong ultranationalist connotations, such as the organic understanding of society, attests to a passage towards an instrumental relation to law. In other words, the law would be henceforth understood not as a form of rationalising state power, but its vector.

The criminal provisions under scrutiny here and the royal dictatorship may have acted rhetorically as a way of limiting the potentialities of time and preventing disaster, but underneath these attempts one may trace the core of the legal intricacies of the interwar period, which are read here as a form of the 'sense-making crisis'.[167] It is no surprise to note that the strategy of suppressing fascism and restating the status quo could not function under the specific historical circumstances pertaining, in that the status of legality in itself was already problematic. Indeed, the facts that the Constitution limited all form of political participation, organised the exercise of power around the central figure of the King, and introduced the state of exception in its conceptual framework, all point to a radical break with modern Romanian constitutionalism. As Vlad Georgescu notes, 'the 1938 Constitution resembled the Organic Statutes [of the 1830s] more closely than it did the constitutions of 1848, 1866 and 1923.'[168]

For its part, the Criminal Code blurred the distinction between politics and criminal action, as well as between lawful and unlawful, through the recourse to open-ended concepts. Moreover, the theoretical structure of interpretation insisted on the centrality of the state and of state power. Consequently, by the same act of containing what was perceived as revolutionary fascism, the legal discourse was itself 'revolutionised', opening the way to full assertions of power.

It is thus worth noting that the Iron Guard was unsuccessfully dissolved several times before the entry into force of the Criminal Code and the institution of dictatorship.[169] Its main leader was tried for treason and rebellion, and killed in what historians describe as a staged shooting while trying to flee custody in late 1938.[170] In retaliation, the fascists proceeded to assassinate the Prime Minister and Minister of the Interior, Armand Calinescu.[171] From this point on, law could not contain historical violence any more, and the dictatorship unleashed the full force of the state.

However, one would be wrong in understanding the overarching royal dictatorship only as a mere attempt to prevent fascist upheaval. In many respects, the Carol regime and its preceding authoritarianism was not only complacent or complicit in fascist ideology and its overtones, but also structurally close.[172] In this

---

[167] GM Platt, 'An Alternative Theory', in R Griffin (ed) *International Fascism* (London, Arnold, 1998 [1980]) 204–15, 208.

[168] Georgescu, *Romanians: A History* 207.

[169] Ibid 196, where he writes 'The Iron Guard was outlawed first in 1931 and again in 1933, but reappeared in 1935 under the name All for the Country'.

[170] Ibid 208.

[171] Ibid.

[172] But see Georgescu, ibid: 'The royal dictatorship was not, however, a fascist or Nazi regime. It was only moderately nationalistic and anti-Semitic'. Whilst Carol II himself was not overtly anti-Semitic,

respect it is significant to note the introduction of the single party, the Front of National Rebirth,[173] as well as the organisation of its structure and propaganda, which mimicked the Legion's public spectacles. The royal dictatorship and its emergence thus appear as a series of extremely ambiguous moments which politically marked the passage from a limited democracy to open authoritarianism. From a juridical perspective, this process reveals the dissolution of the old concepts of form and legality, and the extension of force as a normal response to dissent. State violence thus permeates the very structure of the law and dissolves it. The Criminal Code is both an object and an archive of these dynamics, as it actively took part in the general historical process of the institution of dictatorship, as well as in the later repression organised by the National Legionary State in 1940, continued by Antonescu's military dictatorship through World War II, and arguably further deployed in the first years of the communist regime.

the first steps of the future anti-Semitic legislation date from the beginnings of the royal dictatorship under the Goga cabinet. See for example Decree-Law no 169 for the revision of the citizenship of Jews in Romania, *M Of.*, 21 January 1938. For a comparative analysis of the question of anti-Semitism in interwar Romania and Bulgaria, see WI Brustein and RD King, 'Anti-Semitism as a Response to Perceived Jewish Power' (2004) 83 *Social Forces* 691–708.

[173] Decree-Law no 4321 for the institution of the Front of National Rebirth, *M.Of.*, 16 December 1938.

6

Criminal Law under the Francoist Regime: the Influence of Militarism and National-Catholicism

PASCUAL MARZAL*

General Franco's regime was characterised by a criminal law system, as described in the terms of this chapter, that was influenced by two key conditions, namely militarism and National-Catholicism. First, there was an overriding primacy of military justice rooted in proclamations that continued to be enforced well beyond the end of the Civil War. There were also special courts to punish political enemies. These courts were controlled by and subject to the military courts, a fact that recent literature has graphically referred to as 'the great repression.'[1] Secondly, the common or ordinary criminal law system was based on a series of patriotic, moral and religious principles that the *Nuevo Estado* (New State) propagated to protect the society that came into being after the Civil War, from individuals who were regarded as dangerous. The New State also sought to afford protection from the foes of the official National-Catholic conception of Spain. These two aspects do not, however, encompass all of the multitude of aspects that characterised the substantial penal legislation approved during the 40 years of Francoist dictator-ship. Moreover, the long duration of the legislation in force occurred against a backdrop of profound social changes and a timid opening up of politics that, without a shred of doubt, gradually served to alleviate the penal pressure placed on Spaniards in the final years of the Francoist regime. Nevertheless, my thesis is that the main ideological lines that sustained the regime were based on militarism and National-Catholicism and hence, for the main argumentative thrust of this chapter, I have dispensed with other matters – important in terms of criminal law per se – but nonetheless diverging from my essential line of argument.[2]

---

* All translations are my own.

[1] MN Diaz-Balart, ÁM Dueñas, FE Maestre and JM García Márquez (eds), *La gran represión: los años de plomo del franquismo*, in the series *Colección: Con Franco vivíamos peor* (Barcelona, Ediciones Flor del Viento, 2009).

[2] On the administration of justice in Franco's Spain see M Lanero, *Una milicia de la Justicia. La política judicial del Franquismo (1936–1945)* (Madrid, Centro de Estudios Constitucionales, 1996) especially 318 ff.

A Succinct but Necessary Introduction

The Second Republic was proclaimed on 14 April 1931 as a consequence of the electoral results obtained at the municipal elections held two days earlier. The Republicans were swept into power by voters, particularly in the main cities. The departure and exile of King Alfonso XIII enabled a relatively peaceful change to take place. The Second Republic came into being with an inherited judicial structure that was forced to adapt rapidly to the new political model. In a matter of months, the new constitution was debated and approved. Of greater interest here is the fact that the 1928 *Código Penal* (penal, or criminal law code) as enacted by the then justice minister, Galo Ponte, was repealed. This cancellation was achieved through the Decree of 15 April which resulted in the application of the previous precepts of the former penal code, the already dated Code of 1870; however, its main discrepancies with the Republican system were quickly overcome through the Decree of 2 May 1931.[3] In spite of this, the members of the provisional government wanted a new penal code, and so the old *Comisión de Codificación* (Codification Commission) was replaced with a new body, known as *La Comisión Jurídica Asesora* (Law Reform Commission), spearheaded by the key progressive figure in criminal law, Luis Jiménez de Asúa. The changes he undertook revamped the former commission, which was seen as defunct by progressive members of the judiciary. The new commission guided most of the desired reform in the law.[4] The general guidelines were set forth in the *Ley de Bases* (Law of Basic Principles) of 8 September 1932 and the final provisions of the law were enacted on 5 November 1932. It was de Asúa himself who announced the most important changes in the new text. First, he explained the changes demanded by the Constitution. Among other matters these reforms addressed the roles of civil servants and certain practices deriving from defunct institutions, for example holding duels to settle differences, or the misappropriation of noble titles. Second, the reform dealt with the rectification of material and technical errors and those derived from the incorporation of complementary laws. In this respect, a two-pronged approach prevailed instead of the previous three-pronged approach concerning infringements, as well as the elimination of afflictive and corrective punishments. Third, a more flexible, more humane interpretation of the code was

---

[3] The majority of questions dealt with in this chapter have been taken from L Jiménez de Asúa, *Código Penal Reformado de 27 de octubre de 1932 y disposiciones penales de la República* (Madrid, Editorial Reus, 1934) and *Proceso histórico de la Constitución de la República Española* (Madrid, Editorial Reus, 1932). No bibliography concerning the Second Republic, nor the Civil War, nor the post-war years is presented as they are historical periods that are frequently reviewed by different authors – F Márquez, *La Segunda República española y las izquierdas: unas relaciones turbulentas,* (Madrid, Biblioteca Nueva, 2012), F Luengo and M Aizpuru, *La Segunda República y la Guerra Civil* (Madrid, Editorial Alianza, 2013) and J Guixé, *La República perseguida: exilio y represión en la Francia de Franco (1937–1951)* (Valencia, Universitat de Valencia, 2012).

[4] Jiménez de Asúa first presided over the criminal law section of the commission, and then headed the commission itself.

established. A major consideration in this regard was the abolition of the death penalty and, in addition, those deemed to be suffering from insanity were deemed not to be responsible for their actions; furthermore, the grounds for aggravating circumstances in acts were also significantly reduced. Lastly, reforms were made concerning limits to increases in fines, and greater provisions were made for the crime of usury.[5]

Tensions between different pressure groups, political parties and trade unions that had remained latent during the Republic finally erupted in 1934. The miners' uprising in Asturias and the Catalan anti-government insurrection by conservatives and radical members of the *Confederación Española de Derechas Autónomas* (CEDA) were but two examples of the clear radicalisation of Spanish society, and proved to be a prelude to the bloody unfolding of the Civil War two years later. In criminal law, the main reform was the introduction of the death penalty for acts of terrorism and banditry, set out in the Law of 11 October 1934.[6]

After the electoral victory in February 1936 of the left-leaning coalition of parties known as *La Frente Popular*, a conspiracy was formed against the government; the instigators were the leaders of right-wing parties (CEDA, *Comunión Tradicionalista, Falange*, etc) together with a group of generals that included José Sanjurjo, Emilio Mola and Francisco Franco. The uprising commenced on 18 July and escalated into a fully-fledged civil war that was to see nearly three years of relentless bloodshed in Spain.

Military Justice and Special Courts

We cannot explain or understand the character of criminal law in General Franco's era without going back to the beginning of the Civil War (1936–39) and to the territorial division which split Spain into two distinct areas during the nearly three years of war. Whereas war was not declared in the Republican zone until 23 January 1939, in the Nationalist zone it had already been declared on 28 July 1936. In effect, the state of war continued until July 1948, given that the armed forces had absolute power.[7] Consequently, in the Nationalist area, all Spaniards were under military jurisdiction whether or not they resided in war zones and whether or not they were military personnel. The ordinary courts

---

[5] One of the most recent studies on this text is FJ Genovés Ballester, 'El Código penal de 1932', unpublished doctoral thesis (Valencia, 2006).

[6] *Gaceta de la República*, 17 October 1934.

[7] This exceptional situation was justified for two main reasons: first, to allow the purging of the regime's political enemies and second, the beginning of World War II with the consequent fear of foreign intervention in Spain. The text of the proclamation of 28 July 1936 in the *Boletín Oficial de la Junta de Defensa Nacional de España* was published on 30 July 1936. Recently compendia of the laws of this period have been published, for example in relation to repression see P Pagès i Blanch, *Les Lleis repressives del Franquisme (1936–1975)* in the series *Colección La Memoria* (Valencia, Editorial Tres i Quatre, 2009).

played a secondary role and took on a residual character, as reflected in the afore-mentioned proclamation. In a totally arbitrary fashion the military courts decided which cases would be heard. This resulted in the cases that were rejected by such courts being channelled to the ordinary courts.[8] Consequently, the *Juzgados de Instrucción* (Trial Courts), the *Audiencias Provinciales* (Provincial Courts) and the Supreme Court itself (which had been operating in Nationalist territory since 1938) would only act or desist from acting when the military authority deemed it appropriate. The latter reserved for itself the power to decide arbitrarily and uni-laterally whether the acts of an offender might contravene the law or not accord-ing to the dictates of 'public order.' Logically, there were no conflicts of jurisdiction because in case of doubt, the military court had sole competence.

The primacy of military justice was a reality during and after the war. To illus-trate this situation, we can cite the case of Juan Serna Navarro – Chief Prosecutor of the Court of Valencia and General Prosecutor – who was court-martialled when the Civil War had ended. In his pleading at the *Audiencia Territorial* (Regional Court), he insisted that – in accordance with his status – the competent authority was the Supreme Court, as established in the *Ley Provisional de Organización del Poder Judicial* (Provisional Law on the Organisation of the Judiciary) of 1870, which was in force at that time. The response of the Court shows, once again, the exceptional situation that existed in the Spanish justice system:

> because of the facts, you are subject to proceedings by the Military Authority of the Region, as they occurred during the rebellion, and more specifically, as you had served in it; hence, a special tribunal is the only jurisdiction in accordance with the provisions in the Code of Military Justice . . . and complies with the proclamations of war that were issued to respond to the acts committed by Marxist rebels.[9]

Due to this hegemony, the authorities in Burgos (the Franco regime's capital) did not approve many material or procedural penal rules because the main legal text applicable was the Code of Military Justice of 1890.[10] The harshness of the

---

[8] Art 10 of the Law declaring the state of war, 28 July 1936 (supra n 7).

[9] Letter dated 10 January 1941, see P Marzal Rodríguez, 'Fiscales en guerra: el ejemplo de los tribu-nales valencianos (1936–1939)' in P Marzal Rodríguez, *Matrícula y lecciones*, vol II (Valencia, Servicio de Publicaciones de la Universitat de València, 2012) 59–78.

[10] The 1890 Military Code was hardly reformed during the years of conflict and remained in force, almost intact until the new Code of Military Justice was approved in 1945. Among the few new regula-tions in the years of the conflict were those creating special military tribunals, such as the *Consejos de Guerra Permanentes* (Permanent War Councils) set up by the Decree of 1 November 1936 to 'coordi-nate due process, with the characteristics of speed and an exemplary nature so indispensable in mili-tary justice'; the special courts-martial of Permanent General Officers, set up by the Decree of 5 July 1937 to consider the cases against all officers who had defected to the Republican zone; and a new *Alto Tribunal de Justicia Militar* (High Court of Military Justice) established by the Act of 24 October 1936. It must be remembered that the Second Republic had abolished this latter institution and its powers were attributed to the Sixth Chamber of the Supreme Court. On military criminal law and its strictly military aspects see JM Dávila y Huguet (ed), *Código de Justicia Militar con notas aclaratorias, formu-larios,* 4th edn (Burgos, Imprenta Aldecoa, 1938); FF Tejedor and F Ferreiro, *Derecho Militar* (Valladolid, Talleres Tipográficos Cuesta, 1938) 29–37; and on general questions of the jurisdiction of the High Court (*Tribunal Supremo*) in war, P Marzal Rodríguez, *Magistratura y República: el Tribunal Supremo 1936–1939* (Valencia, Editorial Práctica de Derecho, 2005) 141–44.

articles regarding penalties and procedures was even further accentuated a few weeks after the war began, as was made patent with the Edict of 31 August 1936, whereby summary trials became the procedural norm at courts-martial in order to establish the criminal liability of offenders 'by virtue of the National Movement'. In fact, military authorities regarded such trials as a secondary matter, since they might 'distract from the military duties of service chiefs, officers and lower ranks',[11] so it appears that the question was not so much how to administer justice, but rather how to eliminate 'rapidly' any dissent, preferably with a view to winning the war decisively.

It is not surprising then that the higher military establishment did not pay much attention to the 1938 reform proposal known as the *Anteproyecto de Código Penal Falangista* (Falangist draft penal code) by Antonio Luna García Castejón. The draft – which was not implemented – could have served as an ideological basis for the Francoist State's main code of repression, and was in some ways similar to the 1930 Penal Code of Fascist Italy, and indeed to the legal reforms that took place in Hitler's Germany. The draft also drew ideas from Portugal's Salazar regime in relation to the conception of the 'New State'. The draft proposal abolished the principle of legality in favour of arbitrary judicial power, in that new penal categories could be created. Furthermore, greater emphasis was given to subjectivity with regard to the intent of the perpetrator of a crime, instead of the act per se; this stance was in line with Mezger's 'type of perpetrator', or *Tätertyp*.[12] Spain had already drawn from this conception in the *Ley de Vagos y Maleantes* (law on idle persons and wrongdoers) enacted on 4 August 1933. The author of the *Anteproyecto* had drafted it according to a political doctrine that drew from the realities of Germany and Italy. This inspiration included the idealisation of the leader, the protection of the principles of the regime that were based on moral and religious values, and the idea of historical legacy, all imbued with the significance of fatherland, race, the Catholic religion and honour. To ensure the protection of the moral state, the death penalty was also included in the general range of sentences that a court could hand down.[13]

Returning however to the reality of the administration of justice under the Francoist regime, it must be stressed that unlike the regimes of Hitler, Mussolini and Salazar, Franco had previously fought a civil war in order to gain the reins of power; this undoubtedly had a profound effect on the birth and development of criminal legislation and on those empowered to interpret and apply it. Whereas in other fascist or similar regimes the political courts dealt with the purging of political enemies, in Spain the military courts were assigned this task as yet another

---

[11] The first article of this Proclamation, issued on 4 September, ordered that 'All cases known to the jurisdictions of the army and the navy will be subject to court-martial proceedings.'

[12] On this matter, see for example, E Mezger, 'Die Straftat als Ganzes' (1938) 57 ZStW 675–701.

[13] JR Casabó Ruiz (ed), *The Anteproyecto de Código Penal de 1938 de Falange Española Tradicionalista y de las JONS* (Murcia, Universidad de Murcia, 1978). Also especially A de Luna García, *Justicia*, 2nd edn (Madrid, Editorial Aguilar, 1940) and F Castejón, *Hacia un código penal subjetivo* (Madrid, Estudios Jurídicos, 1944).

duty to be performed. The question was not so much to judge criminals as to eliminate the enemies of the dictatorship. This was largely achieved through the crimes of rebellion or assistance to the rebellion, as reflected in the edict of 28 July 1936, which expanded the content of these types of crimes to numerous additional matters that were not originally included therein in the Republican era; however the edict assumed the free exercise of individual rights such as those of assembly, association, strike, etc.[14] Hence acts of rebellion, sedition, resistance and disobedience to authority or attacks against communications or public buildings were punished, but others were also added, such as those committed against persons or property for political or social reasons, as well as those committed by producing printed material or other advertising media. Similar sanctions applied to those accused of rebellion by publishing false or biased news, those possessing unauthorised firearms or explosives, those holding any unauthorised meeting or conference, those that interfered with the food supply and also those who committed offences against freedom of contract and other employment questions.

During the first months of war, in particular in the Republican area, there was a period of 'red terror' enacted by groups of militants, mainly from the anarchist group *Confederación Nacional de Trabajo – Federación Anarquista Ibérica* (CNT-FAI), who killed people from diverse social backgrounds: landowners, businessmen, priests and nuns, lawyers and right-wing political figures. In a similar fashion, waves of 'blue terror' swept through the areas dominated by the Nationalists, where Falangists, military and other groups killed leftist politicians and trade union leaders on lonely roadsides. After this first phase the Francoist authorities wanted to give an officialised legal standing to repression, so they soon

---

[14] The crime of rebellion was governed by arts 237 et seq of the Military Code of Justice, which included various acts against the legitimate institutions of the state. However, early on, Franco's repressive apparatus gave new meaning to the crimes of rebellion, transforming the rebels led by Franco into defenders of a state threatened by separatist movements, communists, Freemasons, atheists and republicans. In this way Franco's rebels were converted to national heroes. The following words written by members of the national army during the war left no doubt: 'In such cases, despite the existence of an attack on political institutions, there is no criminal or illegal action because there is no attack on any principles or moral values. Indeed, our goal is to re-establish lost values as the attacked institutions do not carry the true state, but simply are an apparent state, a mere façade of a true state and in many cases a real Anti-State. All countries have experienced moments of this kind in their history. Spain lived through this type of moment in 1931 and 1936. The *Alzamiento Nacional* (which was the Francoist expression for the 1936 rebellion against the Spanish Republican Government) on the 18 July 1936, can be considered the prototype of what needs to be done for the survival of a great nation. It did not occur as a simple political reaction. It emerged vigorously as an unstoppable defence movement', Tejedor and Ferreiro, *Derecho Militar* 162. The justification and legal construction of this historical vision was embodied by a Commission created for that purpose by the Decree of 21 December 1938, which included lawyers from different professions, that is law professors, politicians and judges, dedicated to the Nationalist cause. Its name left no doubt: *Comisión sobre ilegitimidad de los poderes públicos actuantes el 18 de julio de 1936* (Commission on the illegitimacy of the public authorities acting on 18 July 1936) and its conclusions, published in 1939, justified the coup of 18 July 1936. Recent revisionist literature continues to justify this viewpoint: see especially Pío Moa, *Orígenes de la Guerra Civil Española* (Madrid, Editorial Encuentro, 1999); *Los mitos de la Guerra Civil* (Madrid, La Esfera de los Libros, 2003).

resorted to a martial strategy.[15] There are many examples of this, but one of the earliest was that involving the Member of Parliament and lawyer, Francisco Casas Sala. He was arrested on 29 July 1936 when heading a column of militiamen and policemen in Puebla de Valverde, Teruel. He was captured together with 40 Republican militiamen by Franco's forces. The arbitrariness of military justice was immediately made patent. The militia members were shot the following day without standing trial, nor any declaration having been made; furthermore no list was made of their names. However, Casas Sala was given a distinct judicial treatment due to his political status. He was subjected to the farce of a summary trial that sentenced him to death on 1 August 1936.[16]

The summary trial and the crime of rebellion, or joining the rebellion, also gave legal cover to repression after the end of the Civil War.[17] Simply having been a member of the Republican *Ejército Popular* (People's Army) resulted in the prosecution of hundreds of thousands of Spaniards. However, there were some exceptions: officers or soldiers who had not been political commissars, soldiers who had not enlisted voluntarily, and soldiers who had not been involved in reprehensible acts at the rear or on the frontline. In these cases they were released quickly from the prison camps after the necessary political endorsements were presented. This was not the case with arrested soldiers and officers who had had any political relevance in or out of the army, nor for those involved in 'blood crimes' or who had been the target of personal revenge. In these cases, the court-martial became the most effective instrument for carrying out Franco's justice.[18] Although changing this system was considered, any possibility of Francoist criminal law reform was then hindered by the outbreak of World War II in September 1939. Perhaps the most notable effort in this regard was reflected in the 1939 *Proyecto de Código Penal* (draft penal code) prepared by the *Comisión General de Codificación* (legal

---

[15] A lawyer who was tried by court-martial summed up Franco's justice as follows: 'The prosecution report, like the whole judgment process, was just an episode of a cruel joke, because everything was already decided beforehand, staged to keep up appearances, giving a mere aura of legality to the monstrous repression, but in a way so blatant that no one could be fooled', MG Corachán, *Memorias de un presidiario (en las cárceles franquistas)* (Valencia, Universitat de Valencia, 2005) 196.

[16] The details of this event as well as a portrait of this character are outlined in my book: *El diputado Casas Sala: una aproximación biográfica* (Castellón, Centre D'Estudis del Maestrat, 2010).

[17] Newly created crimes such as 'providing assistance to the rebellion' or 'joining the rebellion' were criticised by criminal doctrine under Franco as artificial constructions, as reflected in the notion of degrees of complicity in the crime, the penalty for which could be resolved by resorting to other provisions of military and common criminal law: see F Stampa Irueste, *El delito de rebelión* (Madrid, Ediciones de los Estudiantes Españoles, 1945) 79–86.

[18] Revisionist literature, defending the repression carried out by the military, has tried to show that the courts martial only punished those offenders during the three years of war who had stained their hands with innocent blood. Their main evidence was still based on the post-war report made by the Public Prosecutor and deposited in the *Centro Documental de la Memoria Histórica* in Salamanca, whose findings were published as *Causa General. La dominación roja en España. Avance de la información instruida por el Ministerio Público* (Madrid, Ministerio de Justicia, 1943). I do not deny that in many cases the punishment was justified, but in others, the arbitrariness of the repressive system led to many innocent people being put in front of the firing squad; among them was the Valencian University Chancellor, Dr Juan Peset Aleixandre, whose court-martial has been published as *Proceso a Joan B Peset Aleixandre* (Valencia, Universitat de Valencia, 2001).

advisory committee), in which Eugenio Cuello Calón played a key role, but which was not followed through.[19]

The contemplation of any subversive conduct that might warrant punishment by the Francoist regime was repeated again in the main provisions that regulated the crime of rebellion after the war, as reflected in the *Ley de Seguridad del Estado* (State Security Law) adopted on 29 March 1941.[20] This law applied the death penalty to crimes of treason that had previously been regulated by the 1932 Penal Code. Capital punishment was also made applicable to any foreign aggression carried out by Spaniards under another flag, due to the fact that Franco's government feared an intervention by Republican exiles with the help of an allied country. This severity of punishment was also extended to other behaviour that the military considered equally dangerous, such as founding an association, going on strike and demonstrating, as well as logically the most repugnant acts, such as bombing military and civilian targets. These provisions were extended by a further two years in the law of 2 March 1943, which also equated to the crime of military rebellion offences of spreading false or tendentious news, and of possessing any type of weapon. In reality, these rules did not introduce any significant development, but only reiterated in the form of a law the offences and penalties already stipulated under the proclamations of war, and once again ratified the competence of military courts in these matters. This situation was not altered by the Penal Code of 1944 and these provisions were further accentuated in the new Military Penal Code adopted on 17 July 1945.[21]

Despite the terms of these provisions, the reality of the repression carried out by the military during the war is one of the least-known aspects of Franco's era. Historians continue to disagree on the actual numbers of courts-martial, death sentences handed down, prisoners actually executed or indeed those sentences that underwent commutation, as well as the numbers of trials that ended with deprivation of freedom or simply with acquittal.[22]

---

[19] This proposal for law reform was based on the 1932 Penal Code and drew from legislation prior to the Primo de Rivera dictatorship, the 1928 reform and the 19th century Spanish judicial legacy. It protected the Catholic religion, punished continuous extramarital relationships as adultery and reintroduced the death penalty; furthermore, by drawing from subjective legal criteria, it punished attempted crime with a frustration penalty, that is, the intent to carry out an illicit act was sanctioned by the same punishment applicable to the consummated act. See further JR Casabó Ruiz (ed), *El Proyecto de Código Penal de 1939* (Murcia, Universidad de Murcia, 1978).

[20] On this law and its content in terms of criminal law, see J del Rosal, *Acerca del pensamiento penal español y otros problemas penales* (Madrid, Aldecoa, 1942), especially ch III, 'Nuevo sentido defensista del Derecho penal español' 45 ff which recognises and applauds the influence of totalitarian regimes on its preparation: 'The Spanish writers of the Act have taken into account, with a high degree of agreement, comparisons with modern Italian and German criminal law' 51.

[21] The 1945 Code replaced the military codes of the navy and army, respectively valid from 24 August 1889 and 25 June 1890. The merging of the two legal texts, in the opinion of Jiménez de Asúa, occurred in the light of the 'totalitarian character' of the regime and its quest for unity, as it set up the machinery for political repression: see L Jiménez de Asúa, *Tratado de Derecho Penal*, 4th edn (Buenos Aires, Editorial Losada, 1964) 817.

[22] For the tragic consequences and meaning of Francoist military repression, the literature has focused its efforts on providing actual figures of Republican prisoners who were sentenced to death and shot. Vicent Gavarda Cebellán has carried out research for the Valencia region, giving figures of

The Decree of 18 April 1947 repealed the *Ley de Seguridad del Estado* and replaced it with the *Ley de Represión de los Delitos de Bandidaje y Terrorismo* (Law on the Repression of Banditry and Terrorism Offences). This Act provided for trial by court-martial of the perpetrators of such crimes, which were according to the law 'the most serious crimes of all in a post-war situation, the consequence of the relaxation of moral bonds and the exaltation of the impulses of cruelty and aggression of criminals and misfits.' The decree was intended mainly to punish the groups of Maquis (guerrilla fighters) who from the end of World War II had proliferated in Spanish mountainous areas, but also to punish other 'elements' that might oppose the regime with violence. Penalties were severe – death or imprisonment – and the procedure continued to be the summary trial. Only in cases in which the military authorities gave permission could such matters be heard by ordinary courts, but only by those which were considered to be sufficiently rigorous.[23]

This situation continued into the 1950s, which saw the creation of a *Juzgado Militar Especial* (Special Military Court) by a decree dated 24 January 1958. This court had jurisdiction throughout the country to deal with the processing of extremist crimes and operated until 1964 (its head, or *Presidente,* was the fearsome Infantry Colonel, Enrique Eymar). In 1959, and with a view to opening up Spain to Europe, the key *Ley de Orden Público* (Public Order Act) was adopted, the jurisdiction over which was attributed to a court created for that purpose, but integrated in the system of ordinary courts: the *Tribunal de Orden Público* (TOP, or Public Order Tribunal).[24] This law was an important step in transferring repressive jurisdiction over many of the anti-regime political acts to a civil court. Military justice was still hegemonic and did not disappear, however, because the crimes of banditry, terrorism and other acts were included under the crime of military rebellion; such acts included strikes and sabotage and, if they pursued a

6,087 killed, 4,714 of them by firing squad. In Catalonia and thanks to the proximity of the French border, where many Republicans were able to flee, the death sentences were significantly lower. However, in spite of their importance, there is still a lack of reliable figures on the repression carried out in Madrid by courts-martial. See VG Cebellán, *Els afusellaments al País Valencià 1938–1956* (Valencia, Institut Alfons El Magnànim, 1993) and JM Solé i Sabaté, *La repressió franquista a Catalunya, 1938–1956* (Barcelona, Edicions 62, 1985). For an overall picture offering the latest statistics on this issue, see P Preston, *The Spanish Holocaust: Inquisition and Extermination in Twentieth-Century Spain,* (London, Harper Press, 2011).

[23] Many attacks were carried out by the Maquis, and numerous terrorist attacks were silenced by the Francoist regime or simply attributed to common criminals, although in reality military tribunals were acting against their authors. This happened with the murder on the streets of Barcelona of Juan Manuel Piñol, secretary of the *Frente de Juventudes* (Youth Front) in that city, who was shot on 2 March 1949. The news of his death was reported in the press as a 'criminal aggression', but his obituary included the comment: 'foully murdered by the enemies of Spain', see *La Vanguardia,* 3 March 1949 at 8. For its romantic aura, the literature has focused on the study of opposition guerrilla groups in the large cities, for example J Aróstegui and J Marco (eds), *El último frente: la resistencia armada antifranquista en España 1939–1952* (Madrid, La Catarata, 2008).

[24] On the activities of this court, see especially JJ del Águila, *El TOP: La represión de la libertad, 1963–1977* (Barcelona, Editorial Planeta, 2001) and most recently C Fuertes Muñoz, *El Tribunal de Orden Público en el País Valenciano: testimonios de la represión política y el antifranquismo* (Valencia, Fundación de Estudios e iniciativas sociolaborales CCOO PV, Colección Memoria Obrera, 2011).

political purpose or might cause a serious disruption to public order, continued to be tried by the military courts.[25] The Court began operating in 1963 and was abolished during the democratic transition in 1977. However, in only 14 years of existence, it created more than 22,000 records, in which 53,500 people were prosecuted, and where three-quarters of the verdicts handed down were convictions.

Special Jurisdictions

During the years of the Civil War, there was scant evolution and little reform regarding substantive criminal law in Nationalist Spain. This situation began to change in 1938 with the creation of Franco's first government and when the certainty of a speedy victory was in sight. The *Nueva España* of Franco, imitating the Portuguese model of the *Estado Novo* of Salazar, the German Reich and the Italian Fascist state, passed laws and created special courts to purge and remove any political or ideological dissidents. The study of repression across all social classes and institutions in Spain goes beyond the scope of this work, so I shall highlight herein only some key matters relating to the criminal sphere.

In this regard we can highlight the *Ley de Responsabilidades Políticas* (Law on Political Responsibilities) of 9 February 1939 that sought to 'settle political iniquities incurred by those acts or omissions that contributed to forging a network of subversion, to keep it alive for more than two years and to hinder the providential and historically inevitable victory of the National Movement.' These terms were so broad that any act – whether active or passive – carried out by a Spaniard or a legal person that either did not assist or hindered the Francoist victory would necessarily be illegal. Yet most surprising was the fact that any liability that may have been incurred up to two years before the war was sanctionable – the law was applied retroactively to acts dating from 1 October 1934, when a left-wing revolt had hit Spain.

Furthermore, the law specified that mere membership of a political party or labour union forming part of the *Frente Popular* was, in itself, subject to sanctions, even if the accused was under the age of 18, as legal liability was extended back to the age of 14. In addition, the accused's own death or exile did not avoid the sanction. Needless to say, the sentences were compounded when the prisoner was convicted by military courts, had held positions in Republican institutions, or simply had fled abroad during the war. Although this rule included three types of sanction, such as restricting activity (absolute or special disqualification), limiting

---

[25] On 21 September 1960 a decree unified repressive legislation against acts of terrorism and banditry and reiterated these same principles of jurisdiction. The final years of the dictatorship witnessed several courts-martial, such as that held in Burgos in 1970 against ETA or in September 1975 against several FRAP and ETA terrorists that resulted in the execution of the five defendants: see P Pagès, 'Les Claus de la repressió franquista' in P Pagès (ed) *La repressió franquista al País Valencià. Primera trobada d'investigadors de la Comissió de la Veritat* (Valencia, Editorial Tres i Quatre, 2009) 19–46.

freedom of residence (banishment, confinement or exile), and economic (total or partial loss of goods and payment of a penalty), there is no doubt that the primary purpose of the law of 9 February 1939 was to quantify the amount of economic liability of the enemies of the regime, allowing the state to obtain lucrative resources from its political opponents.[26]

To apply the law, a special jurisdiction was set up, composed of courts in a hierarchical, pyramidal structure subservient to Franco, the Head of State. He had the power to appoint or dismiss members. Of all these bodies, the most important was the *Tribunal Nacional de Responsabilidades Políticas* (National Court of Political Responsibilities), composed of senior military officers, professional judges and counsellors of the only party allowed (*Falange Española Tradicionalista y de las JONS*)[27], a composition whose similarity to the German People's Court, or *Volksgerichtshof*, has been stressed by some authors.[28] The *Ley de Responsabilidades Políticas* was in force until 1945, when certain economic reprisals began to be dealt with by the ordinary courts.[29]

However, the main law of revenge introduced by Franco was adopted on 1 March 1940, named the *Ley para la Represión de la Masonería y el Comunismo* (Law for the Repression of Freemasonry and Communism), the two bitter enemies of the regime (Franco's 'real ghosts', according to one author), to whom Franco attributed all of the evil – moral, political and economic – suffered by Spain since the early nineteenth century. In that regard the law mentioned specifically the loss of the Spanish colonial empire and the War of Independence against the French.[30] The mission of the *Estado Nuevo* would thus be to eliminate these organisations, which were described as atheist, materialistic, anti-militarist and anti-Spanish, and which had violated the 'unity, greatness and freedom' of the homeland.

Membership in either of these organisations, or indeed in any other that was deemed harmful to the state – anarchist, Trotskyite or similar – was considered a

---

[26] The prologue of the law impinged on the importance of the damages suffered by Spain, but as happened with other rules of this period, references were made to concepts of justice and Christian piety far from the fierce revenge that its articles contained. It was said that the law was not 'vindictive but constructive', not wanting to 'punish cruelly' or to 'bring misery to households' but to punish violators with 'fairness' and 'humane restraint'.

[27] Some regional courts with political responsibilities were also created, with identical composition. Other ordinary courts also gathered data on defendants' assets.

[28] Cited by Lanero, *Una milicia de la justicia*, 331.

[29] From the extensive bibliography on the implementation of this law see especially MA Dueñas, *Por ministerio de la ley y voluntad del Caudillo. La jurisdicción Especial de Responsabilidades Políticas (1939–1945)* (Madrid, Centro de Estudios Políticos y Constitucionales, 2006) and F Peña Rambla, *El precio de la derrota: la ley de responsabilidades políticas en Castellón 1939–1945* (Castellón, Universitat Jaume I, Servei de Comunicació i Publicacions, 2010).

[30] This law and the court it established to apply it have been the object of numerous studies that in most cases have focused on the suppression of Freemasonry: see especially JA Ferrer Benimeli (ed) *La masonería española: represión y exilios*, 2 vols (Zaragoza, Edición del Gobierno de Aragón, 2011) and V Sampedro, *La maçoneria valenciana i les lògies occidentals durant la guerra civil* (Valencia, Generalitat Valenciana, 1997). On criminal law issues see G Portilla, *La consagración del derecho penal de autor durante el franquismo: el Tribunal Especial para la represión de la masonería y el comunismo* (Granada, Editorial Comares, 2010).

crime. The minimum penalty provided for was 12 years' imprisonment, a sentence that could be harsher depending on the position held in the organisation in question. For the Freemasons, it became an aggravating circumstance to have obtained levels 18 to 33 within their organisational hierarchy, or to have participated in national and international meetings. For the communists, this sentence was harsher if the accused had been involved in national or foreign meetings, had belonged to agitation groups such as Agit Prop, or had been a member of the party executive. Conversely, the treatment for extenuating circumstances went hand in hand with betraying other communists, making a public condemnation of communism, or publicly apologising for past erroneous activity.

To carry out the repression, the law distinguished between the backgrounds of the accused according to whether or not they had belonged to the army. If they were military personnel, they would be tried by military honour courts; if they were not under that jurisdiction, they were tried by an expressly created court which had the same name as the law itself. The composition of this tribunal recalls that of the Political Responsibilities Court: the President was 'freely' appointed by Franco as Head of State and it also included an army general, a high-ranking Falange member and two lawyers, all of them also appointed by Franco. The *Tribunal de Represión de la Masonería y el Comunismo* (Court for the Repression of Freemasonry and Communism) operated until 8 February 1964.

I cannot conclude this section without pausing on an issue to which scant attention has been given in the specialised literature: the repressive machinery of Franco during the war, and especially during the immediate post-war period, was only able to operate thanks to the incorporation of a high number of lawyers into the military justice system. At the beginning of the war, there were only a few dozen members of the military legal corps. The numerous courts-martial demanded the incorporation of lawyers who were given an honorary title. These new legal recruits assumed the duties of prosecutors, auditors and military lawyers; however, unlike the response by lawyers in the Republican area during the war – where most legal professionals avoided collaboration with the *Tribunales Populares* (People's Courts) – the Francoist authorities had no problems in finding volunteers for these legal positions. Most of them were professional lawyers.[31] We must remember that, at the time of the *Alzamiento,* and based on a study of the political affiliation of lawyers, almost 70 per cent were active in right-wing

---

[31] However, the high number of vacancies to be filled, the haste and urgency as to the nomination of candidates and the fact that many files were in areas dominated by Republicans during the war, resulted in law students who had not yet graduated being admitted to these positions. Sometimes this recruitment was done with the tacit approval of the military justice system, while at other times certificates were falsified or those concerned lied about their academic results. So it was with commander Manuel Fernández Martín, known for participating in numerous courts-martial. However, we must qualify an important observation: in military justice, legal charges could fall to be decided by officers without legal qualifications because the question was not so much to do with legal knowledge but rather the accused's rank, ie ensign, lieutenant, captain, etc: Tejedor and Ferreiro, *Derecho Militar,* 38–46. The law of 12 September 1932 in relation to recruitment for judicial positions by the army decided, in line with the above, in art 8 that: 'The staff of Military Justice, if not holding a military status, will be recruited by competitive examination among law graduates'.

parties. They were a target of anarchists during the Red Terror, and several hundred were killed. The rest fled to Nationalist areas or went into hiding. The justice of the new regime gave them the opportunity to take revenge. There is a superb account of what Francoist justice entailed, as documented by the lawyer Manuel García Corachán, who was court-martialled:

> [T]he members of the Court, all military personnel as was later revealed, had no other mission than to merely say 'yes' to what the speaker, their direct superior, had intended. The bloody parody was completed by the *fiscal* [prosecutor] and the *defensor* [defence advocate], both appointed by the Auditor from a special honorary corps. Those concerned with my case were Valencian lawyers who had volunteered for this infamous purpose. The so-called defender never saw us before or after the trial ... the defendants alleged he had not bothered to see them or speak to them at all. What was the use of it as it was all a contrived and wicked mockery of justice?[32]

To complete this brief outline of the human scope of Francoist justice, a passing reference to the judicial career should be made. Although definitive studies are still lacking, we are nonetheless able to state that there were approximately 800 judges and magistrates on the judicial roster at the start of the Civil War, after which 70–80 per cent of them continued unhindered in their positions. Most lawyers, who were mistrusted by the Republican authorities of the *Frente Popular*, preferred to refrain from joining and collaborating with Republican justice during the war. This proved to be to their advantage afterwards and they were generally absolved of collaboration with that system. These lawyers were thus incorporated seamlessly into the ordinary courts of justice.[33]

Ordinary Criminal Law and the Values of the Nuevo Estado

The main policy pillars of what has been called the 'repressive arsenal' of the dictatorship were developed with a multitude of rules focusing on criminal justice, adopted during the war and in the post-war era. Of particular interest and importance is the Penal Code of 1944 that built on previous criminal legislation.[34] Franco took five years to approve a new penal code. The reasons for this relative

---

[32] Corachán, *Memorias de un presidiario* 191.

[33] In the Archive of the *Colegio de Abogados de Valencia* (Valencia Bar Association) is the act of confiscation of the Territorial Court and other courts of the city, written at the beginning of the war by a few (c.30–40 out of c.800) lawyers supporting the *Frente Popular*. The main argument to remove the entire judiciary in Valencia from Republican control was that they were 'notoriously disaffected with the current legal regime in Spain,' *Libro de actas Junta de Gobierno*, Nr 34, ff 90 and 93v.

[34] This Code remained almost unchanged until the 1960s, when a partial revision was enacted in 1963, and 10 years later a new revised text was published. In relation to the criminal law of the latter period, see JF Lasso Gaite, *Crónica de la Codificación Española – 5 Codificación penal* (Madrid, Ministerio de Justicia, 1986) 853–900.

delay are clear and relate to the issues already discussed: ordinary criminal law and justice had a residual status during the first years of Franco's regime due to the primacy of the military courts and special jurisdictions. The insight offered by the criminal law expert, Jimenez de Asúa, in his work *Tratado de Derecho Penal* ('Treatise on Criminal Law') is revealing:

> The regime that was imposed on the Spanish people at the triumph of the insurrection in 1936 actually resulted in the enforcement of the Republican Penal Code of 1932. Strangely enough, the Falange did not immediately repeal laws made by those who were so diametrically opposed to them . . . the real reason for that subsisting law was none other than to attain a more effective instrument for their enforcement purposes. Spain lives under an armed regime and the Code of Military Justice provides its rigorous objectives with the severest arsenal of penalties. The interpretation of the law by judges did the rest.[35]

The Code of 1944 was only a partial reform of the Republican Code of 1932 and a recast of many laws that had emerged during the previous years; it is therefore essential to our arguments to mention some of the many provisions approved prior to its enactment. The characteristics of this body of law were synthesised by Professor Juan del Rosal in 1947[36] in terms of the following principles, some of which have served to structure this section: social defence, protection of political ideas, the religious and social restoration of the Spanish tradition, and adopting the subjectivist approach in courtroom deliberations. In particular, this section focuses on the first two principles, in as much as social defence – the protection afforded by the Franco regime – was parallel to increased penalties and connected with the political, religious and social values of the *Nuevo Estado*. Less attention is paid here to issues relating to the 'restoration of the Spanish tradition' and to 'the adoption of the subjectivist approach'.[37]

In relation to social defence Juan del Rosal stated that the new Code was designed to protect the authoritarian state and its citizens after the war; in short, it was new legislation intended to strengthen 'the socio-political authority of the State relative to the citizen'. Consequently, the legislator expanded the number of criminal offences, aggravated the existing ones and adapted the mitigating and aggravating conditions to give enhanced protection to the values and ideals of the new National-Catholic State. This state – Franco's Spain – had felt enormously threatened for quite some time. Hence, one of its first major steps was to introduce the death penalty, as reflected in the law of 5 July 1938[38] and repeated again

[35] Jiménez de Asúa, *Tratado de Derecho Penal* 809.

[36] J del Rosal, 'Ideas histórico-dogmáticas del Código Penal de 1944' (1947) *Información Jurídica*, 3 ff, reproduced in J del Rosal (ed), *Cosas de Derecho Penal* (Madrid, Universidad Complutense, 1973) 89–132.

[37] With regard to those parts of the Code, Juan del Rosal, ibid, closely examines some formal aspects and criticises the penalisation of impossible attempt. He refers to concepts of malice, social dangerousness, etc, and in doing so he looks to the problematics of suspicion placed upon a person before he or she commits a crime.

[38] Published in the *Bulletin Official del Estado*, 7 July 1938.

in the Penal Code of 1944, and to apply it to the crimes of patricide, murder, and robbery with homicide. The rule itself stated that the introduction of capital punishment did not require 'explanation or justification', given that it was the only penalty compatible 'with the seriousness of a strong and righteous State'.

Together with the death penalty, the Code of 1944 also provided for the loss of Spanish nationality, a penalty that applied to the 'naturalised Spaniard' and could affect thousands of political dissidents, described by the regime as 'undesirable' or as 'traitors' and whom, despite not considering them to have the right to call themselves Spaniards, the Francoist authorities wanted to have court-martialled. Furthermore, the *Ley de Seguridad del Estado* provided in article 42 that Spaniards who committed offences set out in it, could be deprived of Spanish nationality if the crime was committed abroad and the accused failed to present themselves to the Spanish authorities for trial.

It is also important to underline that the Catholic Church supported the regime from the beginning of the war and championed the Nationalist cause, turning the Civil War into a 'real Crusade'.[39] This support was rewarded with various social, political, economic and of course criminal measures. In contrast with the German National-Socialist regime, under which there were racist attacks on Jews and Gypsies, in Spain the racist approach was sublimated to a kind of religious racism, which championed the supremacy of official Catholicism. Attacks on the Masonic movement, the Rotarians, and indeed any kind of association or religion that questioned the pre-eminence of National-Catholicism were never-ending during the dictatorship. Various articles of the Penal Code of 1944 ratified yet again the over-protection of the Catholic Church and all that it represented. Despite provisions made in various articles of this legal text in relation to aggravating circumstances – for instance committing a crime in 'a sacred place' – the main reform was introduced in Chapter II, which regulated 'offences contrary to the exercise of the rights of the person recognised by law'. The second section of that chapter replaced the crimes against freedom of conscience and the free exercise of religion contained in articles 228–36 of the Penal Code of 1932 by the more graphic 'Crimes against the Catholic religion', given that Spain had become a confessional state. This situation affected article 6 of the *Fuero de los Españoles* ('Charter of the Spanish People')[40] and article 205 of the Penal Code, hence '[t]hose who execute any kind of acts aimed at abolishing or diminishing by force the State religion, Roman Catholicism, shall be punished with imprisonment.' This penalty was also applied to any act of prejudice, damage or violence against the Catholic Church, its servants, equipment and any rite or ceremony, even when it was done verbally or in writing. The protection reached such an extent that offences against

---

[39] G Redondo, *Historia de la Iglesia en España: 1931–1939*, 2 vols (Madrid, Ediciones Rialp, 1993).

[40] 'Charter of the Spanish People' (1945) was one of the eight most important laws of the Francoist regime, whereby some rights and liberties of Spaniards were apparently protected. On this matter, see A Sánchez de la Torre, *Comentarios al Fuero de los Españoles* (Madrid, Instituto de Estudios Políticos, 1975).

religious feelings were generally criminalised when made at a sacred place, but no provisions specified the elements of such criminal behaviour.[41]

In a separate chapter, the crime of blasphemy was defined in broad and vague terms and regulated so that: 'Whoever blasphemes by writing and advertising or by words or acts resulting in serious public scandal will be punished by imprisonment and a fine.' Such an offence was not necessary, inasmuch as such acts could be punished under the aforementioned article that provided for attacks against the Catholic religion, or other defamation not specifically involving the Church, so the crime's introduction may be attributable to the pressure of some Catholics in positions of power. In fact, a Supreme Court prosecution circular dated 31 January 1945 ordered that to define the content of the offence, the petitioner should use the definition of the term 'blasphemy' published in the dictionary of the *Real Academia Española* (the Royal Spanish Academy).

The family model protected by the *Nuevo Estado* was the Catholic model and accordingly, provisions against abortion and contraceptive propaganda were adopted in the key law of 24 January 1941. For apparently demographic concerns, the lawmaker punished voluntary premature expulsion of the foetus, its destruction in the womb, and even those who had engaged in abortive practices believing that a woman was pregnant when she was not, a form of *crimen imposible* (impossible crime).[42] The most progressive doctrine considered this regulation and punishment as a fiction and an abuse of the criminal law that meant it was invalid.[43] Regarding contraception, the law punished with imprisonment the public disclosure of contraception or the sale of any method aimed at avoiding procreation. Furthermore, the law of 2 September 1941 provided for the punishment of those who registered children born out of wedlock as legitimate, considering them as perpetrators of the crime of forgery.

---

[41] Art 210 Penal Code. The preamble of the Penal Code of 1944 indicated the influences on this matter, specifically mentioning the 1928 Code of Galo Ponte, the Concordat of 1851 and the Convention of 7 June 1941 between the Holy See and the Spanish Government, although Cuello Calón stressed that the main influence came from the Penal Code of 1848. For a study of the practical application of this legislation, see JR Granados, *Religion y jurisprudencia penal: Un estudio de la jurisprudencia de la Sala 2ª del Tribunal Supremo en el periodo 1930–1995* (Madrid, Editorial Complutense, 1996).

[42] The penalties varied according to whether or not the woman had consented and extended to all those who had directly or indirectly practised an abortion. It punished persons even if they had only assisted or given advice, having indicated 'substances, methods or procedures' to perform an abortion.

[43] Manuel López-Rey y Arrojo clearly explained why this offence was kept in the legislation and why it should be deleted: 'the desire of certain leaders to hold onto a criminal threat, because of a more imagined than real fear of excesses, did not respond to a social demand. The discrepancy between the two positions results in individual and collective attitudes of social tolerance of abortion that occur: a) in that it is not reported or prosecuted in a number of cases, b) that those persons who have the means go ahead with an abortion on medical grounds and in good conditions, and c) that those without such means do so in clandestine conditions with a higher risk of damaging consequences for the mother' in 'El delito de aborto en España y América Latina' (1964) 49 *Boletín del Instituto de Derecho Comparado de México* 31–81. The statistics for the years 1956, 1957 and 1958 published by the *Instituto Nacional de Estadística* seem to agree with López Rey. During the said years, the number tried for this crime were 24,631, 26,895 and 28,867 people respectively. Of these, the majority were women and the most frequent penalties were minimal imprisonments ranging from six months and one day to two years.

The regime's support for the Catholic family model also included the criminalisation of family abandonment in a law enacted on 12 March 1942, in which the short preamble synthesised the values of Francoist Spain:

> The deserving special interest held by the New State for an institution as fundamental as the family, an irreplaceable basis of the social order, cannot remain indifferent to the fact of its criminal neglect that erodes conjugal bonds that are elevated by Religion to Sacrament, and also undermines those other duties inherent to paternity, as understood in natural law as the most sacred of obligations. A Christian society and a Catholic State cannot permit without serious breach of its primary interests that scandalous aggression to its basic principles.

It was a new offence, because never before had these acts been sanctioned by Spanish law and, in the words of Cuello Calón, were necessary because 'between the terrible evils that afflict present-day humanity, one of the most serious is undoubtedly the breakdown of the family, the increasing decline of family [values].'[44]

With undoubted Christian fervour, in that same year the law of 11 May 1942 restored the crimes of adultery and concubinage that the previous Republican legislation had suppressed in the Penal Code (infidelity was considered as the only ground for divorce according to the Divorce Law of 1932). The legal provisions on these crimes were not only unequal in their terms – calling a wife's infidelity 'adultery' and a husband's 'concubinage' – but also in their treatment of men and women, as demonstrated in the privileged position of the husband. In particular, sexual intercourse was insufficient in itself to punish the husband, it being instead necessary to demonstrate that the mistress was present in the marital house, or that the husband had engaged in notorious misconduct outside the marital abode.[45] This law's limited number of precepts was reminiscent of older provisions in Spain centuries before, according to which an adulterous woman and her accomplice were punished with imprisonment. In the case of the husband's infidelity, the husband and the mistress were punished with the same penalty, but his partner was able to avoid prison by exile.[46] The greatest anachronism, which received strong criticism, was article 428, in which male chauvinist Spanish society was clearly reflected. Its content provided that: 'The husband who, surprising his wife in adultery, kills in the adulterous act either of the participants or causes

---

[44] E Cuello Calón, *El delito de abandono de familia o de incumplimiento de los deberes de asistencia familiar* (Barcelona, Editorial Bosch, 1942) 7. Cuello Calón believed that the more correct name would have been that used by the Italian penal code, which criminalised 'non-compliance with the duties pertaining to supporting the family unit.'

[45] About this unequal treatment, Cuello Calón claims that it was justified by the 'different ways of viewing adultery by the collective consciousness and the serious damage caused by uncertainty over the paternity of children.' He also maintained that such conduct constituted an offence against decency, understood as sexual morality, but concluded that the interests injured were public order and family morality, *Derecho penal conforme al nuevo Código penal, texto refundido de 1944*, vol II (Barcelona, Editorial Bosch, 1946) 556 and 568.

[46] The Penal Code reflected the spirit of the law and included provisions against indecency, regulated in arts 449 et seq.

any serious injury, shall be punished with the penalty of banishment. If there were simply injuries, he would be exempt from punishment.' This provision was not suppressed until the Code's reform in 1963.[47]

In contrast it is important to note, as some authors have stressed,[48] that such a puritanical regime with such high Christian values did not punish or ban prostitution until almost two decades after the war ended, in the Decree-Law enacted on 3 March 1956. The justification for this legal measure was outlined in its preamble:

> The undisputed illegality of prostitution in moral theology and natural law has to be reflected in the positive law of a Christian nation for the proper protection of social morality and to attain respect for the dignity of women . . . It is the purpose of the Government to address the whole problem of such damaging moral and social consequences, in its dual aspect of the exploitation and illicit trafficking [of women].[49]

Therefore prostitution was lawfully practised in premises provided for that purpose and which were sometimes referred to as 'brothels and houses of tolerance'. However, only at certain times and in reaction to specific allegations made by influential figures of the regime were charges laid against prostitutes and their procurers by virtue of the articles relating to public scandal offences.[50]

In the 1950s, like prostitutes, homosexuals were also deemed to be 'undesirable' and dangerous. After the war, the Spanish authorities and the regime's media acted as if homosexuality did not exist in the country.[51] However, homosexuals

---

[47] Its demise was justified not so much on the grounds of social progress but because it was regarded as superfluous and unnecessary: see E Vaelio Esquerdo, *Los delitos de adulterio y amancebamiento* (Barcelona, Editorial Bosch, 1976) 35 and MJ Machado Canillo, *El adulterio en Derecho penal: pasado, presente y futuro* (Madrid, Instituto de Criminología de la Universidad Complutense de Madrid, 1978).

[48] Pagès I Blanch, *Les lleis repressives*, 61. On the two-faced morality practised during Franco's era see for example J-L Guereña, *La prostitución en la España contemporánea* (Madrid, Marcial Pons, 2003) and the extensive documentation published by A Roura, *Un inmenso prostíbulo: mujer y moralidad durante el franquismo* (Barcelona, Editorial Base, 2005).

[49] Several authors have seen the connection between this rule and the convention adopted by the UN General Assembly on the suppression of human trafficking and exploitation of prostitution in 1949: see especially J López Luengo, 'Clandestinitat, denuncia i condemna de la prostitució a la ciutat de Castelló durant la repressió franquista (1939–1956)', in P Pagés (ed) *La repressió franquista al País Valencià. Primera trobada d'investigadors de la Comissió de la Veritat* (Valencia, Editorial Tres i Quatre, 2009) 621–50, 628. It seems risky to establish this relationship inasmuch as Franco's government avoided the implementation of international conventions whenever it was convenient. The Decree-Law itself made no mention of it and also legislation against homosexuality had been enacted two years earlier. In my opinion, the wording of this decree-law – in the same way as the one attacking homosexual relations – can be explained by the political mood of members of Franco's government during those years, and in particular the stance of the then Minister of Justice, Antonio Iturmendi, well-known for his Carlist ideology.

[50] Specifically, arts 431(2) and 438(1) were designed to punish those who traded, favoured or cooperated with prostitution and the *Ley de vagos y maleantes* (Vagrancy Act) of 4 August 1933 – in place for many years under the Franco regime – enabled the application of the security measures contained therein to procurers.

[51] Homosexuals were aptly described as *Los invisibles* ('the invisible ones') by Francisco Vázquez García. Even though his study concludes in 1939, this description could very well be extended to this era: see *Los invisibles: una historia de la homosexualidad masculina en España 1850–1939* (Granada, Editorial Comares, 2011). More generally see M Soriano Gil, *Homosexualidad y represión. Iniciación al estudio de la homofilia* (Madrid, Editorial Zero, 1978) although it is of limited interest from a legal history point of view.

were nevertheless abused through humiliation, beatings, discrimination, etc because they deviated from the popular values of the era in terms of the concept of manhood. They also violated the principles and values of the Catholic Church that since the Middle Ages had described sodomy as a sin against nature. Homophobia and the morality of those years were imposed by the law of 15 July 1954, which amended the old *Ley de vagos y maleantes* of 1933. According to the Act, homosexuals threatened the morals and customs of Spain and, thus, with the aim of protecting and reforming the culprit, correction was offered by way of work at agricultural labour camps, but of course 'with absolute separation from others.' Moreover, a homosexual could also be forced to move away from home and to be reachable at any time by the authorities.

Similar values could also be identified in the rationales underlying criminal punishments. For example, the death penalty, as mentioned above, was estab-lished in 1938 and included in the Penal Code of 1944 based on several additional rationales. These included some nuances of Christian piety, as provided for in the penal codes prior to 1932, such as those which regulated the execution of some penalties. Article 83 stipulated that: 'The death penalty shall be executed in accor-dance with regulations. No pregnant woman will be executed.' Of course, this was possible after she had given birth.

Similarly, the *redención de penas por el trabajo* (redemption of sentences by working), stressed by some scholars as a typically Spanish institution, began to be applied by the Spanish authorities shortly before the war ended. There was wide-spread use of it in the prison system by virtue of article 100 of the Penal Code of 1944. Two days worked led to a reduction of one day of sentence. This system was a necessary measure due to the saturation of the prison system, but it was also a measure that generated economic benefits for the state. Similarly, in its inception, there was no questioning of its moral foundation as a way of atoning for sins by the enemies of National-Catholic Spain; indeed it was referred to by Jimenez de Asúa as 'a system devised by a priest'[52] or, as noted by Juan del Rosal, 'the redemp-tion of penalties through work is tinged with a deep religious feeling'.[53]

Finally, a further key concern was the breakdown of the national unity of the homeland, which had been one of the reasons for the *Alzamiento* against the Republic, especially as far as the military establishment was concerned. Spain was the home of the people and as such, there could be only one. The ideological con-struction of the New State was the work of many members of the judiciary, who

---

[52] De Asúa, *Tratado*, 822. Similarly, in a pamphlet published by the *Patronato de Redención de Penas* (Board of Redemption of Penalties) under the title *La justicia de Franco. Redención de penas por el Trabajo* (México, Editora Reconstrucción, 1940) 6, we find that two realities were linked: 'the prisoner must satisfy a dual ransom for his release with full rights: physical salvation by working in seclusion and spiritual salvation by way of a redemptive amendment for positive acts. In this double salvation, the benefit is in terms of a reduction of the sentence and enhancement of personal dignity, support to the absent family, and support and exaltation of the homeland, all of which also involve the convict, and it is one of the most generous social works of Spain, as it is at the heart of Spanish Christian thought and the Redemption of Sentences.'

[53] Del Rosal, 'Ideas histórico-dogmáticas del Código Penal de 1944' 112–32.

were often university law professors aligned with the discourse of the Francoist regime. In this respect Luis del Valle, author of *El Estado Nacionalista Totalitario* ('The Nationalist Totalitarian State')[54] played a decisive role; the work honoured Italian Fascist and German National-Socialist doctrines, offering a conception of the strong state that mercilessly defended itself against its enemies. In this vein, other legal experts included Antonio Royo Villanova, who had written the prologue to *Antiespañolismo: marxistas y separatistas contra España* ('Anti-Spanishness: the Marxists and Separatists who Plot against Spain').[55] Similar arguments were used more explicitly in his later work, *Treinta años de política antiespañola* ('Thirty Years of Anti-Spanish Politics').[56] This conjunction of law and Nationalist ideology was also manifest in repressive measures.

Any separatist conduct, nationalist claim or attacks against the homeland were judged by court-martial as provided for in the *Ley de Seguridad del Estado*,[57] and later taken up into ordinary criminal law. Following on from this, article 123 of the Penal Code of 1944 reflects these feelings in the chapter dealing with treason: 'Outrages committed upon the Spanish Nation, or acting towards its disunity, as well as offences committed against symbols and emblems, are punishable by imprisonment and if they took place with publicity, with rigorous imprisonment.' Article 242 also considered as disrespect any instances of slander against the National Movement, 'embodied in the *FET y de las JONS* and where there is insult or similar hurled at its heroes, its dead, its flags and emblems.' In contrast, when the offenders acted 'on moral, altruistic or patriotic grounds of notorious significance', they had their criminal responsibility lessened. Such vague, broad and subjective concepts enabled judges to dish out penalties in an arbitrary fashion to offenders who might be more ideologically aligned to the regime.

Although it would be possible to extend the analysis of these issues, and to include others that also involved attacks on other democratic principles – inimical to any totalitarian regime – it suffices to recall here from 1940 the words of Isaías Sanchez Tejerina, Professor of Criminal Law at Salamanca University:

> Nothing is worth saying on universal suffrage, the jury, etc because as institutions which are definitely dead, there is no need to note the crimes of all kinds they were responsible for, these defunct political institutions; this is well known by anyone indeed with some

---

[54] L del Valle, *El Estado nacionalista totalitario-autoritario* (Zaragoza, Editorial Athenaeum, 1940).

[55] This work was published in the *Heraldo de Aragon* (Zaragoza, 1935) 4 under the *nom de plume* Pyrene. See also my article 'Juan Galvañ Escutia: catedrático de Derecho administrativo' in M Peset (ed), *Facultades y grados. X Congreso Internacional de Historia de las Universidades Hispánicas* vol II (Valencia, Universitat de Valencia, 2010) 85–107.

[56] A Royo Villanova, *Treinta años de política antiespañola* (Valladolid, Librería Santarén, 1940).

[57] Several of its articles punished, for example, associations to destroy or relax national sentiment, attempts at attacking in any way the unity of the Spanish nation or promoting separatist activities, as set out in arts 7, 30, 32 and 40. Sánchez Tejerina stated that in totalitarian regimes, any criminal activity could threaten the safety of the state and hence all these acts were included in the Penal Code of 1944 within the title relating to crimes against the internal security of the state, together with the crimes of rebellion and sedition, unlike the 1932 Code which classified them as crimes against public order: I Sánchez Tejerina, *Derecho penal español. Parte general, parte especial* (Salamanca, Librería General La Facultad, 1940) 76–104.

learning. Nor is it necessary to mention the countless crimes committed by a press prostituted to the service of the worst instincts and appetites.[58]

Conclusion

Franco's dictatorship and its criminal law model were conceived during the course of the Civil War. This is essential for understanding the decisive manner in which the victors resorted to courts-martial to eliminate their political enemies. The repressive task was rounded off with the creation of courts with a political and military basis that were entrusted with the primary mission of weeding out the biggest enemies of the dictatorship: Freemasons, communists and all manner of political dissidents. Moreover, the threat of the death penalty loomed over Spanish society from its legislative reintroduction in 1938.

The birth of that fascist prototype known as 'New Spain' was also moulded by the ideologies of the Axis powers that threatened Europe in that era. Some ideals were adopted directly and at face value, such as the existence of a sole political party (*FET y de las JONS*) that brought together Falangists and Carlists, the two most important ideological streams of the *Movimiento*; one stream exalted the Head of State almost in the fashion of a deity, while the other drew from principles adapted to Spain's history and traditions, imbued in patriotism, morality and religious conviction. These conditions gave rise to the National-Catholic State headed by Franco. With regard to law reform, the unity of the fatherland and religious puritanism were combined in the spirit of the 1944 reform of the Penal Code. Any attack on patriotic symbols was punished, as were any separatist claims. Also outlawed were any insults directed at the Catholic Church or its ministers. The defence of Christian morality also entailed the punishment of blasphemy, abortion and even the promotion of contraceptives.

The end of World War II, and in particular the onset of the Cold War, was favourable to Franco, in that the United States turned him into one of its European allies. On the one hand, this new setting enabled a certain amount of political openness on an international scale to take place. In Spain, the number of courts-martial diminished, as did attacks by guerrilla groups, Maquis or other terrorists. On the other hand, the authoritarian dictatorship remained intact; the political repression and ideological control over a society that adhered strictly to an exaggerated conception of Catholicism permitted unacceptable legal prescriptions: in the mid-1950s, prostitutes and homosexuals were still included in the category of *vagos y maleantes* – akin to idle scum and wrongdoing degenerates. The 1960s saw enormous economic growth, the massive influx of tourism and the official will to offer another vision of Spain to the world. In terms of the regime's repressive machinery, the period was also marked by one of the biggest legal reforms for

[58] Ibid 95.

many years: the creation of the *Tribunal de Orden Público* (Court of Public Order), made up of civil magistrates, which began to hear cases previously heard by military judges. Consequently, while criminal law under the Franco regime can be seen to have numerous similarities with the penal measures adopted by other broadly contemporaneous fascist and totalitarian regimes, in terms of ideology and motivations, forms and substance, and actual practices, it had its own particular features due to the regime's two key bastions of support: the military and National-Catholicism.

7

When Law and Prerogatives Blend: Generic Fascism in Getulio Vargas's Brazil, 1930–45

ELIZABETH CANCELLI*

This chapter explores the institutionalisation in Brazil between 1930 and 1945 of what some political theorists[1] label 'generic' fascism. Focusing on Brazilian President Getulio Dornelles Vargas's first presidency (1930–45) – which includes his 'provisional government' and *Estado Novo* (New State) – and considering in particular its legal dimensions in the criminal sphere, it will be shown that the major structural girders of Vargas's corporatist state were 'retrofitted'[2] onto existing authoritarian (positivist) legislation, as well as newly created through both presidential 'rule-by-exception', ie top-down executive decrees that bypassed Brazil's Congress, and police repression. The Vargas regime's 'generic' fascism also took form from national political debates about Brazilian 'identity', which included issues such as who was and was not an authentic Brazilian, and what biological and cultural features promoted and hindered Brazilian 'progress'.

Legitimised by means of an emerging positivist (especially in a criminological sense) jurisprudence, Vargas's rule-by-decree, the 'normative' side of his corporatist state, intersected well with, and was fortified by, his state's repressive 'prerogative' side. In fact, it was difficult to find any legislation or police action under Getulio Vargas that did not have his personal imprint and endorsement, another facet of Vargas' generic fascism. Now, while Brazil's politico-cultural version of 'generic' fascism came into being during the same interwar period as that of Benito Mussolini's Italy and Adolf Hitler's Germany, and was in some ways

* Research financed by CNPq. Translation by Susan Casement and technical revision by Ana Vicentini and Martha Huggins.
    [1] Especially R Eatwell, 'On Defining the Fascist Minimum: The Centrality of Ideology' (1996) 1.3 *Journal of Political Ideologies* 303–19; R Eatwell, 'Towards a New Model of Generic Fascism' (1992) 4.2 *Journal of Theoretical Politics* 161–94; R Griffin, 'The Nature of Fascism' in R Griffin with M Feldman (eds) *Fascism: Critical Concepts in Political Science*, vol I (London, Routledge, 2004) 3; A Umland, 'Refining the Concept of Generic Fascism' (2009) 39.2 *European History Quarterly* 298–309.
    [2] The term 'retrofitted' is used because, as this chapter will argue, some initial supports for 'generic' fascism were in place even before Vargas had come to power: he restructured such existing supports to fit the goals of his regime.

influenced by both of them,[3] this chapter recalls – following political theorist Roger Eatwell – that it is 'vital not to adopt too narrow a cultural or chronological conceptualization of fascism'.[4] Taking Eatwell's insight as its starting point, this chapter's historical analysis charts 'generic' fascism's development in Brazil as engineered by Getulio Vargas, especially during his *Estado Novo*.

As a historian of Brazil, I do not intend to enter debates about how various world 'fascisms' should be categorised – 'true European fascism', an 'authoritarian variant', 'something else entirely'. I am comfortable being guided by British political theorist Roger Griffin's assertion that '[t]here are many pieces of the mosaic that comprises fascism'.[5] This chapter therefore argues that in Brazil between 1930 and 1945, a socio-political form of fascism emerged that assumed the form labelled 'generic', with the caveat that, as James Barnes[6] has pointed out, each country makes fascism its own by adopting symbols and tactics that conform to the country's traditions, psychology, and tastes.[7]

Seeking theoretical anchors for this chapter's historical presentation, I turn again to Griffin, who believes that, at a minimum, for a regime to be designated 'fascist', two conditions must exist: core myths about 'national rebirth' ('palingenesis') and 'ultranationalism'.[8] Vargas's *Estado Novo* certainly fostered both ideologies. Roger Eatwell[9] accepts these and adds two additional conditions: a 'polyarchic' corporatist state headed by a 'great leader', who presents himself as ridding the state of its 'old ways' and moving it toward a 'new nation' populated by a politically empowered collectivity of 'new men'. Eatwell points out that 'generic' fascism's 'great leader' must walk an uneasy course, as Vargas often did, in carrying out his socio-economic and political promise to improve the lot of the common man: violence against this constituency, in order to keep newly empow-

---

[3] In a very interesting and recent publication, N dos Reis Cruz brings to light a wide range of historical sources such as government speeches, ministry correspondence, official documents and police reports which show how a fascist frame of government was constructed: 'O governo Vargas e o fascismo' (2013) *Revista do tempo Presente*, www.tempopresente.org/index.php?option=com_content&view=article&id=5824:o-governo-vargas-e-o-fascismo-aproximacao-e-repressao&catid=90:edicao-do-mes-de-dezembro-2013&Itemid=224. The corporatism law that organised labour in Brazil from the early 1930s was directly inspired by Mussolini's 'Carta del Lavoro'. This ideology can be traced in the important work of Vargas's consultant at the Ministery of Labour, Oliveira Vianna: *Problemas de Direito Corporativo* (Rio de Janeiro, José Olympio, 1938), *Problemas de Direito Sindical* (Rio de Janeiro, Max Limonad, 1943) and *Direito do Trabalho e Democracia Social* (Rio de Janeiro, José Olympio, 1951). More recent works about the relationship between Portugal's Salazar regime and the Vargas regime include H Paulo, *Estado Novo e propaganda em Portugal e no Brasil* (Coimbra, Edições Minerva, 1994) and PAM dos Santos, 'As relações luso-brasileiras (1930–1945)' (University of Porto, PhD thesis, 2005); see also PAM dos Santos, 'Relations Between Portugal and Brazil (1930–1945): The Relationship Between the Two National Experiences of the Estado Novo', www.brown.edu/Departments/Portuguese_Brazilian_Studies/ejph/html/issue8/html/psantos_main.html.
[4] Eatwell, 'Towards a New Model of Generic Fascism' 190.
[5] Griffin, 'The Nature of Fascism' 3.
[6] Cited in Eatwell, 'Towards a New Model of Generic Fascism' 190.
[7] This point has also been made by Brazilian political scientist, H Trindade, *Integralismo (O Fascismo Brasileiro na Decada de 30)* (Porto Alegre, Corpo e Alma do Brasil, 1974).
[8] R Griffin, *The Nature of Fascism* (London, Routledge, 1991) 26.
[9] Eatwell, 'Towards a New Model of Generic Fascism' 175–88.

ered masses from becoming a threat to the leader's power, flies in the face of ideologies about the government's 'cooperative partnership' with labour.

Historicising the Getulio Vargas Regime

On 15 November 1889 – 67 years after Brazil had declared independence from
Portugal, and one year after abolishing African slavery – the Brazilian monarchy
was overthrown and a period began that scholars often refer to as Brazil's 'old
republic' (1889–1930). By the 1920s, the old republic, which was itself born of a
coup and maintained its power by force, was experiencing political stirrings,
including from within the Brazilian army. An important element of such dissatis-
faction was the 1920s '*Tenente* [lieutenants] Revolts', which were supported by
the young Getulio Vargas, who although not himself in the army, had a number
of political allies among the rebellious officers .These *Tenentes* – composed largely
of young, idealistic Brazilian army officers, mostly from the lower-middle class –
wanted to rid Brazil of injustice through a series of sweeping national reforms,
including eradicating the old republic's 'decadent liberal traditionalism' and
neglect of the common man, and instituting such wide-reaching socio-economic
changes as agrarian reform and the nationalisation of mines.

In 1930, while Vargas was Governor of the state of Rio Grande do Sul[10] (1928–
30), he and his political confidants launched a coup against the old republic's self-
appointed President, Washington Luis Pereira de Sousa (1926–30). However,
when he assumed Brazil's presidency, Vargas's politics strayed from the earlier
liberal-radical *Tenente* politics, apart from continuing to locate many of Brazil's
problems in political oligarchy and backwardness. For Vargas, these 'old ways'
had to change, but how? Vargas's vision of 'progress' was rooted in the conservative ideas of French philosopher August Comte, especially Comte's pro-science
positivism. Comtean positivism, which had also appealed to some members of the
old republic military, had special cachet for Vargas, due to its appeal to science as
a mechanism for engineering social change. Indeed, Vargas's positivism had
already formed a part of his law-making as Rio Grande do Sul State's Governor.

Holding firm to the belief that Brazil's 'backwardness' was rooted in political
oligarchy, Vargas believed that he could engineer Brazil's 'progress' through 'positivist' state-craft. Legal positivism was the best way for Brazil to achieve 'progress

---

[10] Getulio Vargas, dubbed Brazil's 'Gaucho' President, after the designation given to his state, was
born in Rio Grande do Sul, studied law and received his political education there. An important state
on Brazil's southern border with Uruguay and Argentina, Rio Grande do Sul was at that time the third
most important state politically in Brazil. It represented a kind of counterweight to the strong alliance
of the states of São Paulo and Minas Gerais that supposedly ruled Brazil from 1889 to 1930, and that
many historians call the '*café com leite*' (coffee and milk) period, with café relating to São Paulo and
milk relating to Minas Gerais. Rio Grande do Sul's economy was mainly based on cattle.

with and through order', as Francisco Campos, Vargas's Minister of Justice between 1937 and 1941, explained in an important public speech in 1935:[11]

> [T]otalitarian integration, despite the [negativity associated with this term] . . . does not manage completely to eliminate internal political tensions . . . What the totalitarian State carries out – through the use of violence . . . is [the elimination of] exterior or ostensive forms of political tension.[12]

Campos emphasised that the supreme value of society was not embodied in mankind, but in the nation and state, to which man owed his body and soul. Citing what some called the 'myth of nationalism', Campos applauded its ability to project a nationalist 'mass mentality' through violence.

Positivist Legality in the Service of Power

By the end of the nineteenth century, positivist jurisprudence had already gained importance in Brazil. One variation on Vargas's use of the new legal science of positivism was to employ it to pre-empt social turmoil and promote 'progress' within Brazil's highly unequal and unjust socio-political order.[13] However, as Brazilian sociologist Marcos César Alvarez has observed, the great challenge for positivist law was precisely to 'treat the unequal unequally', not to extend legal equality to the population as a whole.[14] In addition, Alvarez notes that Vargas's positivist legal and institutional reforms broadened the potential for state intervention, an outcome that fitted well with Vargas's preference for top-down governance.[15]

An emerging positivist jurisprudence in the service of national security aided Vargas in appearing to restrict citizens' liberties legally. The 'New State', as ideology would have it, would both be ushered in by and produce a 'new' collective man. This apparently gave working-class Brazilians ample reason to ignore, at least in the short-run, the contradictions between his ideology and presidential practice. In fact, of course, working men and women did benefit from many of Vargas's promises. His *Estado Novo*'s social legislation extended labour and social

---

[11] Campos, one of the most important ideologues of the Vargas regime, enunciated the political and juridical direction of the Vargas regime in his speech on 'The politics of our age', delivered in 1935 and later published in his book, *O Estado Nacional*.

[12] F Campos, *O Estado Nacional*, www.ebooksbrasil.org/eLibris/chicocampos.html.

[13] Political scientist Paulo Sérgio Pinheiro has reflected on the enormous lenience in historiography's treatment of Vargas's power. According to Pinheiro, and we agree with him, Vargas's Provisional Government (1930–34) was a dictatorship, interrupted for a brief period of less than a year, only to have dictatorship re-established with the Vargas regime's 1937 coup and entry into the *Estado Novo*: PS Pinheiro, *Estratégias da ilusão: a Revolução mundial e o Brasil (1922–1935)* (São Paulo, Companhia das letras, 1991) 269.

[14] MC Alvarez, 'A Criminologia no Brasil ou como tratar desigualmente os desiguais' (2002) 45.4 *Dados*, http://dx.doi.org/10.1590/S0011–52582002000400005.

[15] Ibid.

security benefits to previously excluded Brazilians. In particular, women gained the right to vote, and the country's minimum voting age was decreased from 21 to 18 for 'literate' Brazilians – although voting continued to be denied to the illiterate 75 per cent of Brazil's population, thus leaving the approximately 46 million Brazilians who could not read or write disenfranchised. In line with Vargas's progressive discourse about the 'new' worker, his *Estado Novo* government also decreed a minimum wage law, the eight-hour working day, weekly paid leisure-time, and paid holidays, with the stipulation that workers receiving these government-granted privileges were required to be members of an officially (ie Vargas government) recognised union. However, the trade unions, established by Vargas under a 1930 labour law, were required to obtain new legal recognition under his *Estado Novo*, which put them under the almost complete control of Vargas's government. In one example of this, the *Estado Novo*'s 1937 Constitution ended trade union-controlled collective bargaining by directing the Vargas regime's 'labour courts' to arbitrate labour-management disputes. Other aspects of the regime, however, were to be even more repressive.

Criminal Law and Generic Fascism's Constitutional Face

In the area of criminal law, positivism in the Lombrosian, criminological sense was also increasingly present by the end of the 1800s in Brazil.[16] Until then, the Classical School, with its principle of free will, had dominated understanding of criminal behaviour, but clear signs of its waning influence could be seen in the last years of the Empire. In specific legal terms, its principles were partly dropped in favour of those of the Positivist School in the formulation of the 1890 Penal Code and the positivist turn then continued in that Code's replacement of 1942.[17]

The new theoretical outline introduced by the Positivist School was already clear in the 1890 Code, although this Code still included some principles of the Classical School in its terms. It is because of the presence of these two incompatible visions that the 1890 Penal Code came to be seen as a document full of juridical imperfections, technical faults and omissions. Similar criticisms would also be made of its replacement in 1942, but on a lesser scale: the Penal Code in the Vargas era was eminently positivist.

The Positivist School increasingly imposed rigid determinism on Brazil, under the notion that men who had been biologically and socially produced in a certain way would be irresistibly impelled to act in a particular way. Criminals and non-criminals were fundamentally different because of their bio-anthropological

---

[16] E Cancelli, *A cultura do Crime e da Lei* (Brasilia, Editora Universidade de Brasília, 2001) 31–51.

[17] In 1932, the Consolidation of Penal Laws was made, and in 1940 the *Estado Novo* approved the new Code, which was to come into force in 1942. Decree 2848 of 7 December 1940 approved the new Code based on a Bill by Alcântara Machado, reviewed by the commission presided over by the Minister of Justice Francisco Campos. This Code was in force until 1969.

differences. Dividing men into various types, each having an innate tendency, be it total, partial or minimal, the eye of the state was completely fixed on the individual committing the crime and his behaviour. On these bases some crimes, for example crimes of passion, were even considered to have a useful function for society – insofar as they were a type of punishment of socially reprobate actions – and positivist principles also fuelled debates surrounding individual rights, personal liberty and rights to social security.[18]

Issues of criminality were no longer focused on the criminal act, but the individual. A man, or a group, could now be analysed using resources and methods taken from the natural sciences by means of empirical and positivist directives. This was 'more real' and contrary to the eminently 'philosophical' standpoint of the Classical School, with its Enlightenment tradition. In terms of sentencing, the Positivist School did not propose the punishment of the crime, but rather provided preventative or repressive social defence against the criminal himself.[19]

The introduction of the Positivist School at the end of the nineteenth century was therefore a major turning point in Brazil. As well as noting the individual character of the criminal, the Positivist School emerged with a belief in the sociological character of crime. In the genesis of criminal behaviour, nuances were also introduced by climatic and seasonal causes, goitre, as well as the influences of city life, the press, demographic density, immigration and emigration, deprivation, alcohol, and poverty. Man was thus situated in his complex urban environment. These formulations fitted in perfectly with the latest social changes that were taking place in Brazil, especially in the early decades of the twentieth century, when there was the impression that modernisation and mass immigration from Europe were bringing an invasion of innovative new crimes and misdemeanours. In the same way, a clear obsession with observing morality and customs was entrenched in the positivist tradition. On that basis, any type of crime perpetrated against these moral standards constituted an aberration, a primitive manifestation characteristic of abnormal personalities. Defining the type of crime and the criminal would therefore involve the principle of inheritability, manifested in and identifiable by physical characteristics.

Turning from the criminal to the constitutional sphere, during the initial years of Vargas's 'provisional government' (1930–34), the self-appointed Gaucho President dissolved Brazil's national Congress, closed state and municipal legislatures, and sent his appointed 'legislative representatives' to transact state business, all of which was accomplished without formally suspending the old republic's 1891 Constitution. This legal document, seen by Vargas and his political allies as the decadent centrepiece of old republic oligarchical elitism, did not hamstring Vargas's implementation of 'rule-by-decree'. In fact, positivist law, with its aura of being scientific, provided a modern legalistic face for Vargas's

---

[18] See especially E de Moraes, *Criminalidade passional: o homicídio e o homicídio por amor (em face da psicologia criminal e da penalística)* (São Paulo, Livraria Acadêmica, 1933).

[19] See also E de Moraes, *Ensaios de pathologia social* (Rio de Janeiro, Livraria Saraiva de Leite Ribeiro & Maurillo, 1921).

extra-constitutional governance. In turn, the accumulation of 'presidential decrees' provided a legal framework within which Vargas could continue to legis-late in the same way.

Continuing to rule Brazil by executive decree, in 1934, while he was facing spreading political opposition to his government, Vargas set up a 'constituent council' (in other words, a form of constitutional assembly) to draft a new national constitution for Brazil. Institutionalising what he had been doing all along, this constitution, despite retaining on paper the country's federative political system, drastically reduced the autonomy of Brazil's states. Responsibility for making social and economic policy thus fell exclusively to Vargas, with the stipulation that Brazil's Executive, Legislature and Judiciary were to remain con-stitutionally separate.[20]

Along these lines, Brazil's 1934 Constitution mandated citizen ('direct') elec-tions for the executive and legislative branches. Presidential elections were to be held in 1938, but never happened: on 10 November 1937 Vargas launched a coup against himself by nullifying his 1934 Constitution and decreeing the establish-ment of a 'New State' – his *Estado Novo*. His new 1937 Constitution then struck down Brazil's federal system and abolished all state flags and political parties. The Vice-Presidency was eliminated and Congress and all municipal and state legisla-tive chambers were also abolished. Vargas's presidential powers were increased, and the judiciary were formally subordinated to him.

The creation of the Tribunal of National Security on 12 September 1936, one year before the new coup, was in equal measure a show of government force. After lunching at the Ministry of Justice, the Chief of Police and the Ministers of Justice, War and the Navy chose the names of those who would make up the Tribunal. Although at the time Congress was still functioning, neither it nor any juridical entity was consulted. It was decided that the Tribunal's sessions would be public, except in cases in which this was not judged convenient. Yet even when proceed-ings were public, only the accused, his lawyer and authorised people would be allowed to enter. After receiving the report on the crime, the President of the Tribunal was to send it to the prosecutor and designate a judge. The accused was immediately called to be present, and had to appear before the judge within 12 hours. If the accused was not in custody, a note was nailed to the door of the Tribunal headquarters to summon him. In 24 hours, and no more, the formal charges were presented to the accused. After hearing the evidence and examining witnesses on both sides, the prosecution and the defence each had 15 minutes. The accused could not present more than two witnesses, who were allowed no more than five minutes each, and the judge could even dispense with the presence of the accused. The juridical farce which was the Tribunal of National Security granted permission to appeal only to the Military Court, which had no right to suspend any part of the sentence that had already been imposed. In its nine years

---

[20] VVR Miguel, 'Razão de Estado e a defesa da ordem política e social. Arquitetura político-jurídica de Segurança Nacional no Brasil (1934–1938)' (2011) 16 *Jus Navigandi*, http://jus.com.br/artigos/20652.

of existence, the Tribunal judged 6,998 cases, with punishments varying from a simple fine to 27 years in prison.[21]

These were extraordinarily harsh actions for a president who came to be known as Brazil's most important political personality of the twentieth century. Indeed, Vargas held on to Brazil's presidency without interruption for 15 years (1930 to 1945), returning in 1951 as an elected President, and remaining in office until his suicide on 24 August 1954. (Vargas, Brazil's self-proclaimed 'father of the poor' had in fact been pressured to resign the presidency just before his suicide.[22]) Amid growing political crisis that included dissatisfied elites – among them some of his earlier supporters – as well as disillusioned factions of Brazil's organised working class, Vargas ended his presidency as he had ruled the state – his way!

National Identity and Brazil's Generic Fascism

Vargas's particular imprint on Brazil's 'generic' fascism is likely to have been shaped in part by ongoing nineteenth-century debates about the type of society that Brazil should become, the kind of man who would populate it, and government's role in shaping and controlling man and society. Such debates generated idealised political dichotomies: would Brazil become a modern industrialised country, or remain a backward agricultural one? Would workers abdicate their 'free will' and enter into 'class partnership' with their government, or would they launch a divisive 'class-struggle' against government? Would social actors submit to the rational wisdom of a strong leader, or continue to submit to the abstract liberal moralities of decadent elites? The answers to these questions were closely linked to Brazil's obsession about its national 'identity', including concerns with what characterised an 'authentic' Brazilian, whether some people and groups were antithetical to Brazil's economic and social development, and what was the proper role of the state in forging Brazil's 'progress'.

In this context, race assumed an important place among elite Brazilians' ruminations about national identity,[23] with racial differences meriting special attention. On the one hand, Brazil had large numbers of Afro-descendant people[24] and, on the other, Afro-descendant people were seen as problematic for Brazil's social evolution. Blacks were thought to be sensual, with a tendency for servile imitation, to lack initiative and to be lazy.[25] Believed to be a 'lesser' race, there was a fear

---

[21] RP Campos, *Repressão judicial no Estado Novo* (Rio de Janeiro, Achimé, 1982) 123.

[22] Generally R Levine, *Father of the Poor? Vargas and His Era* (Cambridge, Cambridge University Press, 1998).

[23] See especially J Lesser, *Negotiating National Identity: Immigrants, Minorities and the Struggle for Ethnicity in Brazil* (Durham NC, Duke University Press, 1999).

[24] According to IBGE (Brazilian Institute of Statistics and Geography), in 1940 Brazil had 41 million people, 15 million of whom were black or *pardos* (mixed race).

[25] C Motta, *Classificação dos criminosos (Introdução ao estudo do Direito Penal)* (São Paulo, J Rossetti, 1925) 32–50.

among elites that Blacks could carry such degenerative anomalies as 'pragmatism[,] ... a sign of regression to the ancestral type [that] ... is part of the physical constitution of the Negro whose race is inferior because it has remained stationary'.[26] Afro-descendant Brazilians, already second-class citizens, were so marginalised socially, economically, and politically that they were apparently not seen as having the potential to become 'authentic' Brazilians. This made them ineligible to become Brazil's 'new men'.

'Foreigners' were also seen as a threat to Brazil's national identity because, as Brazilian anthropologist Oscar de Godoy explained in the 1940s to his university students, immigrants whose habits differed from Brazil's Portuguese-Catholic tradition or from the social condition of (white educated) Brazilians 'would be expected to manifest negative eugenic characteristics'. Their 'racial formation' might dilute or destroy 'the political stability of nations and the well-being of the individuals [in them]'.[27] Godoy argued that 'imported people [must] have physical, ethnic, and moral qualities that assure their dilution into the mass of the active population'.[28]

Even prior to the Vargas era, and whether copied from or inspired by North American discriminatory immigration laws, or a product of Brazil's independent legal imagination, Brazil's government had already introduced legal means for controlling foreigners in its national territory. In 1907 a Legislative Decree[29] stated in painstaking detail procedures for expelling foreigners from Brazil, and just four months later another Legislative Decree[30] laid out an even more detailed protocol for this purpose. For example a foreigner, who for any reason threatened 'national security' or 'disturbs the peace' could be imprisoned, whether such deviance' was a crime or misdemeanour. A foreigner found guilty by a Brazilian court of 'national security' violations twice or more was to be expelled from Brazil. However, as an ultimate fail-safe against the foreign threat, Brazil's government could employ 'any type of arbitrariness' against a foreigner who threatened Brazil's 'national security'. Some Brazilian jurists and politicians questioned the constitutionality of Brazil's laws allowing the expulsion of foreigners, since banishment had been abolished by Brazil's 1891 Constitution, but to no avail.

The numbers of foreigners deported from Brazil between 1911 and 1930 clearly suggest that critics of Brazil's deportation policies were not successful in blocking the pre-Vargas extra-constitutional deportation laws. In 1911, when anarchist agitation was shaking Brazil's urban areas, the Brazilian government expelled eight foreigners: two Italians, two Russians, two Argentineans, one American and

---

[26] Ibid 31.
[27] O Godoy, Lecture of 2 April 1940, 'Imigração e criminalidade', Gabinete de Investigações, *Arquivos da Polícia e Indentificação*, Vol II (no 2), Separata (1940).
[28] Ibid.
[29] Legislative Decree 1641 of 7 January 1907.
[30] Legislative Decree 8486 of 23 May 1907.

one French national.[31] Foreign expulsions were accelerating as the 1917 anarchist strikes spread: in just one night, and without any formal procedure accessed by the police for doing so, nine working-class activists were arrested and sent out of the country.[32] Such expulsions continued to the extent that, according to Gianpetro Bonfa, approximately 1,130 immigrants were deported from Brazil between 1907 and 1930.[33]

As Vargas consolidated his *Estado Novo*, it became ever more difficult to question legally the rights of the Brazilian State to take action against foreigners who had settled in Brazil. Moreover, under the *Estado Novo*, new categories were added to the growing numbers of 'undesirables' whose 'inauthentic' qualities rendered them bad candidates for inclusion among Brazil's 'new men'. These included Brazil's own communists, foreign spies from Russia's Comintern, and Brazilian liberals, political activists, Jews, and the 'unemployed'. The US Consulate General in São Paulo recorded police persecution of Jews between 1937 and 1945, stating that 'for some time the [Brazilian] police have been operating under secret instructions in relation to the Jews',[34] including refusing to grant Jewish immigrants entry visas.[35] Axis sympathisers joined the Vargas regime's designated 'undesirables' after Brazil joined the Allies in 1942.[36]

State v Citizen

In carrying out his New State's mandate to build an 'organic' society glued together by 'collective nationalism', Vargas took swift action against any ideology or practice that promoted or defended 'class struggle'. Vargas, who sought social 'progress' with 'order', intended to achieve this scientifically through 'class cooperation' – that is, in a 'partnership' between his government and Brazil's state-collectivised common men. The Preamble to Vargas's 1937 Constitution (drafted by Vargas confidant, Francisco Campos) laid out clearly where the *Estado Novo* stood with respect to the ideological war between 'class struggle' and 'class cooperation': 'Communist infiltration . . . demand[s] . . . remedies of a radical and permanent nature', because

[31] Brazilian Ministry of Justice, 'Relatório ao Presidente da República dos Estados Unidos do Brasil pelo ministro de Estado da Justiça e Negócios Interiores, Rivadávia da Cunha Correa' (Rio de Janeiro, Imprensa Nacional, 1912); see also Lesser, *Negotiating National Identity*.

[32] CR Lopreatto, 'O espírito das leis (Anarquismo e repressão política no Brasil)' (2003) 3 *Verve* 86, available at www.nu-sol.org/verve/pdf/verve3.pdf.

[33] RLG Bonfa, *Com lei ou sem lei (A expulsão de estrangeiros e o conflito entre o Executivo e o Judiciário na Primeira República)* (Campinas, Universidade de Campinas, 2008) 143.

[34] NARA (National Archives, Washington), 83200/198 M 147772.

[35] Circulars 1127, 1323, 1328, 1498, 1249, 1127 from Itamaraty. The documents can be found at www.arqshoah.com.br/arquivo/618/. Cf ML Tucci Carneiro, *O anti-semitismo na Era Vargas* (São Paulo, Brasiliense, 1988).

[36] FD McCann, 'Brazil, the United States, and World War II: A Commentary' (1979) 3 *Diplomatic History* 59–76; H Silva, *1944 o Brasil na Guerra* (Rio de Janeiro, Civilização Brasileira, 1974); RE Gertz, *O Perigo alemão* (Porto Alegre, Editora Universidade Federal do Rio Grande do Sul, 1991).

The legitimate aspirations of the Brazilian people to political and social peace, deeply disturbed by known factors of disorder resulting from the increasing action of partisan dissidents, who by means of flagrant demagogic propaganda seek to descend into class struggle ... which tend[s] ... to be resolved by violence [puts] the Nation under the imminent threat of civil war.[37]

Vargas's image of social and political order was supported by a nineteenth-century philosophical treatise written by Emile Durkheim,[38] which narrated the value of social consensus over disruptive social change in creating 'progress'. Building this into a twentieth-century strategy for achieving 'class cooperation', Vargas set his well-oiled propaganda machine to warning Brazilians about the dangers of engaging in violent challenges to his state, while at the same time, Russia's Comintern[39] spread the counter message that 'class struggle' would rid Brazilian workers of their chains. Turning Comintern propaganda on itself, Vargas spread the word that a Communist threat hung over Brazil, warning that Brazilian communists and their Russian Comintern supporters had 'bad habits and other vices that would cause national cultural damage'.

Vargas's resolve to rid his country of left-leaning liberals and communists was very likely nurtured by the fact that in 1935, a broad front composed of the country's liberal National Liberation Alliance Party (ALN) and Brazil's Communist Party – the latter with backing from Russia's Comintern – had opposed him, with the decisive blow coming in that same year when Brazil's Communist Party launched a failed coup against Vargas and his government.[40] The Vargas-controlled national Congress approved exceptional powers for the Presidency, including setting up a strong coordinated pre-emptory machinery for spying on and taking swift action against threats to Brazil's 'national security'. Such changes gained new purpose and strength after 1935, but had already been under construction since the beginning of Vargas's presidency.

For example, in 1930 the police of Brazil's Federal District (DF),[41] then located in Rio de Janeiro's capital district, were subordinated by law to the country's

---

[37] Preamble, 1937 Brazilian Constitution: www2.camara.leg.br/legin/fed/consti/1930-1939/consti tuicao-35093-10-novembro-1937-532849-publicacaooriginal-15246–pe.html.

[38] Durkheim wrote about how societies are held together through different forms of 'solidarity' in the creation of social life, with 'mechanical solidarity' holding social actors together through their 'sameness', and 'organic solidarity' holding actors together through society's division of labour. Vargas and such political allies as Francisco Campos seemed to conflate these two forms of societal order (solidarity) in their belief that social 'sameness' was a precondition for a social order structured by 'organic' solidarity. Vargas's *Estado Novo*, and its corporate state that controlled important elements of workers' lives inside Brazil's economic division of labour, such as workers' unions, clearly took the form of a system of 'solidarity' and social 'order': E Durkheim, *Division of Labor in Society* (New York, Simon & Schuster, 1997 [1893]).

[39] Comintern is the abbreviation for the Communist International, or Third International, created in Moscow (1919–43) to muster all communist parties of the world in order to reach socialism. Under Stalin, the Comintern was the main instrument of Soviet external policy.

[40] See further Pinheiro, *Estratégias da ilusão*.

[41] Rio de Janeiro had been the capital of Brazil since 1763. In the Proclamation of the Republic the Federal District had been denominated the seat of government, which remained in Rio until 1960, when it was transferred to Brasília.

Ministry of Justice. In practice, however, the Federal District's police reported directly to President Vargas, who after his 1930 coup began reorganising them in order to guarantee through legal means his immediate social and political control over them. This wide-reaching change in Brazil's social control apparatus made the Federal District police into an armed wing of the Vargas dictatorship.[42] To understand its importance to Vargas's presidency, between 1933 and 1942, the Federal District police had only one Police Chief, the much-feared Felinto Müller,[43] while during that same nine-year period, Brazil had six different Ministers of Justice and of Home Affairs. Müller's (ie Vargas's) Federal District police then supplanted Brazil's Justice Ministry, putting that force administratively in charge of all other police in Brazil.[44]

As the regime consolidated itself, extra-legal measures taken by the police, such as relatively long detention during inquiries into activities considered to jeopardise public order, were quickly replaced by illegal measures, such as the continued detention of prisoners after the end of their official sentence. The extent of this, however, is hard to establish. The Penitentiary and Statistical Register of Brazil, for example, states that in 1934 there were 6,212 people serving a sentence out of the 46,228,607 inhabitants of the country, which corresponded to 0.000103 per cent of the population.[45] But these numbers supplied by the Penitentiary Council, through its General Inspectorate, did not portray the real criminal situation in Brazil. After all, the police had the power to incarcerate people without formal condemnation by a court, an expedient that was being used increasingly by the police authorities.

To gain an idea of the dimensions of this situation, between 1934 and 1942 in the city of São Paulo alone an average of 47,000 people per year were detained and imprisoned for correction.[46] The number of detentions in 1934 represented more than seven times the total number of people found guilty in court, and the São Paulo statistics did not include detention imposed as a precautionary measure. In the countryside of São Paulo state, the situation was little different from in the capital, for police practice was becoming similar throughout the whole country: 35,039 detentions were recorded in 1942.[47] The greatest percentage of imprisonments in São Paulo's countryside was for running checks on suspects (34 per cent, or 11,761 people). This was an energetic police procedure in a period of heightened vigilance and police repression. This category of imprisonment was followed

---

[42] E Cancelli, *O mundo da violência: a polícia na Era* Vargas (Brasília, Editora Universidade de Brasília, 1991) 47–69.

[43] Felinto Müller was removed from his position as Chief of Police in 1942, but he continued to occupy key posts in the Vargas government. From 1947 he was repeatedly elected Senator until his death in an accident in 1973. He supported the military coup of 1964 and was government leader in the Senate until his death.

[44] Cancelli, *O mundo da violência* 47–69.

[45] CM de Almeida, *Cadastro Penitenciário e Estatístico Criminal do Brasil* (Rio de Janeiro, Imprensa Nacional, 1937). See also AHN: Inspetoria Geral Penitenciária, MJNI, box 80.

[46] *Estatística Criminal do Estado de São Paulo* (São Paulo, Empresa Editora Universal, 1943). In 1940, the city of São Paulo had 1,400,000 inhabitants.

[47] Ibid. In 1940 the state of São Paulo had 7,200,000 inhabitants.

in statistical terms by detention for drunkenness, disorder and idleness. Political prisoners, however, were not included in these data.

The worst situation was in Rio de Janeiro. The main centres where detainees and prisoners were kept were the House of Correction, the House of Detention and the Dois Rios Correctional Colony. All three prisons were closely linked to the Federal District Police and were in a terrible condition. For example, in April 1933, the director of the House of Detention communicated to the Ministry of Justice that the prison was overcrowded, a common complaint. Where there was room for 450 people, 917 prisoners were housed. Of these, 560 were on trial, 162 were there from the House of Correction, 95 detained by order of the chief of police (for the sake of order and public safety) and 40 were imprisoned because they were openly Communists.[48]

According to the Penitentiary Council itself, the living conditions were terrible and overcrowded,[49] and if the situation was already chaotic in 1933, it was to get worse over the years. The number of arrests only increased, as the police worked as the main political arm of repression for the regime, and the descriptions supplied of the conditions in prisons are sickening. The state of an establishment designed for just over 400 inmates[50] makes one despair for the dignity of the prisoners.[51] In particular, the House of Detention had seen no significant renovation in 40 years, but nevertheless went on receiving more and more inmates. In November 1935, the Penitentiary Council confirmed the presence of 911 prisoners, but in December of the same year the number reached 1,480, which was a direct consequence of the arrests that took place after the attempted Communist coup in November 1935. The presence of 50 to 60 prisoners per cell was also recorded there. To be able to sleep, the prisoners had to take turns.[52] In response, the political prisoners participated in a series of riots in May 1937 when the number of detainees in the House of Detention rose to 1,200.

Prison overcrowding and appalling living conditions were common, and the norm was the loss of civilised conduct among prisoners. It is calculated that in the 15 years of the Vargas regime there were 10,000 political prisoners, although it is difficult to be precise because Müller, the chief of police, helped by close colleagues, had the documents from police headquarters burned when he left the post in 1942. These subhuman conditions were made even worse after 1930 when the police introduced torture techniques. Although torture had been officially abolished in Brazil in 1821 as a method of investigation and punishment, it continued to be used and, in most cases, for both common and political prisoners without distinction. There was also censorship and terror by threats. In this situation even jurists from the Penitentiary Council, agents of and nominated by the

[48] AHN (Arquivo Histórico Nacional) MJNI (Ministérios da Justiça e Negócios do Interior), box 15 protocol 1200.

[49] AHN-MJNI, box 79, report of 2 June 1935.

[50] AHN-MJNI, box 79, report of 23 February 1934. The number of prisoners was more than double that planned capacity.

[51] AHN-MJNI box 79.

[52] HP Pinto, *No subsolo do Estado Novo* (Rio de Janeiro, S ed, 1950) 39.

federal government, showed their disapproval of prison conditions and the neglect that led to a series of illnesses among prisoners.[53]

Conclusion

Vargas's power was supported and consolidated by two operational sides of his authoritarian corporatist state. One was the state's positivist 'normative' side that seemingly operated on and through the law. The corporatist state's other side, its 'prerogative' actions, functioned extra-legally outside and around formal laws. These two faces of Vargas's corporatism were the modus operandi of his regime. The 'normative' side gained legitimacy from its position within what sociologist Max Weber would call Brazil's 'legal order', in spite of the fact that Vargas's law-making, which was more political than rational-scientific, had a questionable authoritarian imprint. Vargas, as shown, routinely bypassed Brazil's national Congress, either by ignoring it or by *de jure* nullifying even some of his own laws.

Vargas's corporatist 'State of prerogatives', seemingly (but not really) in contrast to Brazil's allegedly 'normative State', can be seen first and foremost in Vargas's use, whether *de facto* or *de jure*, of presidential law-by-decree. The 'prerogative' side of Vargas's corporatism can be seen as well in his control over Brazil's Federal District police. They operated politically and with impunity among the interstitial spaces variously populated by alleged law violators and deviants whose actions, although not explicitly prohibited by written law, were treated as law-breaking just the same. A fundamental character of both the 'normative' and 'prerogative' sides of Vargas' corporatist state is that he directly controlled both.

Placing theorising about 'generic' fascism within the parameters of this chapter's case study, it has been illustrated that Getulio Vargas shaped a 'generically' fascist New State, his *Estado Novo*, through a core myth of 'national rebirth' (palingenesis) that envisioned his leading Brazil toward 'modernity'. By encouraging his form of 'ultranationalism', Vargas's 'polyarchic' corporatist state would guide socio-political change toward progress with order. Presenting himself ideologically as the nation's 'great leader', Vargas claimed to bring together 'common men' in creating a 'new nation', even as he simultaneously sought to prevent the 'masses' from undermining his state's power. Through a strategy of corporatist power, with its allegedly 'normative' legalist side and its active use of extra-legal 'prerogatives', Vargas mediated the glaring contradictions of his 'generic' fascism.

---

[53] AHN-MJNI, box 79, 220/933.

8

Facilitating Fascism?
The Japanese Peace Preservation Act and the Role of the Judiciary

HIROMI SASAMOTO-COLLINS

Historians and political scientists of modern Japan have often debated whether or not the dominant political orientation in Japan of the 1930s can be described as 'fascist'. For Japan during this period did not have charismatic leaders akin to Hitler or Mussolini, nor a political party which served as a major instrument for harnessing the population. If German or Italian fascism is described as prompted 'from below', Japanese fascism was 'organised from the top by the military establishment'.[1] There was 'no successful takeover of power from below and no formal change in the existing Meiji Constitutional order, no programs and *Gleichschaltung*'.[2] The wartime regime was 'a temporary adaptation' of the political structure responding to 'extraordinary circumstances',[3] but no more. What supported this regime were forces outside the formal politico-legal system, such as traditional modes of communal behaviour, 'culturally ingrained' militarism, and the personality cult of the Emperor. If European fascism preserved as well as perverted some of the features of democratic government, Japanese fascism sprang from the 'undemocratic' aspects of its own society.[4] The Japanese experience has so many distinct peculiarities that it renders 'fascism' ineffective as a comparative concept. It should be understood in its own political, historical and cultural context, according to some observers.[5] Robert Paxton for example

---

[1] Kato Shuichi, 'Taisho Democracy as the Pre-Stage for Japanese Militarism' in B Silberman and H Harootunian (eds), *Japan in Crisis: Essays on Taisho Democracy* (Princeton NJ, Princeton University Press, 1974) 225. Maruyama Masao however distinguishes between a period of 'Japanese fascism from below' (1931–36) and that of 'fascism from above' (1937–45). See my discussion of Maruyama below, text relating to n 20.

[2] Nakamura Kikuo, quoted by GM Wilson, 'A New Look at the Problem of "Japanese Fascism"' (1968) 10.4 *Comparative Studies in Society and History* 401–12, 405.

[3] B-A Shillony, *Politics and Culture in Wartime Japan* (Oxford, Clarendon Press, 1981) 175.

[4] For this view, see for instance R Griffin, *The Nature of Fascism* (London, Routledge, 1993) 153–56.

[5] See for instance P Duus and D Okimoto, 'Fascism and the History of Pre-war Japan: The Failure of a Concept' (1979) 39.1 *Journal of Asian Studies* 65–76, and GJ Kasza, 'Fascism from Above? Japan's *Kakushin* Right in Comparative Perspective' in SU Larsen (ed), *Fascism outside Europe: the European*

withholds the term from the Japanese case and prefers to speak of 'an expansion-ist military dictatorship'.[6]

In my view however the term has still a qualified efficacy, an issue to which I will return later, although this chapter will challenge the usual socio-cultural explanations of Japanese circumstances. My primary focus will be on the behaviour of judges, who might be regarded by such scholars as Itō Takashi, Gordon M Berger, and Gregory Kasza as falling within the ranks of the '*kakushin*' or 'statist reformists'.[7] However, the chapter will also challenge the claims of these critics that there was no apparent break in the structure of the state in the 1930s or even during the war. Prominent court rulings, as this chapter goes on to show, did severely damage the normative structures of the state, a phenomenon also to be found in Nazi Germany and Fascist Italy. By highlighting changes in Japan's national legal structure, my aim is to demonstrate that these changes were not just a reflection of the capricious mood of the time and the inevitable outcome of cultural forces, but were an essential element in the subversion of the country's constitutional arrangements.

Thus, studying the emergence of the Nazi dictatorship within the framework of the Weimar Constitution, the German jurist Ernst Fraenkel observed that there were only two ways for disaffected political groups to take power in a constitutional system: 'Either (a) to establish *praeter legem* a political power outside the legal order and to revise the constitution with the aim of establishing the authoritarian *Machtstaat*, or (b) to substitute *contra legem* a dictatorial state for the rational constitution of the *Rechtsstaat*.'[8] Nazi Germany took the second way, subverting established constitutional and legal arrangements for doubtful (and eventually disastrous) political ends. Paxton notes that both Hitler and Mussolini, brought into the normal politico-legal system by those who were already installed there, soon began to destroy, from within, the established structures of government through various measures, including decisions by the courts.[9] We can observe a similar process within the Japanese State in the 1930s and during the war, whereby incremental legal measures, aided by a complaisant judiciary, furthered the forces of hegemony and repressive rule. In their common deployment of the law, what Gregory Kasza describes as 'functional equivalences'[10] most cer-

---

Impulse against Domestic Conditions in the Diffusion of Global Fascism (Boulder CO, Social Science Monographs, 2001) 183–232. A study of influential *kakushin* (reformist) rightist elites prompted Kasza to conclude that the term fascism does not fully apply to Japan, because their activities did not lead to mass action, did not involve the use of violence, and adhered to traditional values such as the importance of the imperial family, which were all antithetical to the Nazi or Fascist parties.

[6] RO Paxton, *The Anatomy of Fascism* (London, Penguin Books, 2004) 200.

[7] See Itō Takashi, 'Showa Seijishi Kenkyū e no Ichi Shikaku' (1976) 624 *Shisō* 215–28; GM Berger, 'The "New Order Movement"' in *Kodansha Encyclopedia of Japan*, vol V (Tokyo, Kodansha, 1983) 365–66; and Kasza, 'Fascism from Above?'. See also n 5 above.

[8] E Fraenkel, *The Dual State: A Contribution to the History of Dictatorship* (New York, Oxford University Press, 1941) 169.

[9] Paxton, *The Anatomy of Fascism*, 96–104, 119–22.

[10] GJ Kasza, 'Fascism from Below? A Comparative Perspective on the Japanese Right, 1931–1936' (1984) 19.4 *Journal of Contemporary History* 607–29, 627.

tainly exist between Japanese governmental techniques and those that were employed in Europe.

Such similarities stemmed from similarities in state structure and from the regulative power of state law. The operation of a modern nation-state requires concrete and regulative measures to control the population, with state law being one of the most effective and dependable means. This is because state authority in the nation-state is predicated on some form of contractual tie between the holders of that power and their subjects, which state law defines and mediates. If Japan was then not a nation-state as we now understand it, nevertheless the Japanese State operated through a nexus of state laws, which both expressed and transcended cultural factors. The Japanese State required normative means more efficacious than any mere alignment with sentiment and cultural norms, in order to control a population that was both highly literate and increasingly aware of its political rights, especially after the introduction of universal male suffrage in 1925. Cultural factors may intervene in the application of a particular law, but even there, the idea of using a law backed by state authority enables state agents to manage the citizenry with exceptional certitude and claims to efficiency.

In what follows I will focus on a single criminal law, the 1925 Peace Preservation Act (*Chian Ijihō*), to suggest a gradual reconstitution of the country's legal structure. The Act offers an interesting case study which can show that even a highly regulated society may resort to formal means, such as criminal law, for the control of its population. The chapter will trace major court rulings with respect to the Act. The brutality and abuse of power carried out in the name of the law has been well recognised by historians. However, previous work tends to focus on the misuse of the Act by the special police (*tokkō*), military police (*kenpei*), and state prosecutors, but not on the role of the judges who implemented it.[11] By focusing on a sequence of court rulings, I hope to demonstrate the role of the judiciary in transforming the country's constitutional system. Through these rulings judges effectively countermanded legal provisions intended to protect individual citizens from the state's all-inclusive power. The subversion of the Japanese constitutional system therefore took place in the name of the law, although contextual and socio-political factors undoubtedly affected this process.

Before examining major rulings concerning the Peace Preservation Act, it may be appropriate to explain how this approach relates to the core debate in the study of Japanese fascism. For this purpose, I will focus on the work of the Japanese political scientist Maruyama Masao (1914–96), whose earliest contributions shaped the terms of the debate and whose various self-corrections prompted the reassessment of his initial particularist emphasis. Maruyama's own work opened

---

[11] See for instance EK Tipton, *The Japanese Police State: The Tokkō in Interwar Japan* (Honolulu, University of Hawaii Press, 1990); RH Mitchell, *Janus-Faced Justice: Political Criminals in Imperial Japan* (Honolulu, University of Hawaii Press, 1992) especially 51–68; and HP Bix, 'Rethinking "Emperor-System Fascism": Ruptures and Continuities in Modern Japan' (1982) 14.2 *Bulletin of Concerned Asian Scholars* 2–19. Mitchell's book mentions various court cases, but his main emphasis is police brutality. The role of Japanese prosecutors is closely examined by Ogino Fujio, *Shisō Kenji* ['Prosecutors specialising in Political Thought'] (Tokyo, Iwanami Shoten, 2000).

the way for the investigation of law and fascism in a broader historical and comparative perspective. Throughout, however, he highlighted the issue of personal judgement and he begins by examining the grounds of obedience to norms of behaviour. Why did the military leaders and their bureaucrat supporters behave as they did? Maruyama concluded that what determined their behaviour was not a sense of legality but a sense of personal obligation to their immediate superiors and eventually to the Emperor. Maruyama says:

> What determined the behaviour of the bureaucrats and of the military was not primarily a sense of legality, but the consciousness of some force that was higher than they were, in other words, that was nearer the ultimate entity . . . The law was not regarded as some general body of regulations that collectively circumscribed the ruler and the ruled, but simply as a concrete weapon of control operating in the hierarchy of authority of which the Emperor was the head.[12]

Here Maruyama introduces the issue of what legal scholars describe as normativity, the elements directing our behaviour. Maruyama himself never produced a comprehensive study of Japanese fascism and law, and his own analysis of norms of behaviour inevitably admits cultural or sociological forces, which may make it difficult to analyse the issue of personal judgement more precisely. Nevertheless, he suggested the possibility of discussing the issue more formally by pointing to this issue of normativity.

Neil MacCormick has argued that the issue of normativity arises only when we recognise regulatory norms as artificial and malleable rules, as opposed to more deep-rooted patterns of behaviour. Only then can normativity become a valid issue for critical investigation.[13] MacCormick's endeavour has been to keep the issue of personal judgement alive within the highly normative conditions imposed by law. My own objective is not so much to lay the blame on particular individuals but to understand the ways in which individuals contribute to the making and operation of oppressive hegemonic power by deciding how to behave. In my view, despite Maruyama's initiative, the issue of normativity has not yet been fully examined in the analysis of Japanese fascism, partly because empirical or cultural analysis dominates the field, and partly because we have failed to frame the appropriate moral or philosophical questions. I take a normative approach and focus on key court rulings because they epitomise the junction between personal judgement and institutional and cultural forces. Focusing on these rulings, my objective is to highlight a neglected topic in the study of Japanese fascism, and to address the importance of individual judgement and responsibility within the

---

[12] Maruyama, 'Chō-kokkashugi no Ronri to Shinri' in *Maruyama Masao shū* ['Collected Works of Maruyama Masao'], vol III (Tokyo, Iwanami Shoten, 1995) 28. The original was published in *Sekai*, May 1946. Its English translation by I Morris, 'Theory and Psychology of Ultra-Nationalism', is included in Maruyama, *Thought and Behaviour in Modern Japanese Politics* (London, Oxford University Press, 1963) 1–24. The above passage is taken from this collection, 12–13.

[13] '[T]o think normatively is to think judgementally. This is a general and significant truth about all forms of normative order', N MacCormick, *Questioning Sovereignty: Law, State, and Practical Reason* (Oxford, Oxford University Press, 1999) 7.

workings of a key institution. Maruyama's work demonstrates how these issues are intertwined with each other.

Maruyama published the first of his influential articles, 'Chō-kokkashugi no Ronri to Shinri' ['Theory and Psychology of Ultra-Nationalism'] in 1946.[14] In this essay Maruyama grappled with what he saw as the 'lawlessness' of the Japanese Empire. Why was the state allowed to enter into people's private lives so aggressively and so easily? Why were there no clear boundaries between private and public life? Why did the country's leaders so brazenly belittle international law and agreements? The essay tackles the question of normativity head-on.

Maruyama focused on attitudes prevalent within the military and the bureaucracy whom he saw as the main agents of the Japanese Empire, but extended his analysis to the larger society. Among those agents he found a sense of personal loyalty to their immediate superiors, but not to a body of universal principles and regulations that bound them collectively and individually.[15] The Japanese State operated within this hierarchical chain of interpersonal ties. At the top of this chain was the Emperor, but he was neither an absolute monarch nor a modern political leader who sprang from a parliamentary system. The authority of the Japanese Emperor was endorsed by medieval natural law clothed in the country's foundation myths and the title of constitutional monarch. This is because Japan had not experienced its own version of the European Reformation, in which the traditional 'natural' order had been challenged by the new relationship between man and authority. In Europe the abstract notion of the individual began to affect the forms and objectives of government and people's perceptions of these, and eventually led to the emergence of the modern nation-state. Japan had not experienced such a revolution, and perceptions of legitimate authority remained largely hierarchical, communal, and collectivist, but not individualistic.[16] This deep-rooted traditional outlook was reflected in the micro-level operations of the state, including the workings of the law. In this system no one was expected to possess free will, and hence no one was liable to take responsibility for his own action. In this essay Maruyama did not use the term *fuashizumu* (a Japanese transliteration of fascism), although the term itself had become common among those critical of the Japanese Empire in the 1930s. For at this time, for Maruyama and for many like him, the problems of Japanese government and society in the 1930s and during the war were largely exclusive.

Maruyama continued to link the dictatorial Japanese State with the peculiarities of Japanese traditions as shaped by its history and the legacies of its own feudalism. Yet in a second important article, significantly entitled 'Nihon Fuashizumu no Shisō to Undō' ['The Ideology and Dynamics of Japanese Fascism'],[17]

---

[14] *Sekai* (Tokyo, May 1946).

[15] Maruyama, 'Theory and Psychology of Ultra-Nationalism' 13.

[16] Ibid 3. Maruyama develops this comparison in his *Nihon no Shisō* ['Japanese Intellectual Traditions'] (Tokyo, Iwanami Shoten, 1961).

[17] Maruyama, 'Nihon Fuashizumu no Shisō to Undō', in *Maruyama Masao shū*, vol III, 259–322. Its English translation by A Fraser, 'The Ideology and Dynamics of Japanese Fascism', is in *Thought and Behaviour in Modern Japanese Politics* 25–83.

published in 1948, Maruyama singled out the following as the major characteristics of an indigenous Japanese fascism: the tendency to depict the country as a patriarchal family in which the Emperor is the head; a nostalgic yearning for rural life and an emphasis on the importance of agriculture; and pan-Asianism.[18]

Here, the Japanese notion of the family-state differed from the Nazi idea of the *Volksgemeinschaft*. While the German *Volksgemeinschaft* preserved the vision of voluntary cooperation among individuals, the Japanese family-state connoted 'an organic and indivisible' whole. If Hitler was a leader of autonomous individuals, the Japanese Emperor was a patriarchal Confucian father-figure who commanded absolute loyalty.

It is true, Maruyama acknowledges, that many grass-roots groups with noticeably fascist tendencies began to appear in Japan in the first half of the 1930s, as in Germany and Italy. They demanded a radical overhaul of the country's economic system, including a call for state control of the banks, and state protection of workers' and tenant farmers' rights. The need to rescue rural communities from industrialisation and impoverishment was a common demand among these groups. However, after a mutiny by young military officers on 26 February 1936 (the largest ever to occur in modern Japan) these grass-roots groups were subsumed into a new unity movement led by the political elite emerging from within the establishment. In 1940 the movement was taken up by the Prime Minister Konoe Fumimaro and given the name *Shin Taisei Undō* (New Order Movement).[19] Nevertheless from the time of the aborted Mutiny of 1936, Japanese fascism diverged from its European counterparts; it was no longer a movement from below, but from above.[20]

Pan-Asianism, Maruyama finds, was another strand deriving from this movement. That view of Japan as a victim of Western imperialism, and of the country's right to self-defence and its mission to free other Asian countries, was a view which was later formulated as the Greater East Asian Co-Prosperity Principle by the government.[21]

Observing these phenomena, Maruyama nevertheless describes Japanese fascism as a socio-political phenomenon based on weak individualism prevailing in both the establishment and the larger society. It was not a conscious political movement from below, as in Germany and Italy.[22] It was never a mass movement prompted by the lower-middle class and workers, and led by leaders with modern political consciousness who claimed to be their willed representatives. Maruyama's

---

[18] Maruyama, 'The Ideology and Dynamics of Japanese Fascism' 36–37, 51.

[19] See Berger, 'The "New Order Movement"' and M Fletcher, 'Intellectuals and Fascism in Early Showa Japan' (1979) 39.1 *Journal of Asian Studies* 39–63 at 56–60.

[20] Maruyama, 'The Ideology and Dynamics of Japanese Fascism' 33.

[21] Maruyama, 'The Ideology and Dynamics of Japanese Fascism' 56. Japanese Pan-Asianism has received wide scholarly attention. For general perspectives and recent work see S Saaler and JV Koschmann (eds), *Pan-Asianism in Modern Japanese History* (London, Routledge, 2007).

[22] 'In Germany and Italy, as everywhere else, fascism was a movement of the lower-middle class', Maruyama, 'The Ideology and Dynamics of Japanese Fascism' 59.

analysis became the cornerstone of subsequent culture-based analysis of Japanese fascism, adopted by Roger Griffin and many others.

At the same time, Maruyama was becoming more alert to the historical backgrounds of these phenomena. The strong agrarian emphasis, for instance, was clearly attributable to Japan's relentless industrialisation after the Meiji Restoration which took place at the expense of agriculture and rural welfare.[23] Such an element had more to do with the country's immediate political and economic conditions than with static traditions and established forms of behaviour.

This latter perspective led Maruyama to realise some basic similarities between Japan, Germany, and Italy, and he summarises them as follows:

> the rejection of the world view of individualistic liberalism, opposition to parliamentary politics ... insistence on foreign expansion, a tendency to glorify military build-up and war, a strong emphasis on racial myths and the national essence, a rejection of class warfare based on totalitarianism, and the struggle against Marxism.[24]

Anti-liberalism, anti-individualism, and anti-Marxism were common features. His paradigm here is now in line with those of leading scholars of European fascism such as Ernst Nolte, Stanley G Payne, and (later) Robert Paxton.[25]

Maruyama developed this universal definition of fascism in an article of 1952 entitled 'Fuashizumu no Sho-Mondai' ['Fascism – Some Problems: A Consideration of Its Political Dynamics'], written at the height of McCarthyism in the United States, and inspired by those critical of it.[26] After examining some features common to war-time Germany, Italy, Japan, and McCarthyist America, Maruyama now defines fascism as 'the twentieth century's most acute and most aggressive form of counter-revolution',[27] that is, an authoritarian response to new social forces that challenge the status quo. Here some features of fascism are shaped by the increasingly atomised and industrialised societies of the late nineteenth and twentieth centuries, with communists and socialists being seen as threatening new forces.

There were always reactionary responses to new assertive forces historically, as in the case of the Counter-Reformation in sixteenth-century Europe, and Metternich's conservatism in the early nineteenth century, according to Maruyama. Such movements are prompted by fear.[28] As such they do not have a

---

[23] Ibid 42. The impact of this lopsided development on the emergence of militaristic government has been examined by B Moore, Jr, *Social Origins of Dictatorship and Democracy* (Boston MA, Beacon Press, 1966) 228–313.

[24] Maruyama, 'The Ideology and Dynamics of Japanese Fascism', 35.

[25] See E Nolte (L Vennewitz, trans), *Three Faces of Fascism* (London, Weidenfeld & Nicolson, 1965) 429–30; SG Payne, *Fascism: Comparison and Definition* (Madison WI, University of Wisconsin Press, 1980) 6–8; and Paxton, *The Anatomy of Fascism* 32, 41.

[26] Maruyama, 'Fuashizumu no Sho-Mondai' in *Maruyama Masao shū*, vol V, 253–77. The original was published in *Shisō*, October 1952. The English translation by R Dore, 'Fascism–Some Problems: A Consideration of Its Political Dynamics' is in *Thought and Behaviour in Modern Japanese Politics* 157–76.

[27] Maruyama, 'Fascism – Some Problems' 159.

[28] Ibid 165: fear is the main theme of this essay and Maruyama discusses various kinds which he thinks 'open the way for fascism'. These fears include not only the ruling class's fear of revolution but

coherent ideology, but have a strong aversion to anything which appears to challenge group or communal ethos. There is a strong mistrust of man's ability to judge rationally. Individualism and liberalism are therefore their enemies. In any society at any time, some people always have such anti-individualistic attitudes. Yet there is a crucial difference between such personal taste and state-sponsored persecution of those who advocate new views about authority and social organisation. Japanese fascism, while tinged deeply with the country's traditions and culture, emerged in the twentieth century when state-sponsored violence and mass mobilisation became possible.[29] How such a reactionary movement is actually manifested in society may be determined by state structure, socio-economic arrangements, and cultural traditions, as well as by more contingent and personal factors. Nevertheless, there is a commonality in all these phenomena, which is to eliminate minority opinion, suppress civil liberties, and impose crippling conformity on individuals.[30]

This broad view reflects Maruyama's position as a Japanese humanist who remained loyal to the traditions of post-Reformation European political thought and the Enlightenment. For him, the essential element of a progressive political community is the individual capable of rational thought and mutual understanding of others, and he came to ground his analysis of Japanese fascism on this liberal assumption. Maruyama's later normative approach therefore stands in sharp contrast to views expressed by other leading scholars of Japanese fascism who try to explain the Japanese case as a self-contained development.[31] Maruyama went beyond describing the Japanese case as an inevitable consequence of cultural orientation, political calculation or utilitarianism, and arrived at a view of Japanese fascism as a deliberate form of oppression and a failure to live up to universal moral principles. Liberal individualism is central to his understanding of Japanese fascism, and he criticises Japanese fascism from this 'modernist' position.

It is true, Maruyama acknowledges, that inherited modes of behaviour, values and political arrangements shaped the course of the Japanese polity in the 1930s and the war period. As a socio-political phenomenon, Japanese fascism was an expression of the collective response to the political situation of the period. However, it also betrays a familiar anti-humanist reaction to a new political situation and consciousness, and was guided by a particular group of people who had a strong personal investment in such behaviour. In this sense, Japanese fascism

also fears of loss of security and livelihood, and the fear of 'foreign' elements in society, to which the larger population is equally susceptible. Here the influence on Maruyama of psycho-sociological analysis by Erich Fromm and others is apparent, but this and other essays show that he was also influenced by a wide range of authors who defended individual freedom and liberal pluralism, such as Harold Laski and the theologian John Macquarrie.

[29] Maruyama, 'Fascism – Some Problems' 166–67.
[30] Ibid 176.
[31] Here I am referring especially to the '*kakushin*' argument proposed by Itō Takashi, Kasza and others, and also to the 'total-war' theory of Yamanouchi Yasushi. Yamanouchi proposes to explain the mechanism of national mobilisation using Talcott Parsons's utilitarian social theory. See Yamanouchi, 'Total-war and System Integration: A Methodological Introduction' in Yamanouchi, JV Koschmann and Narita Ryūichi (eds), *Total War and 'Modernization'* (New York, Cornell University, 1998) 1–39.

was an Asian variant of a global trend in the early twentieth century. It was a movement to crush freedom of thought and expression by obliterating the boundaries between the prerogatives of the state and the rights of the individual, a distinction based on natural law. The manner in which each government unleashed its violence towards individuals was shaped by its own decision-making institutions, such as parliament, the level of its industrialisation, and the relative development of mass society. Yet anti-humanist strands link the variants.

This chapter shares Maruyama's modernist position, recognising the anti-humanist stance as the core of these variants, and uses the term fascism to mean an ideology or policy that claims, in part, that localised group interests outweigh individual rights, and that the latter can be sacrificed to the former. This conclusion accords with an emphasis of many others, including Paxton.[32] 'Fascism' therefore, considered as it was by Maruyama as implying an abuse of the commonality, has connotations of general utility and is most certainly applicable to the Japanese case.[33]

However, other than by hinting at the use of coercive forces, such as outright violence, intimidation, and family and peer pressures, Maruyama's work does not explore the processes by which state authority comes to violate the private space of the individual. By so doing, he obscures the formal and social dynamics of the dictatorial Japanese State. Hence, following in Fraenkel's footsteps, I now propose to examine actual court rulings to show that the disappearance of legal norms meant to protect individuals from the state's coercive power was the work not just of contextual and extra-legal forces but of the judiciary itself. In the formation of Japanese fascism, and in its operations, criminal law played a central part.

The Peace Preservation Act and the Judiciary

The Peace Preservation Act was enacted in 1925 as a special criminal law to deal with growing labour and social protest movements and the perceived threat of the spread of communism after the Russian Revolution. Japan already had a substantive general criminal law, and also strict press and assembly regulations, to control the dissemination of radical ideas. However, conservative forces, including some members of the non-elected House of Peers, as well as bureaucrats at the Home

---

[32] Paxton notes 'the right of the chosen people to dominate others without restraint from any kind of human or divine law, right being decided by the sole criterion of the group's prowess within a Darwinian struggle', *The Anatomy of Fascism* 220.

[33] Miles Fletcher, unusually for a scholar in the English-speaking academy, also supports the use of the term fascist in discussions of Japan. He says: 'First, fascism was a meaningful term to Japanese during the pre-war era; the nature and implication of fascism in Europe, as well as the possible rise of fascism in Japan, were discussed and debated often in the Japanese media. Second, since historians still use the concept of fascism to analyse European political trends during the 1930s, it provides a context for comparative studies of events during that period': Fletcher, 'Intellectuals and Fascism in Early Showa Japan' 41.

Affairs and Justice Ministries, were so alarmed by the frequency of organised protest movements by workers, tenant farmers, and other social and economic groups that they felt the country needed a new law that could more directly suppress such activity.[34]

The original Peace Preservation Act had just seven articles. Article 1 made it illegal to organise a group for the purpose of changing the national polity (*kokutai*) or denying the private property system. Anyone who knowingly participated in such a group would be punished with imprisonment. Article 2 made it illegal to consult with others to achieve such objectives, and to instigate (*sendō*) others to do so was banned by article 3. Article 4 punished those who provoked public disturbance to achieve the objectives mentioned in article 1 and harm others and damage property. Article 5 criminalised the exchange of money or goods to achieve these objectives. In keeping with Confucian tradition, article 6 pardoned those who confessed to the authorities after committing one of the aforementioned crimes, while article 7 proclaimed that the law should be applied to anyone who committed such crimes even 'outside the jurisdiction of this law'. This in effect expanded the applicability of the law to independence activities in Korea and Taiwan,[35] to Japanese left-wing activists abroad,[36] to active soldiers,[37] to judges,[38] and to members of Parliament.[39]

The real novelty of the law was that people could be charged even if there was no actual disturbance, as long as it was confirmed that they had the purpose of changing the national polity or denying private property. This was a major departure from the provisions of the Japanese Criminal Code which required evidence of actual disturbance. The law was so radical that even the government felt it necessary to distribute pamphlets explaining its own interpretation of the law among law enforcement officers, including judges and prosecutors.[40] To punish someone without concrete evidence was thought to be a progressive measure by some bureaucrats, which had already been introduced by other countries, including various states of the United States. In particular, the law's emphasis on private property derived from the provisions of these US laws and from the anti-anarchist

---

[34] Japanese historians have identified large quantities of governmental documents concerning the Peace Preservation Act, including transcriptions and minutes of meetings of bureaucrats and public prosecutors discussing its application: see especially Okudaira Yasuhiro (ed), *Chian Ijihō* ['The Peace Preservation Act'] (Tokyo, Misuzu Shobō, 1973). The four volumes of Ogino Fujio (ed), *Chian Ijihō Kankei Shiryōshū* ['Primary Sources concerning the Peace Preservation Act'] (Tokyo, Shinnippon Shuppan, 1996) expanded those sources. Many primary sources, such as pre-war court rulings, are now available online via the website of the National Diet Library of Japan, Tokyo (www.ndl.go.jp). For a detailed analysis of the political background of the Act, see RH Mitchell, 'Japan's Peace Preservation Law of 1925: Its Origins and Significance' (1973) 28.3 *Monumenta Nipponica* 317–45 and Tipton, *The Japanese Police State* 22, 62–65, 110–14. See also n 44 below.

[35] *Yomiuri Shinbun* (Tokyo, 19 October 1936). See also Mizuno Naoki, 'Chian Ijihō to Chosen Oboegaki' (1979) 188 *Chosen Kenkyū* 45–53.

[36] *Yomiuri Shinbun* (Tokyo, 21 June 1933).

[37] *Yomiuri Shinbun* (Tokyo, 15 April 1933).

[38] *Tokyo Asahi Shinbun* (Tokyo, 18 January 1933).

[39] See Mitchell, *Janus-Faced Justice*, 97.

[40] *Tokyo Asahi Shinbun* (Tokyo, 8 May 1925).

bill submitted to the US Congress by the Senate Committee on the Judiciary in October 1919.[41] Despite these similarities, though, the Japanese law did not include any provision intended to protect the rights of the suspect, such as the right to seek judicial review of the law itself and the right not to testify against oneself. The legislation of some US states, such as that of Kentucky enacted in March 1920, included some protective provisions, although their provisions too were severely curtailed.[42] Hence, the Peace Preservation Act expressed what the ruling elite saw as the essential national interests of the period, and combined the anti-Bolshevik legislation of many industrial, capitalist countries, the preservation of confession as a basis to determine punishment, and the colonial power's need to extend its criminalising power beyond the national boundaries.

The initial bill submitted to the House of Representatives in 1922 banned the dissemination of anarchism and communism, and punished anyone who organised a mass rally or formed a group 'aimed at violating State law'. Opposition to the bill was strong both in and outside Parliament, and the House of Representatives voted it down. However, when the Peace Preservation Bill was re-submitted in 1925, it came with a universal male suffrage bill. The progressive forces of Parliament who had once opposed the bill now accepted it because it was thought to be a compromise worth making in order to win the support of the conservatives for the passage of universal male suffrage. Ironically, the Peace Preservation Act began life as part of a package of liberal measures.[43]

The law however soon became a means to alter the normative legal structure. This was possible through a combination of dogmatic interpretation (thanks to the ambiguity of its wording) and incremental revision. The death penalty was added in 1928, and in 1941 the police power of preventive detention. An estimated 70,000 people were arrested under the Act in Japan alone, and 23,000 in Korea, then Japan's colony, before the Act was repealed in 1945.[44] The Peace Preservation Act clearly worked to contain dissent within the country and in its colonies. Yet the effective use of the Act was only possible with judges' active participation. A series of rulings by the Supreme Court reveals the break-down of the natural-law principle of legality in the courts' own hands.

There were three ways in which the courts enacted and made concrete the law's repressive potential: giving words a strict, positivist meaning, using 'reason by

---

[41] The US bill was one of a number of foreign laws used by Japanese bureaucrats at the Ministry of Home Affairs in drafting the Peace Preservation Act and its predecessors. Its Japanese translation is found in Ogino (ed), *Chian Ijihō Kanren Shiryōshū*, vol I, 61–64, especially 64. Translations of the remaining laws are also found in the volume.

[42] Ibid 56–61.

[43] For the simultaneous passage of universal male suffrage and the Peace Preservation Act, see H Sasamoto-Collins, *Power and Dissent in Imperial Japan: Three Forms of Political Engagement* (Copenhagen, NIAS Press, 2013) 38–39, 237.

[44] Nagahara Kenji (ed) *Iwanami Nihonshi Jiten* (Tokyo, Iwanami Shoten, 1999) 748. The original Act of 1925 and its revisions of 1928 and 1941 are included in Wagatsuma Sakae (ed), *Kyū Hōrei Shū* ['A Collection of Defunct Japanese Laws'] (Tokyo, Yūhikaku, 1968) 451–54. An English translation of the original Act is included in DJ Lu (ed), *Japan: A Documentary History* (New York, ME Sharp, 1997) 397–98, a modified version of which is reproduced at the end of this chapter.

analogy' rather than deferring to concrete evidence, and interpreting law as a body of internal rules rather than as an instrument to protect the individual's right to basic autonomy. These interpretations will feature in what follows, and they were reinforced as precedents over time.

Here the highly emotive term *kokutai,* or 'national polity', proved most important. Neither the earlier bill which was rejected by Parliament in 1922 nor the various earlier drafts prepared by the Home Affairs Ministry and the Justice Ministry included the term. *Kokutai* was deployed during a brief period of intense negotiations involving government leaders, bureaucrats, and opposition members of Parliament about the law's objectives just before its enactment.[45]

Nevertheless the term *kokutai* had been used already in various governmental texts intended to extol public morality, such as the Imperial Rescript on Education of 1890, in order to suggest the supposed unity and uniqueness of Japanese statehood. The term was extremely popular among bureaucrats, politicians, military men, and civilian ideologues when justifying their arguments without the need for further elaboration.[46] Yet its meaning was never clear and it was never in vernacular use. Neither the Criminal Code nor the Code of Criminal Procedure, even after their revision in 1907, contained the term.

The legal standing of *kokutai* was confirmed by the Supreme Court on 31 May 1929.[47] The Court ruled on an appeal brought by five members of the regional branch of the Japanese Farmers Union in Hokkaido, northern Japan. They were arrested the previous year for participating in the illegal Japanese Communist Party, and helping to expand its support base, through distributing the party's newspaper *Akahata* ['Red Flag'] and holding meetings to discuss strategy. The District Court found them guilty, which was confirmed by the Regional Appeals Court. The defendants appealed.

The defendants asserted that national polity was not a legal term, but a term of general sociology. For them it referred to the fact that the Japanese State was a composite reality shaped by its own 'traditional customs, habits and mores'. Such cultural and social traits, they said, have their own organic momentum. It is impossible to change them forcibly. Therefore there is no such crime as changing the national polity, which is ineffable. For the defendants, the courts had failed to establish that there had been any significant damage to person or public.

Equally the defendants asserted that such a phrase as 'to deny the private property system' cannot constitute a crime, because this term too is imprecise and logically flawed. There is no such single descriptive social system as the private property system. Some forms of private ownership have long existed in human history, and even in communist countries such as the Soviet Union, private prop-

---

[45] The earlier bills contain more familiar terms already used in the Criminal Code of 1880, the revised Code of 1907 and the Press Law of 1909, such as *chōken no binran* (destroying or changing the national law) and *seitai no henkaku* (subverting the political structure).

[46] See for instance Kasza, 'Fascism from Above?' 214.

[47] *Japan v Yamana* et al, Great Court of Judicature (Supreme Court), 4th Criminal Department, 31 May 1929, 8 Dai Shin In Keiji Hanrei Shū ['A Collection of Criminal Cases of the Great Court of Judicature'] (hereafter cited as Dai-Han Keishū) 318–34.

erty has been recognised to a degree. The defendants insisted that the courts had failed to show exactly which aspect of the private property system it was possible to destroy in twentieth-century Japan.

The Supreme Court was not at all inclined to entertain such questions, nor willing to discuss the validity of the law at the same conceptual level. Instead, it said that the legal status of *kokutai* should be upheld so as to confirm the Emperor's sovereign status. It also said that no system, including the private property system, existed outside state law, and therefore it was possible to say that the private property system, which did exist, was under the law's protection.[48]

From these arguments the Court decreed that communism was against the law because it rejected the Emperor's sovereign status inherited from his ancestors and confirmed by the country's Constitution. The Communist idea of the common ownership of production was also against the law because it tried to remove the state protection of private ownership. The defendants' confirmed tie with the Communist Party was enough to incriminate them under the Peace Preservation Act.

Hence the Court's ruling gave these two ambiguous terms, *kokutai* and the private property system, a definitive meaning, clear but very narrow. The national polity became synonymous with the fact of the Emperor's sovereign status, and the private property system was assured of state protection. Such judgments however only hindered the careful calibration of law and available evidence, and some jurists objected to their use in legal debate.[49] The ruling, moreover, suggests the triumph of an unsecured form of legal positivism, in which legal and non-legal terms were juxtaposed with each other without strict demarcation and where key terms, previously imprecise and contentious, were given new standing. Of paramount importance, within the freshly politicised judicial vocabulary, was *kokutai*.[50]

According to Griffin, *kokutai* facilitated mass mobilisation, because it was 'steeped in a mystical sense of the indivisible unity between the emperor and his subjects . . . reinforced by such deeply rooted and pervasive structures of Japanese cultural life as Confucianism, Buddhism, the samurai ethos of *bushido*, emperor worship, "familism", militarism and, above all, Shintoism'.[51] Rikki Kersten also assumes that the term epitomises the Japanese psyche, and states that '[t]he core of notions embedded in the sphere of *kokutai* were: the divine origins of the imperial family; the essential racial and spiritual homogeneity of the Japanese; the notion of the emperor as the father of the nation; and a continuous ("unbroken") line of emperors from ancient times'.[52]

---

[48] *Japan v Yamana* et al, 8 Dai-Han Keishū 330–34.

[49] See for instance Minobe Tatsukichi, *Nihon Kenpō no Kihonshugi* ['Fundamental Principles of the Japanese Constitution'] (Tokyo, Nihon Hyōronsha, 1934) 9–17.

[50] Richard Mitchell however says that the inclusion of *kokutai* in the Act, which was a parliamentary decision, forced judges to enter 'a hazy area', and made their decisions unduly vulnerable to criticisms from outside the courts. See Mitchell, 'Japan's Peace Preservation Law' 345.

[51] Griffin, *The Nature of Fascism* 153.

[52] R Kersten, 'Japan' in RJB Bosworth (ed), *The Oxford Handbook of Fascism* (Oxford, Oxford University Press, 2009) 531.

Such explanations may help us to understand the larger cultural and social backgrounds of Japan's metamorphosis into a totalitarian state. However, to make the term *kokutai* central to overarching cultural analysis ignores the fact that at the time of its most important deployment its meanings were far from settled. They were contested, by defendants in the courts, as well as by some Japanese scholars and judges, even despite the government's announcement of its own interpretation in 1935, an interpretation that Griffin and Kersten nevertheless use for their analysis. Even then, some judges remained reluctant to use *kokutai* in their rulings.[53] The 31 May 1929 ruling however became a key precedent to be followed by many.[54] *Kokutai* was given formalised expression by the courts, in ways that were both arbitrary and normative, and that is why the term became so effective in eliminating those critical of the emerging hegemonic state power. The oppressive potential of the term was institutionalised by the law, and activated by the judges. Counter-arguments were foreclosed by court-imposed readings of essential concepts.

Illiberal tendencies are also discernible in the removal of a jury from cases involving the Peace Preservation Act in 1929. With Parliament's backing, the government revised the law concerning the jury system so that defendants charged with violating the Act were no longer entitled to a trial by jury.[55] Defendants would now have to confront an increasingly intractable judiciary without having their actions assessed in a broader context. From now on such decisions would seriously impede any critical debate about the political role of the Emperor, or a political decision or activity carried out in his name, and the social and economic system of the country. Labour activists, religious organisations, and the forces of political dissent all fell foul of the law's remit in the 1930s.[56]

Still compliant, on 17 November 1930 the Supreme Court confirmed lower courts' rulings that actual membership of the Communist Party was no longer necessary to establish the relevant political criminality.[57] A shop assistant who had no formal connection with the Communist Party was arrested for distributing a proletarian newspaper. The Court said that as long as the defendant had sympathy with some ideas advocated by the party and he distributed the newspaper to help disseminate those ideas, his activity fell into the category banned by the Peace Preservation Act, even if there was no factual evidence that he was a member of the party or that he intended to change the national polity or destroy the private property system.

---

[53] See Mitchell, *Janus-Faced Justice* 150.

[54] Such rulings include: *Japan v Yamashiro*, Great Court of Judicature, 1st Criminal Department, 9 July 1932, 10 Dai-Han Keishū 325–37, and *Japan v Yasuda*, Great Court of Judicature, 2nd Criminal Department, 1 September 1943, 22 Dai-Han Keishū 241–47.

[55] *Tokyo Asahi Shinbun* (Tokyo, 6 April 1929). Japan retained a jury system between 1923 and 1943, although it was highly restricted in terms of eligibility and the power of the jury vis-à-vis the judges.

[56] For the use of the law in the prosecution of followers of the Ōmoto religion, a new Shinto-inspired sect, see Mitchell, *Janus-Faced Justice* 150.

[57] *Japan v Yoshida*, Great Court of Judicature, 5th Criminal Department, 17 November 1930, 9 Dai-Han Keishū 788–801.

The case was representative. At a time of increasing social unrest and political instability amid the widespread economic difficulties after the US Stock Market Crash of 1929, the authorities had become ever more zealous in invoking the Act, and the judiciary in augmenting it. Henceforth insufficient examination of actual objective evidence and insufficient protection of the rights of the individual seriously disadvantaged many. Thus on 21 May 1931 the Supreme Court confirmed that a labour union activist who was not a member of the Communist Party was guilty of violating the Act.[58] The man had printed 80 copies of a campaign pamphlet for a municipal election at his workplace and distributed them. The pamphlet contained phrases that indicated his sympathy with communism. The man claimed that the lower courts' rulings were unjust because he was not a member of the Communist Party and had no direct link with it. The Supreme Court rejected his appeal, confirming once more that 'any conduct which appears to be assisting an organisation banned under the law' should be punishable under the law.[59] The ruling was now able to draw upon precedent and further weakened the position of the individual within the legal system.

The potential area of activities which came under the jurisdiction of the Peace Preservation Act was now expanding. This occurred against the backdrop of the civilian government's increasing loss of control over the military. In September 1931 Japan's Kwantung Army had begun its unauthorised conquest of southern Manchuria. For Maruyama this is also the beginning of the period of 'Japanese fascism from below'.[60] Yet the judiciary too was also becoming increasingly reactionary. On 26 November 1931, in another case involving radical politics, the Supreme Court ruled that joining a subversive group and helping the group to achieve its objectives constituted a single crime.[61] Until this ruling, the two were thought to be separate.[62] The Court also asserted that it was valid to apply the new law to this sequence of crimes even if some crimes had taken place before the law was changed. Article 6 of the Criminal Code specifically stipulated that if punishment was altered by a change in the relevant law, the lighter punishment of the two (under the old and new law) should be applied. To override this provision, the Court referred to article 55 of the Criminal Code, which stated that if a series of activities facilitated the same kind of crime, they should be regarded as one crime, and the perpetrators punished accordingly. However, the defendants claimed joining the group and helping its activities should be discussed separately, as the Peace Preservation Act stipulated that joining such a group is a more serious crime than the other and the defendants had joined the group before the law

[58] *Japan v Ishimura*, Great Court of Judicature, 1 Criminal Department, 21 May 1931, 10 Dai-Han Keishū 239–45.

[59] *Japan v Ishimura*, 10 Dai-Han Keishū, 245.

[60] Maruyama, 'The Ideology and Dynamics of Japanese Fascism' 33.

[61] *Japan v Nishiyama*, Great Court of Judicature, 1st Criminal Department, 26 November 1931, 10 Dai-Han Keishū, 634–46.

[62] *Yomiuri Shinbun* (Tokyo, 29 November 1931). The case attracted wide attention as the first case in which the revised Peace Preservation Act was used. The newspaper reported the ruling as 'a new interpretation by the courts' (*shin-hanrei*).

was revised. Thus they insisted that article 54, not article 55, should be applied to their case.[63]

Articles 54 and 55 represent a deep ideological schism present in the Japanese Criminal Code. Article 54 states that if an act concerns more than one specific crime and touches on other specific crimes because of its means or consequences, the most serious crime should determine punishment. The principal subject of this provision is the individual, and the article can be paraphrased thus: if a person commits a crime which can be related to other crimes, he will be punished with the severest punishment of all punishments that can be meted out for these crimes variously. However, an equivalent paraphrasing is not possible for article 55, which says: if a series of acts concern the same specific crime, they shall be treated as one crime. This is because the primary emphasis of the provision is not on the individual. The aim of this provision is systematisation of crime-types and attendant punishments. Implicit in the Court's preference for article 55 is a significant shift in Japanese legal thinking. For the way in which crime and punishment are linked is less predicated on the individual than on their inner logic. The kind of individualism which is so prominent in article 54 has no bearing on article 55.

Article 54 was introduced into the Japanese Criminal Code in 1880 under the strong influence of Enlightenment precepts present in the French Criminal Code of 1810.[64] In contrast, article 55 was introduced into the Japanese Criminal Code in 1907 when it was revised under the influence of the so-called Modern (or 'Positivist') School of Criminal Law and Criminology, which embraced scientific notions of crime and the criminal as well as utilitarian notions of law as an instrument of social reform. The view that the law was an instrument of individual justice was now contested by the 'modern' view that the individual was a member of a sovereign state and a socially and biologically conditioned being, and so the law can treat him as such.[65]

This decline in concern with individual rights, even those of the criminal, is directly relevant to the many years of abuse suffered by Japanese dissidents in the 1930s. Article 55 was abolished after the war,[66] and the article may indicate some patterns of thought among previous Japanese jurists as to how they understood the principle of legality. Japanese legal culture during this period strongly points at the decline of the notions of natural law and individual rights which earlier

---

[63] _Japan v Nishiyama_, 10 Dai-Han Keishū, 639–41.

[64] The Japanese Criminal Code of 1880 is included in Wagatsuma (ed), _Kyū Hōrei Shū_ 431–45. In this code, the original terms of art 54 are found in the chapter dealing with the concurrence of offences (arts 100–03). When the code was revised in 1907, these articles were modified. Some revised wording of art 54 reflects later influence, but the article preserves the original principle. The revised Code of 1907 is found in _Hōrei Zensho_, a monthly-based compilation of laws and regulations enforced by the Japanese government since 1867.

[65] Representative of the modern school is Eiichi Makino (1878–1970). The influence on Makino of the Modern School of criminal law and criminology, which included Cesare Lombroso (1835–1909), Enrico Ferri (1856–1929), and Franz V Liszt (1851–1919), is apparent. See Makino, _Keihō no Sanjūnen_ ['30 years of the Criminal Code'] (Tokyo, Yūhikaku, 1938) 16–19, 45.

[66] Dandō Shigemitsu, _Keihō Kōyō Sōron_ ['A Commentary on the Japanese Criminal Code'], 3rd edn (Tokyo, Sōbunsha, 1990) 444.

Japanese jurists had attempted to implement in the country's legal system, as demonstrated in the case of article 54. Instead it saw the rise of more mechanical and authoritative, less humanistic notions of legality.

The idea that the primary focus of punishment was the individual now became increasingly remote. The case just discussed is symptomatic of the narrow, formalistic notions of legality applied at this time by the Japanese judiciary. The case also highlights the failure of the Japanese judiciary to meet a fundamental challenge of modern criminal law, that is, to find an adequate balance between the need to protect the public good, and the need to protect the uniqueness of the individual subject. By conflating a series of activities into a single crime motivated by the same intention, the Japanese Supreme Court effectively dissolved this tension. By paying only lip-service to the notion of the individuality of free will, the Court in fact deprived the defendants of opportunities to defend their intrinsic selfhood. Even more importantly, by interpreting 'purpose' excessively broadly, the courts could now criminalise even basic and commonplace activities. In this way the range of illegal activities could be expanded, arbitrarily, by the courts' own rulings, a phenomenon Ernst Fraenkel also observed in Nazi Germany.[67] Thus on 28 April 1932, the Supreme Court ruled that labour activism, which was unlikely to achieve anything concrete on its own, also fell into the category banned by the Peace Preservation Act, 'as long as it shares objectives stipulated by the Act with other groups'.[68]

This unlimited expansion of criminality under the law was combined with other forms of arbitrary justice. State prosecutors and judges would pardon those who voluntarily acknowledged their guilt and repented. Here the traditional Confucian-influenced emphasis on confession and rehabilitation, articulated in article 6 of the Act, became an instrument of social control, while also blurring the distinctions between law and morality, judicial punishment and educational rehabilitation.[69]

State pardons also explain the huge disparity between the number of arrests and the number of indictments. The average indictment rate between 1928 and 1943 is a little less than 20 per cent. In 1931, when about 10,400 people were arrested for violation of the Peace Preservation Act, only 307, or 3.0 per cent, were indicted (see Table 1).[70] Many of those who were arrested denounced their ties with the Communist Party during interrogation, which may have involved the use of torture for die-hard activists. Pardons, however, combined with indiscriminate evidence to subvert dialectic, weakened dissent and facilitated the ends of those in power.[71]

---

[67] Fraenkel, *The Dual State*, 18–19, 42–45, 50–55.

[68] *Japan v Abe* et al, Great Court of Judicature, 28 April 1932, 11 Dai-Han Keishū, 530–58.

[69] Mitchell, *Janus-faced Justice* 5, 103–04.

[70] Elise Tipton however relates the markedly low indictment ratio after a rise in the number of arrests in 1931 to a shift in the actual terms of jurisdiction of the Peace Preservation Act from criminal to administrative law. See Tipton, *The Japanese Police State* 28.

[71] In 1933 the government announced the defections from the Communist Party of two imprisoned leaders, Sano Manabu and Nabeyama Sadachika. Their conversions, *tenkō* in Japanese, prompted many to follow suit, and led to the collapse of the communist movement in pre-war Japan. See ibid 26.

Table 1. Arrests and Indictments under the Peace Preservation Act

Year	1928	1929	1930	1931	1932	1933	1934	1935
No of arrests:								
Left-wing	3,426	4,942	6,124	10,422	13,938	14,622	3,994	1,718
Independence	0	0	0	0	0	0	0	0
Religious	0	0	0	0	0	0	0	67
Total	3,426	4,942	6,124	10,422	13,938	14,622	3,994	1,785
No of indictments:								
Left-wing	525	339	461	307	646	1,285	496	113
Independence	0	0	0	0	0	0	0	0
Religious	0	0	0	0	0	0	0	0
Total	525	339	461	307	646	1,285	496	113

Year	1936	1937	1938	1939	1940	1941	1942	1943*
No of arrests:								
Left-wing	1,207	1,292	789	389	713	849	332	87
Independence	0	7	0	8	71	256	203	53
Religious	860	13	193	325	33	107	163	19
Total	2,067	1,312	982	722	817	1,212	698	159
No of indictments:								
Left-wing	97	210	237	163	128	205	217	18
Independence	0	0	3	0	12	29	62	15
Religious	61	0	0	225	89	2	60	19
Total	158	210	240	388	229	236	339	52

* As of 30 April 1943.
Source: Okudaira Yasuhiro (ed) *Chian Ijihō* ['The Peace Preservation Act'] (Tokyo, Misuzu Shobō, 1973)

Other judicial procedures employed at this time also seem to serve the ends of those in power. Thus, as a symbolic gesture, in 1934 the Supreme Court publicly announced that it had reduced a sentence for a defendant accused of violation of the Peace Preservation Act who claimed the sentence given by the lower courts was too heavy despite his admission of guilt.[72] Later, in November 1938, after the outbreak of full-blown war with China, the Supreme Court announced that the criminal record of another political defendant who became a soldier would be deleted from official records.[73] In what was now the period of 'fascism from above', the judiciary's compliance with government policy is clear. For if the judiciary appears to modify its own policies the ends those policies serve remain unchallenged.

The Peace Preservation Act was particularly effective, and painful, for students and academics committed to self-expression. The newly fluid notion of purpose

[72] *Yomiuri Shinbun* (Tokyo, 14 October 1934).
[73] *Yomiuri Shinbun* (Tokyo, 13 November 1938).

could allow state prosecutors to discuss one's past indiscriminately, tearing down one's personal and intellectual history, identity, conscience, and friendships. The realisation that the authorities did not recognise the boundaries between the inner world and external conduct was a matter of grave concern for those intellectuals who took such boundaries for granted. For example, Kuno Osamu, arrested in 1937 and indicted later for publishing a critical magazine, learnt to his cost how flimsy were the protections of the law when in prison.[74] Kamei Katsuichirō, who spent two and a half years in prison after being arrested in 1928 for violation of the Peace Preservation Act, speaks vividly of the 'anxiety and despair' of prison life.[75]

In fact many leftist intellectuals now experienced long periods of detention without clear charge or knowledge of the future. They felt their fate was entirely in the hands of prosecutors and judges, who now employed the flimsiest kind of legal argument. Incrimination was all too easy, and the law was increasingly an instrument of hegemony: definitions of illegality were now in the hands of the courts, and these were not at all inclined to promote the necessary discriminations.

This break-down of the legal structure intensified as the country entered into a state of war. In 1933, after Japan's invasion of Manchuria in 1931, 17 prominent lawyers acting on behalf of defendants who had been arrested in the large-scale crackdown on communists in 1928 and charged under the Peace Preservation Act were themselves arrested for violating the Act, and 13 of those lawyers were found guilty in May 1935.[76] In 1941 the Peace Preservation Act was expanded into 65 articles, radically increasing the grounds of arrest. The right to appeal was suspended. The number of defence lawyers in cases involving the Act was restricted to one. The investigative power of state prosecutors was increased, including the extension of a detention period without charge. Following in Germany's footsteps, the police power of preventive detention was also added. Always repressive, the original law had now expanded to become a tool of dictatorial government.[77]

Antecedents

Why then did the Japanese judges so willingly collude with the break-down of the legal structure? In particular, why did they reject so blatantly the competing principle of legality based on the notion of individual rights?

---

[74] Kuno is quoted by Aoki Eigorō, *Saibankan no Sensō Sekinin* ['War Responsibilities of the Judges'], 2nd edn (Tokyo, Nihon Hyōronsha, 1971) 28.

[75] Kamei, quoted by Yamaryō Kenji, 'Nihon Romanha' ['The Japanese Romantic School'] in Shisō no Kagaku Kenkyūkai (ed), *Tenkō* ['Political Apostasy'] vol I (Tokyo, Heibonsha, 1959, 2000) 270.

[76] *Yomiuri Shinbun* (Tokyo, 3 May 1935).

[77] Aoki Eigorō, *Saibankan no Sensō Sekinin* ['War Responsibilities of the Judges'] 18.

Part of the answer seems to lie within Japanese legal history. Such judges came from a tradition that sponsored neither their professional autonomy nor the notion of individual rights as a realistic principle, as we have seen. Thus until the Meiji legal reforms of the late nineteenth century, there had been no clear distinction between the civic administration and the judiciary in both criminal and civil cases in Japan. Investigation and trial were part of a single administrative action taken by the same group of people. When Japan introduced the Continental European inquisitorial system, it reinforced the old practice. In the new European-style judicature, state prosecutors were given disproportionately large powers. They interrogated a suspect and decided whether or not to indict him. They had close contact with judges, as their offices were attached to each court. They would influence rulings if not guide them. Such a system would not promote the idea that law should be respected for its own intrinsic value, or to protect the rights of the individual. This close collaboration between justice and administration was therefore prone to abuse.[78]

Nevertheless, the global trends to which they were increasingly exposed and their own understanding of law and justice also moved the late nineteenth-century Japanese judiciary to accept the need for reconstruction. Meiji legal reforms brought in the notions of judicial independence and of inalienable rights, and transformed some of the conditions that had constrained Japanese judges. In 1871 the Justice Ministry was established, absorbing the *Keibu Shō* (Ministry of Punishment) and the *Danjō Dai*, which was responsible for internal security. A national judiciary was now conceived as something that transcended the traditional role of the judicature, which was to punish criminals and ensure public security. The edict entitled *Shihō Shokumu Teisei* (Standing Regulations concerning the Functions of the Judiciary) issued in 1872 introduced a national structure of courts and divisions of judges, prosecutors, and lawyers based on the French model. In 1875, the *Daishin'in* (the Great Court of Judicature, the present-day Supreme Court) was also established, marking the first clear separation between the executive and the judiciary in Japanese history. In the same year regulations on more specific trial procedures such as appeals and retrials were implemented. By the late 1870s an 'independent' national judiciary was clearly emerging.

The most crucial event in this respect was the introduction of the dialectics of natural law. The notions of inalienable rights and equitable justice were brought to Japanese jurisprudence by foreign advisers, such as Gustave Émile Boissonade de Fontarabie (1825–1910) and Japanese students who had studied law abroad.[79] Nishi Amane (1829–97) studied law in Holland from 1862 to 1865, and translated many European legal texts into Japanese. Nishi was one of the first Japanese who

---

[78] See Ienaga Saburō, *Shihōken Dokuritsu no Rekishiteki Kōsatsu* ['A Historical Study of Japanese Judicial Independence'], 2nd edn (Tokyo, Nihon Hyōronsha, 1967) 28–32 and Tipton, *The Japanese Police State* 52–61.

[79] For Boissonade's contribution to disseminating European natural law, see J-P Lehmann, 'Native Custom and Legal Codification: Boissonade's Introduction of Western Law to Japan' in G Daniels (ed) (1979) 4.1 *Proceedings of the British Association for Japanese Studies* 33–72, 41–44.

saw law in tandem with the natural-law notion of justice, emphasising the limits of positive law and admitting the notion of inalienable rights.[80] A fledgling contractual tie between governmental power and the citizenry was now entering Japanese legal discourse.

The Criminal Code of 1880 is redolent of the impact of the natural-law notion of justice influenced by the Enlightenment movement. The Code introduced the principle of legality which ensured that 'to be punishable, an act must be explicitly forbidden by a law which was in force at the time it was committed'.[81] The principle underlines the Enlightenment notions of the autonomous individual and individual liberty. Anyone, even a criminal, possesses autonomy and a unique inner life independent of external force. Therefore, if one is punished for a crime he has committed, a clear distinction should be made between the interiority of the mind of the criminal and outward signs of the crime itself. What the law can punish, however, is only the latter. Therefore, extreme care should be taken to assess evidence of a crime objectively. Such an emphasis remains in keeping with universal individualism. The law is for punishing criminals but also for protecting individuals from arbitrary persecution. This new principle of legality was also furthered by the establishment of the Justice Ministry and of the Supreme Court in the 1870s which helped to disseminate the notion of judicial independence. Legality now ensured that no one should be punished without a law enacted prior to the crime; judges must rule strictly according to written laws and reject political interference. The *Ōtsu* case in 1891 was widely hailed as an exercise of this principle by a Japanese judge.[82]

However, the erosion of this individualistic, natural-law notion of justice soon began. There were two forces ranged against it. One is the notion of law and justice based on the superiority of the state. According to this view, 'the aim of criminal law is to maintain the security and peace of the country, and any rules can be introduced in order to achieve this objective'.[83] Here a valid law is a command of the state, and the notion of crime's relation to free will and individual liberty is without validity in a well-structured society. The other objection depends on 'scientific' notions of crime and the criminal. In that light the criminal is considered to have committed a crime because of various personal factors, including psychological and sociological reasons. The aim of criminal law is to re-educate the criminal so that he is no longer a threat to society. The rise of these two schools reflects

---

[80] RH Minear, 'Nishi Amane and the Reception of Western Law in Japan' (1973) 28.2 *Monumenta Nipponica* 151–75.

[81] Art 2. For the background to its introduction, see H Sasamoto-Collins, 'Progress Impeded: Constraints on Legal Equality in Post-Restoration Japan' (2008) 20.3 *Japan Forum* 337–60.

[82] When he was visiting Japan in 1891, the Russian Crown Prince Nicholas Alexandrovitch was wounded by a policeman who was escorting him. Concerned with the possible negative impact on the bilateral relationship, the government put pressure on judges to apply the death penalty. The chief justice, Kojima Iken (1837–1908) rejected the government's interference and sentenced the accused to life imprisonment, as the Criminal Code demanded for attempted murder.

[83] Tomii Masaaki (1858–1935) in a lecture at the Kokka Gakkai in 1891, quoted by Saeki Chihiro and Kobayashi Yoshinobu, 'Keihōgaku-shi' ['A History of Japanese Criminal Law'] in Nobushige Ukai et al (eds), *Nihon Kindaihō Hattatsushi*, vol XI (Tokyo, Keisō Shobō, 1967) 229–30.

the completion of the structure of the state, the popularity of the new science, such as biology, physiology, and anthropology, and the emergence of mass society in Japan at the turn of the century. Such trends were not unique to Japan at that time, but their impact on Japanese criminal law was especially potent, because the natural-law tradition was still only recently established.[84]

The influence of these two trends was apparent when the Criminal Code was revised in 1907. The natural-law notion of justice – one is punished for what one has done as a free-willed, autonomous individual – was seriously weakened. The dialectical relationship between the natural law notion of justice and the principle of legality was further damaged. As a result, a more radical interpretation of law, more mechanical and authoritative, less humanistic, gained support. Socio-cultural factors were highly relevant but not paramount.

In 1925 the Peace Preservation Act was introduced in this climate, where individualistic notions of legality were steadily overtaken by extremely positivistic notions of legality, both new and old. The principle of legality no longer meant that law was there to protect the rights of the individual, and those rights were now subordinated to the workings of the law. However, some judges who had subscribed to the natural-law notion of individualism were deeply troubled by this trend and their conflicting roles. In 1907 when the Criminal Code of 1880 was revised, signalling a clear shift in Japanese perceptions of law and justice, one judge published a piece pointedly entitled 'The difficulties that judges face'. Here Judge Imai Kyōtarō complains that the new code has reduced the number of articles which clearly spell out the relationship between crime and punishment and therefore the principles of legality. Gone with them is the extreme care attached to these principles in order to protect individual freedom. Expanded instead is judges' discretionary power. But judges do not have 'proper standards' for using that power.[85] For this perceptive judge, the removal of clear provisions on legality was a form of judicial disablement.

Twenty years later, for other judges, the natural-law notion of individualism would prove increasingly expendable, an imperative they might easily discard. One judge was faced with the task of handing down rulings to nearly 200 defendants who had been arrested during a large-scale crackdown on communists in 1929, but in 17 separate cases. The judge combined these cases into one and handed down his rulings to them, all on the same day. Such a mass trial was unprecedented. Asked why he resorted to such a radical measure, the judge explained:

> The Japanese criminal procedure is based on individualism deriving from the liberalism of post-Revolution France. Its principle is that individuals should be tried separately and treated individually. But the Peace Preservation Act targets the Communist Party which is an organisation of individuals. The law is intended as a check on collective

---

[84] The American philosopher MR Cohen is quoted as saying in 1914: 'To defend a doctrine of natural rights today requires either insensibility of the world's progress or else considerable courage in the face of it' in Fraenkel, *Dual State* 111.

[85] Imai Kyōtarō, quoted by Saeki and Kobayashi, 'Keihōgaku-shi' 246.

activities, but [its objective] is incompatible with the present Code of Criminal Procedure. It [the disparity] has given me great trouble.[86]

Nevertheless, for this judge, the recognition of disparity did not preclude the implementation of the Act. For him, the legality that cherished natural-law justice was not an unquestionable value. Collective imperatives triumph despite inconsistencies in the law. The passage seems at one with the difficulties, but also the compliance, of the Japanese judge-bureaucrat of the period. For this judge abets the regime even as he complains of his own dilemma. In addition the outlook and wavering doubts about liberal individualism expressed here echo the sentiments of the '*kakushin*' elite whom Kasza identifies as the main contributors to the inception and operation of Japan's 'military-bureaucratic regime'.[87]

This attenuation of the principle of legality complements the co-option of the criminal law into the war-time structure. In July 1940 the Justice Ministry helped to form a panel of 30 leading pro-government legal scholars, judges and prosecutors to discuss criminal law. Clearly the move was in keeping with the New Order Movement led by the former Prime Minister Konoe Fumimaro to strengthen national unity by intensifying censorship, increasing state control of economic activities, and promoting the dissolution of political parties, all in an attempt to prepare the country for imminent war. Although the movement never achieved all of its aims, as Parliament just managed to survive, its programme anticipated the establishment of the war-time 'totalitarian' structure. The outline of a study of Japanese criminal law announced by the Ministry panel in July 1941 aligns itself with the same objectives, and signals the outright rejection of the principle of legality altogether. It says:

The substance [*jittai*] of Japanese law is the spontaneous evolution of the imperial national polity itself. Statutes are external forms which express this substance. Thus, as long as the substance of law is concerned, how it is expressed is not restricted to any provisions of actual statutes. The essential and noble role of judicial officers is to interpret the law as close to its substance as possible . . . even if it may involve 'reason by analogy' [*ruisui*] [rather than by referring to specific laws].[88]

This statement shows no hint of trying to preserve the legal order for its own intrinsic value, or for defending individual rights. These leading judges, jurists and prosecutors endorse an extremely teleological interpretation of the law, prioritising a malleable and highly convenient 'substance' rather than statute. Their seeming expression of judicial discretion is, however, inseparable from their reliance on state policy and vocational solidarity. By their training and institutional arrangements, these men were unlikely to promote judicial review. And the more they identified with state policy, the more they lost their ability to judge independently. The judiciary who speak to us here were no longer the servants of society

---

[86] *Tokyo Asahi Shinbun* (Tokyo, 28 October 1932).
[87] See Kasza, 'Fascism from Above?' 208–10.
[88] 'Nihon Keiji Hōri Yōkō' ['The Outline of A Study of Japanese Criminal Law'], in Aoki Eigorō, *Saibankan no Sensō Sekinin* 106.

but of state. The constitutional structures which the early Japanese jurists had tried to implement were no longer there. Robbed of those elements meant to defend the contractual tie between the state and the individual, the law had turned into a unilateral tool of coercion.

The Post-War Judiciary

The Peace Preservation Act was repealed in 1945 shortly after Japan's unconditional surrender. Some personnel of the special police (*tokkō*) accused of using torture against suspects were brought to justice after the war, although their number was very small. In contrast, the responsibilities of the judiciary went unexamined until quite recently.

In 2008 the Supreme Court dismissed a request for a retrial made by the former defendants and bereaved families of other defendants in the so-called Yokohama case. In 1942 the editors and journalists of the magazine *Kaizō* were arrested for violation of the Peace Preservation Act after they had published an article by a political scientist which the special police (*tokkō*) deemed to be disseminating communist ideas. Between 1942 and 1945, about 90 people were arrested in connection with the case. Four of them were tortured to death during detention. About 30 people were found guilty based on evidence which one lower-court judge in a separate retrial suit described as 'extremely flimsy'. However, the Supreme Court rejected the request, saying that the case legally ceased to exist when the defendants were released through pardon when the law was repealed. The lawsuit was filed in 1986, followed by three more similar suits connected to the case.[89]

In 2010, however, the Yokohama District Court granted five of the former defendants in one of the follow-up suits the legal right to seek state compensation, a right of those who are acquitted in criminal cases. Thus, although it stopped short of declaring them not guilty, the court did so in effect. The presiding Judge, Ōshima Takaaki, condemned the use of torture in the case, which along with the fabrication of evidence, meant that it involved 'a malicious violation of even the war-time Code of Criminal Procedure'. The judge also added that the publication of the article did not automatically lead to an attempt to re-establish the illegal Communist Party as the prosecution had claimed, for interpreting the article would depend on the reader.[90] Here the judge recognised the inviolability of private thought, and upheld the limitations of a criminal law which abused this principle. Partially restoring the natural-law aspirations of the Meiji legal reforms,

---

[89] *Asahi Shinbun* (Tokyo, 2 July 1986). The first of the four suits was filed with the Yokohama District Court on 3 July 1986 by six former defendants and the family members of another three who were already deceased, including the family of the deceased US trained economist Kawata Hisashi, his surviving wife Kawata Sadako, and journalists Kimura Tōru and Hatanaka Shigeo.

[90] *Asahi Shinbun* (Tokyo, 4 February 2010).

Ōshima ruled that the war-time rulings were unfair and the police had acted illegally. Encouraged by this ruling, other litigants in the Yokohama case are now filing similar lawsuits to seek state compensation, although most of the original defendants, including those who were granted state compensation in the 2010 ruling, have passed away.

Such a ruling was made possible because of post-war legal reforms which strengthened judicial independence, and the right to judicial review. Individual rights such as freedom of thought and conscience are now enshrined as inalienable in the new Constitution which came into force in 1947. Initially, however, the Japanese judiciary struggled to make human rights an absolute principle in its rulings. Yet in an epoch-making ruling in 1975, the Supreme Court adopted the principle that a retrial may be granted on the basis of fresh evidence if it points at 'reasonable doubt' about the ascertainment of facts in a previous trial. This was to ensure that the interests of the suspect should be protected rather than impeded in the absence of proof.[91] This newly affirmed independence of the judiciary and its willingness to uphold people's basic rights have allowed Japanese judges to recognise the illegality of the Peace Preservation Act, and their predecessors' role in its operation. The courts were now more willing to grant a retrial in the interest of justice.

Equally important was the determination of the former defendants and their families to keep alive the memories of the state violence under the Peace Preservation Act. In the 1980s the government of the hawkish Prime Minister Nakasone Yasuhiro attempted to increase the country's military strength and its security ties with the United States. One of the proposals to this end was to tighten anti-espionage measures in a new state secrecy law. Like many citizens across the country, the defendants saw the bill as echoing the terms of the Peace Preservation Act, seriously affecting freedom of thought and association. The first suit seeking a retrial, filed in 1986 as noted above, was a direct response to the proposed security bill.[92]

Serious issues remain, however. Many former defendants and victims of the Act have already passed away uncompensated, to say nothing of those who had suffered from the law in Korea and Taiwan, then Japan's colonies. These issues are entangled with the larger question of Japan's war responsibilities. However, legal questions are just as challenging as political adjustments. How, for example, can we criminalise the behaviour of the state in time of war? Who adjudicates between the prerogatives of state power and the individual's private life into which state power should not be able to enter? From our twenty-first-century perspective, the Peace Preservation Act was poorly conceived and deplorably implemented, yet it

---

[91] *Murakami and Murata v Japan* (the Shiratori case), Supreme Court, First Petty Bench, 20 May 1975, 29 Saikō Saibansho Keiji Hanreishū ['A Collection of Criminal Cases of the Supreme Court'] no 5, 177.

[92] Such a bill was passed only in December 2013 however, when Parliament (with the Liberal Democratic Party having a strong majority) passed the Special State Security Law (*Tokutei Himitsu Hogohō*) despite strong civic protests. Once again, the need for vigilance has returned to Japan with the passage of new laws of constraint and surveillance.

remains a touchstone at the forefront of negotiations between central power and the individual, and between law and justice. Through the mirror of this Act, we can observe calamitous violence in the name of law and speculate on the necessary boundary between the prerogatives of the state and the rights of the individual that would be worthy and suitable for our time.

Conclusion

This chapter has sought to explore the links between an indigenous Japanese fascism and a deeply flawed legal system. Fascism, especially considered as a violation of the private sphere, is deeply entrenched in Japan's wartime record. Japanese fascism is therefore both highly particularist *and* generic. It is not *sui generis*. Accordingly there still seems to be a strong case for using Maruyama's universal and historical notions of fascism and aligning the Japanese experience with global experience in the twentieth century. For if it is used as Maruyama defines, the term can provide us with a useful vantage point where we can observe historically and comparatively the vulnerability of the private sphere in the face of intrusive state power. And law as we have seen can undermine the private sphere all too effectively. For state law is intertwined with other state institutions, such as the police, the executive, and the judiciary. State laws however need human agents to activate and implement them. Paramount among such agents are the judges. It is they who bear the heaviest responsibility. For embedded as they are in the state structure, they are also part of the larger society and their judgments inevitably affect the values of the majority. All too often, however, in the years before and during the war, Japanese judges not only helped to implement a pernicious law but seriously extended its reach.

Even so pockets of personal judgement most certainly existed. As Richard Mitchell shows, some judges hesitated to apply the charge of violating *kokutai*, and others resisted the bullying of the government and public prosecutors.[93] Their principled attitudes contrast sharply with those of the majority of the judges, who were content to follow the 1930/31 precedents mechanically. Nevertheless, pre-war Japanese legal history shows, for the most part, that the Peace Preservation Act was applied excessively formalistically. As individuals are not only normatively but also emotionally tied to the state structure by a legal system, the law became a highly effective means to violate individual rights and well-being. Abetting rather than resisting the political forces of the time, many Japanese judges colluded with oppression. Their behaviour therefore has a significance beyond the history of Japanese fascism. For without a dedicated and unwavering commitment to basic rights, on the part of those who implement the law, criminal law and public law as a whole can become lethal instruments. Only careful

---

[93] Mitchell, *Janus-Faced Justice* 80, 150–51.

monitoring and intervention by individuals, either judges, lawyers, or ordinary citizens, can check the forces of hegemony and social control. Japanese fascism, whatever the uniqueness of the cultural forces active within it, has this abiding relevance.

Appendix

The Peace Preservation Act 1925[94]

Article 1: Anyone who organises a group for the purpose of changing the national polity [*kokutai*] or of denying the private property system [*shiyū zaisan seido*], or anyone who knowingly participates in said group, shall be sentenced to penal servitude or imprisonment not exceeding ten years. An offence not actually carried out shall also be subject to punishment.

Article 2: Anyone who consults with another person on matters relating to the implementation of these objectives described in clause 1 of the preceding article shall be sentenced to penal servitude or imprisonment not exceeding seven years.

Article 3: Anyone who instigates others for the purpose of implementing those objectives described in clause 1, article 1, shall be sentenced to penal servitude or imprisonment not exceeding seven years.

Article 4: Anyone who instigates others to engage in rioting or assault or other crimes inflicting harm on life, person, or property for the purpose of attaining the objectives of clause 1, article 1, shall be sentenced to penal servitude or imprisonment not exceeding ten years.

Article 5: Anyone who, for the purpose of committing those crimes described in clause 1, article 1, and in the preceding three articles, provides money and goods or other financial advantage for others, or makes an offer or commitment for same, shall be sentenced to penal servitude or imprisonment not exceeding five years. Anyone who knowingly receives such considerations, or makes demand or commitment for same, shall be punished in a similar manner.

Article 6: Anyone who has committed the crimes described in the three preceding articles and has surrendered himself voluntarily to authorities shall have his sentence reduced or be granted immunity from prosecution.

Article 7: This law shall be made applicable to anyone who commits crimes described in this law outside of the jurisdiction in which this law is in effect.

---

[94] Taken from Lu, *Japan: A Documentary History*, vol II, 397–98.

Conclusion: Repression and Legality

STEPHEN SKINNER

When the Fascist and other regimes considered in this collection sought to con-solidate their power, repress their opponents, and stamp their version of order on society, key instruments among the various means adopted were criminal law and related institutions, including primary codes and courts, as well as related ad hoc or extraordinary laws and specialised tribunals using the conceptual order of criminality. Yet despite accompanying bombastic claims to uniqueness and supe-riority in the criminal law sphere, the Fascist regime did not start with an entirely blank slate, or radically reinvent criminal regulation, and other related regimes also drew on existing norms and modes of criminal law. All of them used similar institutional structures to give repression an appearance of legality through judi-cial processes, and to execute it through a semblance of justice. Reading the chap-ters collected here, some common issues concerning values and professional actors need to be underlined, together with three key themes. These three themes are the issue of form, particularly duality; the instrumentalisation, or functional-ity of criminal law and criminal justice; and connections through criminal law among these regimes and other legal orders, including the recurrent problem of temporal continuity with preceding and subsequent systems, as well as trans-systemic similarities with external legal orders. As each chapter situates its argu-ments in relation to the existing literature, the aim here is to summarise and underline these possible interconnections.

With regard to the matter of values, and risking a statement of the obvious, it is important to recall that the Fascist and other regimes that emerged in the interwar period, borne of what Chapter 5 identifies as the 'crisis of authority' engendered by the First World War, sought to construct their criminal law around a broadly shared set of values. As indicated by some of the commentaries outlined in Chapter 3, the modern(ist) concerns with declining standards and the perceived threat to society meant that such systems rallied around religion, predominantly Catholicism, family and moral values, the protection of youth, or the regime's future, together with – as flagged in Chapters 4 and 7 – issues of national purity, national preservation and race. Although not unique to these extreme regimes, but shared with contemporaneous democracies, and not in themselves determi-nate of 'fascistic' identity, they nevertheless constitute a common ground of criminal law's protected goods that indicate important features of the period's landscape of crisis and reaction. Also in this respect, as discussed in all of the chapters, but perhaps especially Chapters 1, 5, 6, 7 and 8, all of these regimes shared a concern with perceived threats from enemies of the state, or 'dangerous elements' in society, a common refrain in state discourse in the interwar period and beyond.[1] Almost always linked to the fear of communism and cast in terms of dangers to the state's internal security, even its personality, many of the chapters here show how these regimes sought to use the language and mechanisms of criminal law to construct and present responses to such menaces as social protection.

The other preliminary point to be noted is the important role of two professional bodies in the rise and operation of these regimes. One of these bodies is the military, essential to the development and survival of all of the regimes discussed here. This is, of course, a well-known historical fact, given these regimes' close ties with the armed forces, including the regimes' emergence from the First World War and the grievances of veterans, or in the case of Spain, the role of the military in the coup and subsequent bloody civil war. However, in connection with criminal law it is important to underline, especially as in Chapters 1 and 6, as well as 5 and 8, the influence of the armed forces' own values and priorities, particularly in relation to the defence of the state, and the connection between military institutions and the construction of a penal discourse of internal combat against enemies, with its symbolic advantages.[2]

The other professional body is that of lawyers and judges. While perhaps the recurrent significance of such actors is not surprising, given the collection's focus on criminal law and justice, several chapters have emphasised how lawyers were all too often complicit in the rise of these regimes and, through techniques of interpretative distancing, in the application of their law irrespective of its origins and impact. This has largely been due to the political sympathies of lawyers and their class or economic interests, as suggested in Chapter 6 on Spain, but also as indicated in relation to Italy in Chapters 2 and 3, where lawyers favoured a legally positivist, or technical-legal interpretation that ignored political foundations and practical effects.[3] Furthermore judges, as in Chapter 8, when willing to comply with authority or turn a blind eye to the effect of their judgments by applying repressive law without demur, cease acting as a filter between state and citizens, and become active in the former's exertion of power to 'violate the private space' of individual life.[4]

---

[1] See also text relating to n 114 in Ch 2, and further E De Cristofaro, 'Legalità e pericolosità. La penalistica nazifascista e la dialettica tra retribuzione e difesa dello stato' (2007) 36 *Quaderni fiorentini per la storia del pensiero giuridico moderno* 1031–82.

[2] See especially text relating to nn 64 and 84 in Ch 1.

[3] Note particularly M Sbriccoli, 'Le mani nella pasta e gli occhi al cielo. La penalistica italiana negli anni del fascismo', in M Sbriccoli (ed), *Storia del diritto penale e della giustizia. Scritti editi e inediti 1972–2007*, vol II (Milan, Giuffrè, 2009) 1015.

[4] Text following n 33 and the conclusion in Ch 8.

Turning to the three key themes emerging from the collection, the first involves questions of form, especially duality, albeit not always precisely as Fraenkel argued.[5] Perhaps closest to Fraenkel's model of a system based on law and prerogatives, Chapter 7 suggests how the Vargas regime constructed itself and furthered its aims through criminal law and related repressive measures by combining legal and discretionary prerogative measures. Vargas both used law based on positivist principles and directed elements of policing and crime control through personal, dictatorial powers. The chapter thus argues that through this dual and mutually reinforcing exercise of authority, the regime was able to rely on apparently legal measures to legitimate its broader, authoritarian dimensions. Ultimately, the chapter argues, this combination supported the regime's fascistic focus on ultra-nationalist concerns with identity, rebirth and control.

Similarly, Chapters 6 and 8 also point to the dual operation of criminal law and special law. Under the Francoist regime, military law and justice retained the upper hand even though ordinary criminal law was gradually revised and consolidated. Indeed, as Chapter 6 highlights, the regime's military dimensions, paralleling the laws and institutions of the ordinary state the dictatorship purportedly sought to save, were a defining aspect of its identity. In Japan – as in the other systems considered – Chapter 8 shows that ordinary criminal law was also supplemented by the special provisions of the Peace Preservation Act targeting labour and social protest movements. The open-textured terms and provisions of that Act lent themselves, through willing judicial interpretation, to fierce repression.

Other forms of duality highlighted in Chapter 5 are of particular significance, involving both (and in a different sense) the binary construction of law and exception in order to buttress authority, and the internalisation within law of state violence, which 'permeates the very structure of the law and dissolves it'.[6] A core duality in the interwar period, the relationship between law and exception is also central to Chapter 1, in which the 'paradox of freedom' is identified as a characteristic problem in liberal orders, in response to which the twin track of rule/exception, or law/discretion, comes into play and challenges the myth of monolithic legality.[7] The latter's appearance, as observed in Chapter 3, was recognised as an ideological device masking a different intention even as Fascism stormed towards its downfall, albeit if, as both that chapter and Chapter 4 show, subsequent legal analysis has at times struggled to break free of its illusory nature and accept that law may not be the dominant reality, but the thrust of politics beneath it.

A further form of duality, or more accurately hybridity, is emphasised in Chapter 2, in terms of the Rocco Code's splicing of liberal, positivist and Fascist values and objectives. Although this could be seen as an illustration of what has generally been perceived as Fascism's eclectic mix of influences, it can also be seen as an example of the regime's merging of such influences into an instrument

---

[5] E Fraenkel, *The Dual State: A Contribution to the Theory of Dictatorship* (New York, Oxford University Press, 1941).

[6] Text following n 172 and relating to nn 5–11 in Ch 5.

[7] Text relating to nn 4–6 in Ch 1.

better suited to its repressive goals. Whereas Arturo and Alfredo Rocco claimed to have rejected both positivist and classical influences, the chapter shows this was not the case in the Rocco Code, even if its intended objectives differed from those of both criminological schools.

Finally, that coexistence of claim and reality (a further form of duality, it is suggested here, in fascist systems) – as studies of fascism often recall[8] – also requires attention here. Usually used to underline the difference between fascist belief and action, the distinction between what such regimes said they were doing and what they did is apparent here, both as Chapter 2 shows in the Rocco Code's mixed bases, and as Chapter 6 points out in the ways such regimes' brutal conduct belied claims to the contrary. In that sense Franco's rhetoric of humane justice was clearly at odds with the repressive actions the regime carried out.[9]

The second theme is the issue of function, that is the instrumentalisation of criminal law and criminal justice under Fascism and the other systems discussed. Setting up this theme, Chapter 1 argues that the Special Tribunal for the Defence of the State in Fascist Italy was a 'space' in which the 'falsification of justice'[10] served to give the regime's repressive and preventive activities a veneer of acceptability, or a stamp of authenticity.[11] Pointing to the 'symbolic function' of courts, the chapter argues that the Special Tribunal was used to tap into pre-existing authoritarian tendencies and the perceived value of juridical structures in order to drive forward the totalitarian agenda. Similarly, Chapter 6 on the Francoist regime also points to the reliance on military courts, borne of the regime's military foundations and emergence through civil war, as well as specialised courts with a specific repressive focus on the regime's enemies. Here too, the trappings of judicial justice were used to give 'a mere aura of legality to the monstrous repression.'[12] Even though proceedings in such courts may have been a 'contrived and wicked mockery of justice',[13] acted out as part of the process of eliminating the Franco regime's enemies, it is significant that the trappings of justice were nevertheless retained. The particular importance of courts and judges in contributing to, even building, a repressive regime's manipulation of the legal order is highlighted in Chapter 8, focusing on the instrumental role of the judiciary in interwar Japan and their interpretation of the Peace Preservation Act. Situated in relation to the fundamental nature of normativity, the latter analysis argues not only that judges played a central role in the development of Japan's form of fascism, but also that the questions of legality and belief in the force of law need to be central to our understanding of how legality operates to achieve repression.[14]

---

[8] AJ Gregor, *Mussolini's Intellectuals: Fascist Social and Political Thought* (Princeton NJ, Princeton University Press, 2005) 248–49.

[9] n 26 in Ch 6.

[10] n 68 and related text in Ch 1.

[11] Compare O Kirchheimer, *Political Justice: the Use of Legal Proceedings for Political Ends* (Princeton NJ, Princeton University Press, 1961) 5–6.

[12] MG Corachán, n 15 in Ch 6.

[13] Text relating to n 32 in Ch 6.

[14] Text relating to n 12 and 13 in Ch 8.

With regard to substantive criminal law, both Chapter 2 and Chapter 7 underline the relationship between forms of positivism and repressive criminal law under Italian Fascism and the Vargas regime in Brazil. Whereas Chapter 2 argues that the Rocco Code adopted a corrupted form of positivist criminological concepts to serve the regime's ends, Chapter 7 suggests that positivist tendencies were relied on in order to build a harsh legalism to impose order and bolster the regime. Both chapters therefore point to the direct control function of criminal law, enhanced by shaping the ideological foundations, content and application of legal norms. Contextually, Chapter 5 argues that the repressive turn in criminal law in interwar Romania reflected a more widespread authoritarian turn in that period due to a general 'crisis of authority', in which states sought to strengthen control in the face of rapid change.[15] Similarly, Chapter 3 indicates how such a tendency in criminal law, towards tighter controls over perceived deviance from a desired norm, morals and perceived threats of disorder, was seen by some contemporaneous commentators as a recurrent pressure, even need, across a range of systems, Fascist and democratic. Consequently, criminal law and criminal justice were important instruments of control in these repressive politico-legal orders, but it is crucial to note that the legal and judicial form was important in achieving that control both due to the ways in which it allowed the direct application of power, and – as in Chapters 1 and 7 – because of its facilitative or apparently legitimating effects; in other words, law and courts were instrumentalised as conduits and masks for power.

The third major theme running through the collection concerns the questions of continuity and connectedness, with various points emerging from the chapters. Importantly, Chapter 4 highlights that the question of continuity and connection with a darker past is not unique to fascist and authoritarian systems, and requires careful engagement both with the nature of such links and the ways in which we may seek to address them critically. In that regard the chapter also emphasises the dynamism of such continuity, in that the process of identifying and evaluating such contestable politico-legal legacies changes over time and requires analysis at several levels, from the internal interpretative practices of law to the external political context. As Chapters 1 and 2 illustrate, the construction of Fascist criminal justice and criminal law built on core elements of the previous liberal order, while Chapter 7 suggests how the Vargas regime was able to build on pre-existing authoritarian tendencies in Brazilian law. In that sense, elements of penality under fascism were maintained from before and, as Chapter 3 indicates, lasted beyond the regime's fall due to a lack of institutional renewal and the Rocco Code's preservation, thus pointing to clear leakage beyond the perceived historical parenthesis problematised in Chapter 4.

Significantly, Chapters 5, 6, and 8 also underline the continuity of criminal law from their chosen historical periods into subsequent times. Chapters 5 and 6 both indicate how the conceptual substrata and institutional structures of criminal law

---

[15] Text relating to nn 1 and 6–10 in Ch 5.

and justice that were formulated in interwar Romania and under Franco respectively lasted beyond their selected periods of study. The 1936 Romanian Penal Code influenced penality in that state over subsequent decades, including under Communism.[16] The Francoist laws and courts continued to exert an influence long after their genesis in and after the Civil War, due to that regime's particularly long life (and their impact and residue after the end of the regime are still being explored). Chapter 8 provides an important outline of the legacy of judicial decisions under the Peace Preservation Act and the continuing pursuit of justice in its aftermath in Japan today, highlighting the social resonance and significance of such decisions even long after the law in question has ceased to be applied. However, Chapter 8 also includes a call for vigilance as similar concerns with internal order and security to those raised at the time of the Peace Preservation Act creep back into current Japanese political discourse and legislative responses[17] (although Japan is not alone in this experience). Along similar lines, Chapter 2 reminds us that the influence of positivist criminology may still be felt in current forensic practices, although perhaps not quite yet with a 'fascistic' focus on controlling deviance and dangerousness.[18]

Lastly here, as Chapter 3 has suggested, the connectedness of Fascist criminal law also includes trans-systemic questions involving similarities in terms of substance and methods, as well as apparently contiguous legality, across systems of different political complexions. Given such continuities, and in light of the call for vigilance raised in Chapter 8, the questions in Chapter 3 about how we may identify and respond to the emergence – or recurrence – of such problematic regimes, and evaluate similar characteristics in the criminal law sphere, remain salient.

Overall, the chapters in the collection draw our attention to a central idea of a rearranged relationship between law and political power. In the context of a time of crisis in authority, perceived threats and a reliance on law and legality to authenticate state responses to constructed dangers, law ceases to operate as a restraint and a protection – albeit imperfectly – and is reduced to a mere instrument of power. Yet, that instrument retains recognisable features, namely apparent legality and the (hollowed out) mechanisms of justice. Hopefully, the chapters' outlines of how we might understand the politico-legal dimensions of these sorts of regimes, trace their objectives in the legal sphere, and assess their reliance on law as a pillar and channel of power, will support further analysis of such matters, both historically and as an ongoing concern.

---

[16] nn 84–85 and related text in Ch 5.
[17] n 92 in Ch 8.
[18] nn 23 and 27 in Ch 2 and related text.

Afterword
Through the Looking Glass: Thinking About and Working Through Fascist Criminal Law

DAVID FRASER

'It's a poor sort of memory that only works backwards,' says the White Queen to Alice.

Finally, in 2014, in this book, we have a set of English-language essays dealing, for the first time, with the ideas, practices, and ideologies of criminal law within various totalitarian legal systems that are conveniently, if not always with total taxonomical comfort, described as fascist. For this, the editor and contributors are to be congratulated and we readers must be grateful. It is not my intention, given the blank canvas afforded to me by the editor, to engage with the various constituent parts of the present volume with any specificity or in any detail. Instead, I want to address several interconnected issues and concerns inspired by the contributors, and in doing so, to both highlight the significance of this volume, and to trace some key concepts and ideas which might, indeed I believe should, serve as guideposts along the trail of future research engagement with the central idea presented throughout this book, the conceptual and historical reality of totalitarian criminal law.

As Michael Stolleis has highlighted, this historical and intellectual reality, of law divorced from Enlightenment concepts of justice, of judges, lawyers, and law professors dedicated to a legal system embodying the counter-narratives of reaction, repression, exclusion, and in the end, mass extermination, has served as an almost insurmountable roadblock to concerted and collective efforts to confront the legal history of the twentieth century. Indeed, as he also argues, this common psychological blockage is perhaps a fortiori evident when we consider the difficult, tragic, irreconcilable and inevitable issue of continuity, in ideological concepts, normative rules, institutional and individual roles, in the various temporal and geographical manifestations of the 'post-totalitarian' manifestations of legality.[1] But the time has come for just these kinds of confrontations, for this type

---

[1] M Stolleis, 'Reluctance to Glance in the Mirror: The Changing Face of German Jurisprudence After 1933 and Post-1945' in C Joerges and N Singh Ghaleigh (eds), *Darker Legacies of Law in Europe: the Shadow of National Socialism and Fascism over Europe and its Legal Traditions* (Oxford, Hart Publishing, 2003) 1–18, 16–17.

of engagement with the critical history of law, and in this case, criminal law, within and at the foundational core of fascist regimes. It may never be possible to avoid ideological and disciplinary biases in such socio-legal historical confrontations with totalitarian legalities, but it is no longer possible, nor is it acceptable, to hide behind arguments about conceptual difficulties, jurisprudentially nebulous constructions of 'law', historical complexity and incommensurability, or finally the always present and inevitable accusation of subjective interpretation, to avoid our own legal historical coming to terms with our 'criminal' past, our fascist criminal law *Vergangenheitsbewältigung* (coming to terms with, working through, the past).[2]

I begin this project of sketching my tentative and preliminary research programme by eschewing, as do the contributors to the present volume, any detailed or final discussion of the ideas and taxonomies that might inform studies of Fascist, fascist, totalitarian, or National Socialist, criminal law regimes. I am not suggesting that such debates and examinations are not useful, or necessary. Instead, I limit myself here to the simple declaration that such taxonomical inquiries will always be part of any intellectually sophisticated socio-legal history of criminal law in the relevant jurisdictions. At the same time, while definitional accuracy and comparative possibility are laudable goals, history also shows that squabbles over definitional purity or comparative veracity can and do sometimes serve as effective barriers to other significant avenues of inquiry. Indeed, such taxonomical debates also show themselves as concrete manifestations of deeper ideological and political biases that have prevented fruitful scholarship. One need only remember the controversies of Germany's *Historikerstreit* to see that debates about necessary historical inquiry and valuable comparative history can hide and mask more profound issues.[3]

My first proposal for future research on totalitarian criminal law systems is that we return to the key insight into the unique political place occupied by criminal law offered by French philosopher Louis Althusser. I invoke Althusser here not because I seek an intellectual return to a structuralist Marxism, from which even Althusser partially resiled.[4] Or, to be less kind, I am not seeking to invoke as an intellectual model what his critics labelled 'one-dimensional Marxism'.[5] To continue the theme of limitation, but in the obverse, I am not suggesting that debates and studies of the place of Althusserian Marxism in the French philosophical tradition are not of current importance.[6] Indeed, more generally, there is an argument to be made that many of our insights and concerns over the apparent disjunction between 'justice' and law which can be said to be central to totalitar-

[2] M Stolleis, *The Law Under the Swastika: Studies on Legal History in Nazi Germany* (Chicago IL, University of Chicago Press, 1998) 30–31.
[3] J Habermas, *The New Conservatism: Cultural Criticism and the Historians' Debate* (Cambridge, Polity, 1994).
[4] L Althusser, *On the Reproduction of Capitalism* (London, Verso, 2014).
[5] S Clarke et al, *One-Dimensional Marxism: Althusser and the Politics of Culture* (London, Allison & Busby, 1980).
[6] P Dardot and C Laval, 'Après Althusser, quelle actualité de Marx?' (2013) 56 *Cités* 77.

ian criminal law, and our studies of fascist criminal law, stem from, and are informed by the practices and insights derived from more general Hegelian Marxist traditions of immanent critique.[7] But my interest and my focus here are more limited. I want merely to suggest that what we can take from Althusser's work on ideology in particular is a key way of entering upon an intellectual path that might lead us to a further series of informative pathways for the study of fascist criminal law.

I am thinking specifically of Althusser's exposition of the nature and role of the state and its 'apparatuses'. For him, the capitalist state in particular maintained itself as the superstructure for capitalist production through a complex array of mechanisms, or apparatuses, which, as a highlighted signpost for possible future research, he usefully divided into Repressive State Apparatuses (RSAs) and Ideological State Apparatuses (ISAs).[8] The key for beginning to understand, or at least to inquire into, the nature and role of criminal law in fascist legal systems is to be found in footnote 8 of his text, where he tells us that 'the "Law" belongs to both the (Repressive) State Apparatus and to the system of ISAs'.[9] This idea that law has both a repressive function, epitomised in criminal law sanctions, and an ideological function, again embodied in the criminal law's role in instantiating categories of social, political, and cultural exclusion, in modern criminological terms in labelling, is, I believe, invaluable in analysing and understanding criminal law in the context of historical fascist regimes. It allows a way into developing understandings of, and exploring, the different instances in which fascist criminal law both repressed enemies/criminals and succeeded in constructing the synonymous ideological relationships between criminals and enemies of the state/people/*Volk*/Nation etc. The ideological/repressive vortex of mutually reinforcing practices of exclusion of a criminal Other and the protection of the Nation can be seen at the heart of criminal law in fascist regimes.

The utility of this intellectual framework becomes more apparent when one examines in more detail the Althusserian tropes of RSAs and ISAs. Key for Althusser was the idea that both forms of state activity were essential to the strength and survival of the state and therefore of the system of the relations of production, ie in this instance capitalism. But more profoundly, Althusser was keen to highlight the ways in which for ISAs in particular, much of their power appeared to derive from the fact that they were not 'public' or state-based in nature. Most of the organs identified as belonging to the ISA structure were 'private' bodies – the Church, schools, the family, trade unions, political parties etc. Of all these, law most clearly fits into the 'public' domain, although as we as jurists are aware, the distinction between public and private is a powerful and persistent one in legal theory and practice. The real practical power of ideology for Althusser in this understanding lies in its 'private' nature, but its truly repressive function,

---

[7] J Derrida, *Specters of Marx* (London and New York, Routledge, 1994) 88–92.

[8] L Althusser, 'Ideology and Ideological State Apparatuses (Notes towards an Investigation)', in *Lenin and Philosophy and other essays* (New York and London, Monthly Review Press, 1971) 127.

[9] Ibid 143.

perhaps in the sense of 'false consciousness', is located not just in the coexistence of RSA/ISA characteristics in 'law', but in the foundational fact of the contingency of the public/private distinction itself. The line between that which is 'private' and that which is 'public' is not a normatively rigid, inflexible, or unbreachable one. It is dependent, among other things and especially for Althusser, on decisions emanating from the state itself. The very existence of the public/private distinction depends on the 'public' in both its repressive and its ideological manifestations. Of course, we now live in a world in which both feminist critique and the work of Critical Legal scholars have unveiled the constructedness of the public/private distinction, but Althusser got there first and most persuasively in relation to the RSA/ISA nature of criminal law.[10]

These Althusserian insights are however important for more than the RSA/ISA taxonomies, or synonymous categories selected from other historical intellectual traditions for research purposes, which can lead to potentially fruitful investigations of the ways in which criminal law and criminal justice systems, including those which established special or exceptional jurisdictions, operated and were understood in fascist regimes. The emphasis on the public/private distinction and its relationship with the RSAs and ISAs, whether again we chose to adopt Althusserian terminology or adapt other categories of analysis to the same substantive effect, also leads to other paths of inquiry into criminal law under fascism.

Althusser and his followers, like other Marxist theoreticians, constructed law, RSAs, ISAs, criminal law, etc, in foundational terms and within normatively unswerving understandings of base and superstructure and, most importantly, of the capitalist mode of production. The state, and all its apparatuses, always in the final analysis served to preserve and protect that mode of production. Law, and criminal law in particular, with its dual characteristics, was always capitalist law in a capitalist state.[11] In a similar vein, structuralists like Althusser and Poulantzas, along with other Marxists from different intellectual strains within the broad Marxist tradition, and as a consequence of this rigid ideological normative frame, also saw fascism as a more specific (totalitarian) manifestation of the capitalist order. I would not suggest that a research project targeted at any fascist or totalitarian criminal law system with this particular narrow, and indeed reductionist, understanding is likely to be fruitful. However, hidden within the Marxist reductionist vision of fascism are other important insights from which we might learn and which we might apply, with the necessary intellectual and normative caveats.

The first point that emerges from these intellectual engagements with fascism, and with fascist criminal law, is the apparently obvious, but too often overlooked,

---

[10] D Kennedy, 'Stages of the Decline of the Public/Private Distinction' (1982) 130 *University of Pennsylvania Law Review* 1349; MJ Horwitz, 'The History of the Public/Private Distinction' (1982) 130 *University of Pennsylvania Law Review* 1423; R Gavison, 'Feminism and the Public/Private Distinction' (1992) 45 *Stanford Law Review* 1.

[11] For example N Poulantzas, *State Power Socialism* (London, Verso, 1978) especially at 76 et seq for the classic embodiment of this view.

idea of periodisation. Fascism, whatever its particular variant, or national context, did not emerge out of nothing.[12] Whether the particular analytical frame which one adopts will turn out to be one of revolutionary caesura or of radical continuity, or some more complex combination in terms of the sovereign constitutive moment of the fascist regime in question, fascism and fascist criminal law can only be understood in terms of that which preceded them. Moreover, in keeping with the periodisation imperative, it seems obvious historically and as a matter of sound legal scientific analysis, as our Continental colleagues would have it, that we must engage with fascist criminal law as it appeared and as it evolved. The Hitler regime of 1933 was not the same as it was in 1940, nor was Pétain's Vichy the same in 1940 as in 1943. Its political and social circumstances evolved, as did its criminal law. Perhaps the better examples of this will turn out to be Fascist Italy, or Francoist Spain, or Salazar's Portugal, with their longer life spans. Whichever regime is being examined, the general importance of keeping a periodised historical perspective in mind must be central to our future research agendas.[13] National revolution and renewal were often key elements in fascist ideology, and they manifested themselves in criminal law norms, practices, and institutional arrangements, but not identically and not all at once.

Periodisation is therefore a minimum intellectual and methodological component of any future research on fascist criminality. But it can be more than that. A periodisation approach might lead to a more careful and subtle analysis of changes in the legal regime, from identifying traces of remaining liberal legality to a time when a criminal system can be said to be more or less fully fascisised. It might also lead in other directions, such as the one adopted by Kristen Rundle in her study of law in Nazi Germany.[14] Rundle argues that a periodisation approach in that context leads to the conclusion that at a certain point the Nazi regime ceased to be one that applied 'law', when it began the push to the Final Solution. While I think this is a misconceived conclusion about the nature of law in the Nazi state,[15] and has been since Radbruch made a similar jurisprudential proposal,[16] I accept the fact that a more complex temporal focus on law as it evolves during a totalitarian period can only ever be useful to those of us who seek to understand and grasp the central concepts and operational realities of fascist criminal law. Fascist criminal law had origins and it had a political and ideological teleology. The intellectual history of totalitarian legal systems and accurate understandings of their normative content demand historical and taxonomical awareness informed by a clear vision of the contexts in which they arose and developed.

[12] Ibid, and N Poulantzas, *Fascism and Dictatorship* (London, Verso, 1979).

[13] See generally K Hite and P Cesarini (eds), *Authoritarian Legacies and Democracy in Latin America and Southern Europe* (Notre Dame IN, University of Notre Dame Press, 2004).

[14] K Rundle, 'The Impossibility of an Exterminatory Legality: Law and the Holocaust' (2009) 59 *University of Toronto Law Journal* 65.

[15] D Fraser, *Law After Auschwitz: Towards A Jurisprudence of the Holocaust* (Durham NC, Carolina Academic Press, 2005).

[16] G Radbruch, 'Gesetzliches Unrecht und übergesetzliches Recht' (1946) *Süddeutsche Juristenzeitung* 107.

To return to the ideological and repressive functions of fascist criminal law, and to the centrality of the public/private distinction, another research focus should also be highlighted. While capitalist or liberal legality can be said, with the appropriate reservations, to be characterised by the distinction between the public and the private, with its concomitant emphasis on autonomy and citizenship in an individualised sense, a sense which derives from the very notion of the public and the private, and from which also flows our understanding of state and civil society, it seems quite clear that a core characteristic of fascist law, and of fascist criminal law in particular, is the erosion, if not the elimination, of the public/private distinction. The line between state and civil society is blurred or restructured under National Socialist, fascist, syndicalist, etc understandings of the Nation. In a similar fashion, criminal law becomes much more clearly and almost self-avowedly a unitary system where the ideological and the repressive become ever more symbiotic and eventually perhaps indistinguishable. From special courts and special laws meant to deal with particular dangers to the nation, to an evolutionary system in which the dream is of a new man under a new fascist law, totalitarian criminal law brings together ideology and repression in ways which require close and careful examination. One might choose to identify these in terms of continuity with some of the elements already present and inherent even within liberal legality,[17] or conversely, or more fundamentally, to identify some forms of Benjaminian rupture and continuity in the very nature of law's foundational violence.[18]

Once more, however, it seems to be obligatory for our future and ongoing intellectual engagements with the subject that one must place fascist criminal law in the intellectual and normative context of the public/private, repression/ideology dyads and seek to explore and explicate various elements of substance, procedure, and institutional arrangements through at least a preliminary deployment of these tropes. Derrida suggests that the spectre that haunts us from National Socialist law to today is the spectre of 'police', a looming presence that does not even require an actual police presence.[19] In following the critical socio-legal historical path of investigating the ideological and repressive, often murderous, practices of fascist criminal law, we may indeed go through a looking glass to a place where the sentence precedes the verdict and the private is subsumed by a psychologically omnipresent public police, where law is indeed both total and totalitarian.

It is, I would suggest, of vital importance to explore the ways in which fascist criminal law came to embody, to a greater or lesser extent, at different times and in different historical, cultural, and political circumstances and contexts, interesting

---

[17] L Lustgarten, '"A Distorted Image of Ourselves": Nazism, "Liberal" Societies and the Qualities of Difference', in Joerges and Ghaleigh, *Darker Legacies of Law in Europe* 113.

[18] G Agamben, *Homo Sacer: Sovereign Power and Bare Life* (Stanford CT, Stanford University Press, 1998).

[19] J Derrida, 'Force of Law: The Mystical Foundation of Authority' (1990) 11 *Cardozo Law Review* 921, 1011.

variants of the gradual disappearance of the very dyadic structures on which liberal legality apparently depends. This is, as Vivian Curran has so carefully and thoughtfully established, not a question of different jurisprudential schools of thought informing judicial technique, or broader intellectual understandings of law and legality. Instead fascist law can be grasped, however tentatively, in Curran's deployment of the concept of unicity.[20] Dyadic relationality as embodied in such different concepts as public/private, repression/ideology, or multiform complexity of social life, are replaced in fascist law by a single vision, a single point of legitimation, and a single function. The *Duce*, the *Führer*, the General, the Emperor, all embody a single crudely devised source of sovereign power flowing perhaps from the masses, the *Volk*, the Nation, or a national derivative thereof. Repression and ideology as embodied in fascist criminal law then come to perform the singularity, the unified one, by identifying, excluding, and perhaps exterminating those who do not belong in the imagined and indeed spectral unitary whole.

This might be the point at which the structuralist Marxist critique loses its usefulness as a guide to our research paths. It is difficult, if not impossible in some cases, for example, to justify and reconcile fascist criminal law with models invoking the economic rationality of capitalism, with the rent-seeking behaviour of monopolists, or with the creation of an industrial reserve army in the tradition of *Capital*.[21] The Shoah was perhaps informed by modernist rationality and ideals of efficiency in its attempts to reach its end goals,[22] but it cannot plausibly be explained simply or comprehensively, let alone convincingly, by any understanding of fascist legality as a slightly more focused form of capitalist state repression and ideology.

Indeed, it is perhaps at this point that any proposal for future research agendas such as I have been tentatively suggesting here, should begin once again to emphasise the need not just for periodisation, but the absolute necessity of an historically and methodologically focused specificity in any analysis of fascist legality. While Brazil and Japan have not historically been immune from anti-semitism, the criminalisation, repression and exclusion of Jews are not central elements of the history of totalitarian criminal law in those countries. Unicity, however potentially universal as a way of beginning to understand variants of fascist criminal law, is not univocal. Enemies can be found even if only in order to eliminate them. With regard to Romania and Italy on the other hand, I would suggest that it would be a serious mistake, and a flawed effort at understanding, to ignore the role played by anti-semitism and the subsequent introduction of anti-Jewish measures as core elements of fascist legality in those two countries.[23] At the same time and

---

[20] V Curran, 'Formalism and Anti-Formalism in French and German Judicial Methodology', in Joerges and Ghaleigh, *Darker Legacies of Law in Europe* 208.

[21] K Marx, *Das Kapital* (Hamburg, Verlag von Otto Meissner, 1867); *Capital: A Critique of Political Economy* (New York, Modern Library, 1906).

[22] Z Bauman, *Modernity and the Holocaust* (Cornell, Cornell University Press, 1989).

[23] For Italy, MA Livingston, *The Fascists and the Jews of Italy: Mussolini's Race Laws, 1938–1943* (Cambridge, Cambridge University Press, 2014). For Romania, C Cercel, 'The "Right" Side of the Law. State of Siege and the Rise of Fascism in Interwar Romania' (2013) 2 *Fascism* 203.

again, a periodisation and careful attention to context and nuance will be required in any further exploration of the centrality (or not) of anti-semitism to fascist criminal legality both in these two countries and elsewhere in Europe.

I return to a theme indicated in the earlier discussion, the ideological role and nature of fascist criminal law. Here, however, I want to focus on the place and nature of legal education as a potential locus for future research projects. Universities in general, and faculties of law in particular, fit comfortably and precisely into the Althusserian ISA model, and other models of fascist state practice. Under fascism, I would suggest that they are also very likely to fit into any methodological model or ideological approach that would try to understand the unifying vision and function of the fascist state and its institutions. In other words, university law faculties which function in fascist states serve the function of forming professional judges and lawyers in the Continental system, lawyers and judges who will then serve as other relay points in the concretisation and further institutionalisation of fascist criminal law practice and ideology.

Work which has been undertaken in relation to legal education in Vichy France may well serve here as a guide to the ways in which our understanding of the unicity of fascist criminal law, as a repressive practice with clear ideological purposes, was instituted in the contexts of totalitarian legal systems that will be the object of future study. Dominique Gros has already offered a detailed study of the ways in which legal education was adapted to legitimise juridified anti-semitism through the normal and normalising practice of teaching texts.[24] More recently, Silvia Falconieri has examined and explored the way in which 'racial law' became an unremarkable and ordinary part of legal education in France.[25] Still, most work even on Vichy universities focuses mostly on anti-semitism either within institutions in general, particularly on the exclusion of Jewish professors and students under the *numerus clausus* provisions,[26] or as with Gros and Falconieri, on the normativity and normalcy of legalised anti-semitism within law faculties. Studies of Italian universities likewise appear to focus on the application of racial laws against Jewish students or on the position of Jewish faculty, under Fascism and in the immediate post-war period.[27] To broaden and deepen our understanding of the ways in which fascist criminal law functioned, we must continue not just to examine these central questions, but to look at legal education, and education in criminal law, in much more detail. How were issues of continuity and tradition taught? How were new matters of fascist law introduced into the system of forming legal professionals? How was the nature of law in the new system explained?

---

[24] D Gros, 'Le statut des juifs et les manuels en usage dans les facultés de Droit (1940–1944)' in P Braud (ed), *La violence politique dans les démocraties européennes occidentales* (Paris, L'Harmattan, 1992) 139, available online at http://conflits.revues.org/415 and http://conflits.revues.org/415?lang=en.

[25] S Falonieri, 'Le "droit de la race". Apprendre l'antisémitisme à la faculté de droit de Paris (1940–1944)', available online at www.cliothemis.com/Le-droit-de-la-race-Apprendre.

[26] C Singer, *Vichy, l'université et les Juifs* (Paris, Belles lettres, 1992).

[27] GP Brizzi, *Bologna 1938: Silence and Remembering: the Racial Laws and Foreign Jewish Students at the University of Bologna* (Bologna, CLUEB, 2002); D Gagliani (ed), *Il difficile rientro: Il ritorno dei docenti ebrei nell'università del dopoguerra* (Bologna, CLUEB, 2004).

What did the doctrinal texts say? Who went to law school? Who taught in law schools? Did the central authorities place their faith in the ideological purity and rectitude of the professoriate, or was there a deeper implication of the state in university matters?[28] These are all important questions if we are to come to understand fascist criminal law in its fullness, as repression and as ideology.

Such questions and such a particular focus may well give rise to existential crises among researchers and their colleagues. The very concept of fascist law is troubling enough for those who now work in a world of liberal higher education, where we experience the unifying impulses of the Bologna process, and a certain hegemony of liberal democratic, human rights infused legal education. But any attempt to engage in truly critical socio-legal research on these questions, whether more broadly focused on the normative and ideological practices of the repressive manifestations of fascist criminal law, or on the historical institutional embodiments of the ideology of fascism in legal education, will, as I believe it should, trouble our colleagues. They should be troubled by a carefully contextualised legal history that will inevitably reveal both continuities in the origins of fascist criminal law with more 'liberal' traditions, and continuities within our current jurisprudential and juridical structures with the 'darker legacies' of the legal past. When the focus shifts away from fascist legality in the legal system of legislatures, courts, government agencies, and law offices and shines a penetrating light on institutional practices closer to our academic lives, on legal pedagogy, and legal pedagogues, as embodiments and agents of fascist criminal law, our colleagues should be and will be troubled.

The process of engaging along the research paths suggested here is likely to be an arduous one. It involves a self-awareness of one's own institutional and ideological embeddedness in 'law' with all that that entails for any study of fascist criminal law. It requires long and laborious time spent with archival material or now seemingly ancient texts, as well as the effort to be expended in coming to terms, however tentatively, with the broader context in which the texts were produced and applied. It involves a conscious dedication to follow the path to its end. Most significantly perhaps, it involves a clear choice to enter into the study of subjects and materials that others have consciously ignored. The amnesia of the legal academy about fascist or totalitarian criminal law is a state arrived at, I believe, not unwillingly or unknowingly, but at a minimum by wilful blindness, and more probably by a set of conscious individual and collective choices about what should or can be remembered. In other words, I suggest that future research, of which this volume is an excellent example and starting point, along a trail of other scholars who have initiated similar studies, will occur in a context not of academic amnesia but of an historical pedagogical amnesty which must itself be deconstructed.

There is abroad in the world of law a now well-developed discourse about and practice of memory laws. These laws embody, in their best form, the highest

---

[28] M Escoli, 'Education in Fascist Italy' (1937) 4 *Social Research* 336.

recognition of historical injustices and carry with them a conscious avoidance of collective amnesia. But for the most part, this discourse of memory laws tends to ignore the part played by law and by lawyers, by legalised repression and juridical ideology, in the commission of the atrocities, and in attempts to achieve their historical, juridified erasure.[29] Memory laws quite simply tend to forget law. The task of those of us who really want to see a connection between law and memory when it comes to the fascist past, must face up to both the intellectual and ideological resistance of our colleagues and our peers, and to the further complications imposed by legal history itself.

Even if we can legitimately, for reasons of time constraints or limits on work length imposed by publishers, decide that we 'only' want to study or write about fascist criminal law from the 1920s to the 1940s, the methodological and ethical demands of periodisation and context will be omnipresent. Fascism was succeeded by something else, and that something else also suffered from, or was informed by, its own issues of rupture, continuity and context. In some countries, like Romania, fascist criminal law was replaced by Communist criminal law.[30] In others, such as Spain, fascism had a longer lifespan. As Michael Stolleis has argued, if we have any desire or intention to attempt some kind of legal history of the twentieth century, as colleagues have done for preceding epochs, we must confront fascist, totalitarian and National Socialist legality.[31] More significantly as Stolleis sets out, in many cases we must also be willing to confront the continuities of criminal law, for example in Communist Romania, or the rehabilitation of fascists in the Italian political, legal and university systems.[32] Moreover, from this perspective, any real legal history of Italy, for example, would then have to include the relationship of Western 'democratic' Communists with Stalinism and the Soviet Union, or the continuities with the Red Brigades and the 'years of lead'.[33] In addition, I would suggest that any such complete legal history of the twentieth century would also have to explore the continuities in political and legal practice, ideology, and jurisprudential understandings of the post-war Italian and German legal systems, for example, by the Red Brigades and the Red Army Faction.[34] It is not a historical accident or a coincidence that groups such as these portrayed self-described liberal democracies as 'fascist' regimes, or that the legal reaction by

---

[29] For an exploration of this point in another context, see D Fraser, 'Law's Holocaust Denial: State, Memory, Legality', in L Hennebel and T Hochmann (eds), *Genocide Denials and the Law* (New York and Oxford, Oxford University Press, 2011) 3.

[30] See generally F Turcanu, 'D'une dictature à l'autre: Droit et politique en Roumanie de 1938 à 1948', in MO Baruch (ed), *Faire des choix?: Les fonctionnaires dans l'Europe des dictatures, 1933–1948* (Paris, La documentation Française, 2014) 127.

[31] Stolleis, 'Reluctance to Glance in the Mirror' 17–18.

[32] G Montori, 'The professors in and after the fascist regime. The purges in the universities of Italy, 1944–46' (2009) 14 *Journal of Modern Italian Studies* 305.

[33] Ibid.

[34] Historians and sociologists have now begun to some extent to look at the period with some critical distance and insight. See for example K Hanshew, *Terror and Democracy in West Germany* (Cambridge & New York, Cambridge University Press, 2012); J Varon, *Bringing the War Home* (Berkeley and Los Angeles CA, University of California Press, 2004); M Lazar and M-A Matard-Bonucci, *L'Italie des années de plomb: le terrorisme entre histoire et mémoire* (Paris, Autrement, 2010).

those regimes to armed struggle, or political violence, was the invocation of special police regimes, limits on civil liberties, and the right to legal representation, and special systems of isolation within the prison system. When we expand our jurisdictional focus, other similar issues, with their own contextual and historical specificities and contexts, will similarly trouble any idea that the history of twentieth-century criminal law is one of liberalism, republicanism, and democratic values.

I am not suggesting that we all engage in such a 'global' legal history of the twentieth century. I invoke Stolleis's crucial insights to highlight the ideas of contingency, contextualisation, and periodisation, as well as the vital tropes of rupture and continuity, to signal again that the research process that could be inspired by this volume, indeed that could be seen to have been begun by the contributors, is an important and a complex one. We must never be paralysed by the complexities of context or periodisation. We can and should be aware of them, but at the same time we must draw our inspiration from the importance of offering a socio-legal history of fascist criminal law in all its breadth and depth.

Of course, any such process, both because of our contemporary temporal position, and the ideological and institutional disciplinary practices and discourses in which we are inevitably implicated, will always be present in our legal historical endeavours. We can, and must, be aware that our socio-legal histories will inevitably take on the characteristics of ethnography with all the pitfalls and dangers of imposing a subjective hermeneutic frame on the texts we read and interpret.[35] But as with the complexities of periodisation and context, hermeneutic dangers can never stand in the way of our ethical research project. If we are impelled and compelled by any sense of the centrality of some conceptual frame of 'justice' to our work, the examination of the socio-legal history of fascist criminal law begins to take on the form of an imperative from which we cannot resile. When we study fascist criminal law, as the contributors to this volume have, we examine the collapse in radical form of any idea that law and justice are synonymous, or correlated. Most significantly, perhaps, we confront real contexts and historical examples in which the idea that justice is a goal worth contemplating within legality was itself radically questioned. We become implicated in the explication and examination of a system in which a process of unicity imposed in a violent repressive fashion was at the core of the criminal law. Law became a central discourse, among other discourses of ideology and repression, the aim of which was often simple (if it is ever simple) murder. Our task on the other hand is a truly simple one. We must engage with a sordid legal history in order to offer evidence for the prosecution of 'law' itself. Not only must we overcome our reluctance to look in the mirror,[36] we step through the looking glass into the strange and strangely alluring wonderland of fascist criminal law. Derrida wrote in the context of the Final Solution and law, but his identification of the frame within which we work,

---

[35] Stolleis, *Law Under the Swastika* 6–7.
[36] Stolleis, 'Reluctance to Glance in the Mirror'.

in any process of examining what we call in our own studies 'fascist criminal law', entails an inescapable ethical imperative:

> we must think, know, represent for ourselves, formalize, judge the possible complicity between all these discourses and the worst (here the final solution).[37]

Onward comrades; *no pasarán.*

---

[37] Derrida, 'Force of Law' 1045.

INDEX